THE
INTERNET

AT YOUR FINGERTIPS

THE INTERNET

AT YOUR FINGERTIPS

Michael Miller

ALPHA

A member of Penguin Group (USA) Inc.

ALPHA BOOKS

Published by the Penguin Group

Penguin Group (USA) Inc., 375 Hudson Street, New York, New York 10014, USA

Penguin Group (Canada), 90 Eglinton Avenue East, Suite 700, Toronto, Ontario M4P 2Y3, Canada (a division of Pearson Penguin Canada Inc.)

Penguin Books Ltd., 80 Strand, London WC2R 0RL, England

Penguin Ireland, 25 St. Stephen's Green, Dublin 2, Ireland (a division of Penguin Books Ltd.)

Penguin Group (Australia), 250 Camberwell Road, Camberwell, Victoria 3124, Australia (a division of Pearson Australia Group Pty. Ltd.)

Penguin Books India Pvt. Ltd., 11 Community Centre, Panchsheel Park, New Delhi—110 017, India

Penguin Group (NZ), 67 Apollo Drive, Rosedale, North Shore, Auckland 1311, New Zealand (a division of Pearson New Zealand Ltd.)

Penguin Books (South Africa) (Pty.) Ltd., 24 Sturdee Avenue, Rosebank, Johannesburg 2196, South Africa

Penguin Books Ltd., Registered Offices: 80 Strand, London WC2R 0RL, England

Copyright © 2009 Michael Miller

International Standard Book Number: 978-1-59257-927-3
Library of Congress Catalog Card Number: 2009923296

11   10   09   8   7   6   5   4   3   2   1

Interpretation of the printing code: The rightmost number of the first series of numbers is the year of the book's printing; the rightmost number of the second series of numbers is the number of the book's printing. For example, a printing code of 09-1 shows that the first printing occurred in 2009.

Printed in the United States of America

Publisher: **Marie Butler-Knight**

Editorial Director: **Mike Sanders**

Senior Managing Editor: **Billy Fields**

Acquisitions Editor: **Tom Stevens**

Development Editor: **Jennifer Moore**

Production Editor: **Kayla Dugger**

Copy Editor: **Amy Lepore**

Cover and Book Designer: **Kurt Owens**

Indexer: **Tonya Heard**

Layout: **Brian Massey**

Proofreader: **John Etchison**

To Sherry, one year down and counting.

CONTENTS

INTRODUCTION

The Internet is a big topic to discuss and an even bigger thing to learn. It's a combination of many pieces and parts, from e-mail and the web to instant messaging and social networking. Even if you master one piece of the puzzle, there's more out there to learn.

That's why I wrote this book. *The Internet at Your Fingertips* attempts to explain a little bit about a lot of things that are all Internet related. Want to know how the Internet assigns domain names? Need to set up a new e-mail account? Want to instant message or chat or social network with friends and family? Need advice on how to set up your own blog or upload videos to YouTube? It's all here in an easily referenced format. It's a lot of information, hopefully presented in a way that makes it easy to find what you need to know.

You no longer have to spend time and effort researching multiple books or surfing numerous websites to find condensed, organized, and understandable information about the Internet. Use this book as your primary reference as you progress through your Internet experience. You now have *The Internet at Your Fingertips*.

How This Book Is Organized

The Internet at Your Fingertips is meant to be a comprehensive reference to the Internet—those parts that make up the Internet and the things you do online. As such, you don't have to read it front to back; it's perfectly okay to dip into and out of the book to find specific information.

To that end, here is how we've organized the information in this book:

▶ Each chapter provides a table of contents so you can quickly see the areas that are covered. You can choose to read the entire chapter or flip to the particular subject of interest.

▶ This book was written without assuming any prior Internet experience or technical expertise on the part of the reader.

◀ SEE ALSO references are used to quickly find other sections of the book that pertain to the same subject and may further explain the topic. ▶

WARNING . . .WARNING . . .WARNING

These sidebars present cautionary advice on the topic at hand.

WORDS TO GO . . .WORDS TO GO . . .WORDS TO GO

Words to Go are short sidebar definitions of Internet-related terms presented in each chapter. They are provided to further clarify the material covered.

Acknowledgments

Thanks to the usual suspects at Alpha Books, including but not limited to Tom Stevens, Jennifer Moore, Kayla Dugger, Amy Lepore, and Marie Butler-Knight.

Special Thanks to the Technical Editor

The Internet at Your Fingertips was reviewed by an expert who double-checked the accuracy of what you'll learn here, to help ensure that this book gives you everything you need to know about using the Internet. Special thanks are extended to Rolf Crozier, who provided his technical skills in this regard.

Trademarks

All terms mentioned in this book that are known to be or are suspected of being trademarks or service marks have been appropriately capitalized. Alpha Books and Penguin Group (USA) Inc. cannot attest to the accuracy of this information. Use of a term in this book should not be regarded as affecting the validity of any trademark or service mark.

1

CONNECTING TO THE INTERNET

HOW THE INTERNET WORKS

Pieces and Parts of the Internet

The Internet Backbone

Connecting to the Internet

Domain Names and URLs

For most of us, the Internet is an important part of our lives. We use the Internet to communicate with others, to read the latest news, to shop, to search for information, and more. But just what is the Internet—and how does it work?

Pieces and Parts of the Internet

The Internet is nothing more than a big computer network. In fact, it's a computer network that connects other computer networks—what some would call a "network of networks."

There are a variety of different services that are offered over the Internet. The Internet itself doesn't actually provide any of these services, but it does *enable* these services to occur. When you connect to the Internet through your personal computer, you have access to all these services and more.

What are the pieces and parts of the Internet? While there are many, most everything you do on the Internet today is part of just three of these services—the web, **e-mail,** and **instant messaging.** E-mail and instant messaging, of course, are used to communicate with other users. The web is used for just about everything else, from searching for information to watching videos to blogging to doing online banking. All of these web-based activities are accomplished on **web pages** viewed in a **web browser.**

The Web

The **World Wide Web** is the most popular part of the Internet, the place where information of all types is presented in a highly visual format, using a combination of text, images, audio, and even video.

Information on the web is presented in web pages; each page is composed of text, graphics, and links to other web pages. A web page resides at a **website,** which is nothing more than a collection of web pages residing on a host computer. The host computer is connected full-time to the Internet so that you can access the website—and all its web pages—anytime you access the Internet.

The main page at a website is called a home page, and it often serves as an opening screen that provides a brief overview and a sort of menu of everything you can find at that site. You view web pages with a software application called a web browser such as Internet Explorer or Safari.

◀ *SEE ALSO 2.3, "Browsing Web Pages"* ▶

E-mail

Electronic mail (e-mail) is a means of communicating with other Internet users via letters written and delivered electronically over the Internet. Although e-mail messages look a lot like traditional letters, e-mail itself is considerably different from the so-called "snail mail" delivered by the U.S. Postal Service.

When you send an electronic letter to another Internet user, that letter travels from your computer to your recipient's computer (via the Internet) almost instantly. Your messages travel at the speed of electrons over a number of Internet connections, automatically routed to the right place just about as fast as you can click the Send button. That's a *lot* different from using the U.S. Postal Service, which can take days to deliver a similar message.

◀ *SEE ALSO 12.2, "Choosing an E-mail Program"* ▶

Instant Messaging

Instant messaging (IM) is a method for one-on-one text conversations between two Internet users in real time. It's the Internet equivalent of cell phone text messaging—sometimes accompanied by audio or video conversations.

◀ *SEE ALSO 13.2, "Instant Messaging"* ▶

FTP

The **File Transfer Protocol** (FTP) is a means of downloading files from dedicated file **servers.** FTP servers can be accessed with dedicated FTP software or by entering the FTP server's address in a web browser.

◀ *SEE ALSO 5.2, "Downloading Files"* ▶

Usenet Newsgroups

A **newsgroup** is a type of public bulletin board that you can use to read messages from and post messages to other users interested in a particular topic.

◀ *SEE ALSO 11.5, "Using Usenet Newsgroups"* ▶

Social Networks

A social network is a web-based community where users can interact with friends, colleagues, and acquaintances. These communities, such as Facebook and MySpace, are not separate parts of the web per se, as they operate on the web through any web browser, but they are fast becoming a dominant channel for personal communication and interaction.

SEE ALSO 11.1, "Understanding Social Networking" ▶

The Internet Backbone

Everything you access on the Internet is hosted on a computer; these computers are called servers because they serve information and services to users. The Internet itself comprises tens of millions of individual servers, each connected by a high-capacity data backbone. This backbone routes data and communications from one server to another at near-instantaneous speeds.

Each server and device connected to the Internet is identified by a specific address, called an **Internet Protocol (IP) address.** An IP address is specified using dot-decimal notation with a series of numbers divided by dots, like this:

123.45.678.9

The Internet uses an underlying networking technology called Transmission Control Protocol/Internet Protocol (TCP/IP) to manage data transmission and communications between Internet servers. To contact a given server, your web browser or other software specifies an IP address; the communication is then routed to the Internet server that uses that specific IP address.

Connecting to the Internet

As you can now see, when you connect to the Internet, you're connecting your computer to tens of millions of other computers—and the information that resides on all those other computers. But before you can contact those other computers, you first have to gain access to the Internet.

Since your computer does not connect directly to the Internet backbone, you instead connect to a company that serves as an Internet service provider (ISP)—that is, a company that is directly connected to the Internet backbone and provides Internet service for you and other consumers. The connection to your ISP can be via phone line, cable line, or even satellite communication. Your computer connects to the ISP, the ISP connects to the Internet, and thus you are connected to the Internet.

Once you're connected, you can access any site or service on the Internet as well as any mail or news servers run by your ISP. You do this by specifying the IP address of the website or server—or, more commonly, by specifying the site's **domain name** or URL.

Domain Names and URLs

While all Internet servers have IP addresses, most servers assign their IP addresses to a more easily remembered address called a domain name. Domain names are translated into IP addresses via the Internet's Domain Name System (DNS)—essentially a large database that associates IP addresses with their corresponding domain names.

A domain name includes the domain and a suffix separated by a dot, like this:

domain.com

The first part of the domain name, to the left of the dot, is the **second-level domain,** assigned to a specific server or website. The second part of the domain, to the right of the dot, is the **top-level domain,** which is one of a short list of names used to identity a type of server or territory. For example, most commercial websites are assigned the .com domain, educational websites are assigned the .edu domain, and websites in the country of Canada are assigned the .ca domain.

The domain name typically is part of a larger address called the **uniform resource locator (URL).** To access a particular Internet server or website, you can enter the name of the URL instead of the complex series of numbers in an IP address.

A URL consists of two parts and looks like this:

http://www.domain.com

The first part of the URL (http://) is called the **protocol identifier,** and it identifies the protocol, or type of server, used. For example, the http:// scheme is used for web servers; the ftp:// scheme is used for FTP servers. The second part of the URL is called the **resource name** and consists of an additional protocol identifier (www. for World Wide Web; ftp. for FTP sites) and the domain name.

Most web browsers don't require you to enter the URL's protocol identifiers. So for example, you can enter **domain.com** instead of the full **http://www.domain.com.**

Individual pages or files on a website or server are noted to the right of the domain name in the URL, separated by a forward slash. Directories and subdirectories are noted by additional forward slashes. So for example, if you want to access the webpage called **page.html** in the directory **maindirectory** on the website located at the **domain.com** domain, you'd use the following URL:

http://www.domain.com/maindirectory/page.html

A **domain name** is an easily remembered Internet address that is associated with a specific IP address.

E-mail is a means of communicating with other Internet users via electronic letters.

File Transfer Protocol (FTP) is a means of downloading files from dedicated file servers on the Internet.

Instant messaging is a method for one-on-one, real-time text conversations between two Internet users.

An **Internet Protocol (IP) address** is used to identify each server and device connected to the Internet.

A **newsgroup** is an electronic bulletin board dedicated to a particular topic.

The **protocol identifier** is the part of a URL that identifies the protocol used by a given site or server; it's the http:// part of a website URL.

The **resource name** is the second part of a URL, to the right of the //, and it contains the domain name.

The **second-level domain** is the part of a domain name, to the left of the dot, assigned to a specific server or website.

A **server** is a computer connected to the Internet that serves information and services to users.

The **top-level domain** is the part of a domain name, to the right of the dot, that identifies the type of website or server.

The **uniform resource locator (URL)** is the full address of a website or server, including the protocol identifier and the resource name.

A **web browser,** such as Microsoft's Internet Explorer, is a piece of software used to browse the web.

A **web page** is a single document on the web, typically housed on a website.

A **website** is an organized collection of pages on the web.

The **World Wide Web** is a collection of linked websites and pages hosted on servers connected to the Internet.

1.2 BROADBAND VS. DIAL-UP

Dial-Up Connections

Broadband Connections

The first step toward surfing the web is to establish a connection between your computer and an **Internet service provider (ISP).** Different ISPs offer different ways to connect.

The two primary types of connections are **dial-up** and **broadband.** Dial-up is the older and much slower technology, while broadband connections are significantly faster.

◀ *SEE ALSO 1.3, "Choosing an Internet Service Provider"* ▶

Dial-Up Connections

In years past, dial-up was the only type of connection available. A dial-up connection works by connecting your PC to a normal phone line using a piece of hardware called a **modem.**

A modem—internal or external—is so named because it modulates and demodulates transmitted data. (The word "modem" comes from the *mo* in modulate and the *dem* in demodulate.) The modulating process involves taking the digital signal from your computer and then modulating it into an analog signal to transmit the data over the analog medium of the phone line. Demodulation is the same process in reverse, as analog information is demodulated into digital pulses and fed back into a computer.

The modem, which physically connects between your PC and your phone line, dials in to your ISP and logs in to your personal account. Your ISP plugs the signal from your computer into the Internet so that your computer is now connected to the Internet through your ISP. When you're done surfing the web, you disconnect from the ISP by essentially hanging up the phone line.

Dial-up connections are less than ideal for two reasons. First, you have to connect and disconnect to the ISP manually; you don't have an always-on connection. This makes sharing a connection over a home network problematic, as you need to be connected all the time—and you can't make or receive phone calls when you're online.

Second, and most important, a dial-up connection is extremely slow—transferring data at no more than 56.6 kilobytes per second (Kbps). Given the increasing size of files found on most web pages today, the 56.6 Kbps dial-up pipeline isn't big enough to download everything instantaneously. This results in web pages that take a very long time to load and e-mails with large attachments that take forever to reach your inbox.

The slow speed of a dial-up connection also makes it impractical for some web-based activities. For example, the large file sizes associated with streaming video from sites such as YouTube make it next to impossible to watch video on a dial-up connection. Likewise, a dial-up connection is simply not fast enough to enable participation in real-time online games.

Broadband Connections

In the late 1990s, slow dial-up connections began to be supplanted by faster broadband connections. Unlike an analog dial-up connection, a broadband connection is an end-to-end digital connection. When you don't have to modulate and demodulate the data from digital to analog (and back again), the all-digital data can travel much faster from your computer to other points on the Internet.

Broadband connections are most commonly available from either your telephone company, via what is called a **digital subscriber line (DSL)** connection, or your cable company via **cable Internet.** Broadband speeds are considerably faster than dial-up connections, 3 Mbps (3,000 Kbps) or more for DSL and 6 Mbps or more for cable Internet. At the lowest speeds, a DSL connection is 60 times faster than a dial-up connection—and most cable Internet connections are 120 times faster!

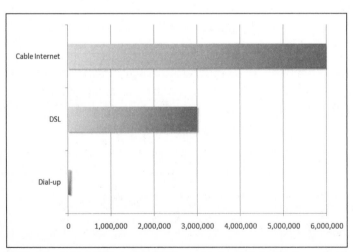

Comparing dial-up, DSL, and cable Internet connection speeds.

In addition to speed, a broadband connection is an always-on connection. You don't have to manually connect and log on when you want to go online, which makes using the Internet much more convenient.

For both of these reasons, a broadband connection is better for sharing on a home network than is a dial-up connection. If you try to share a dial-up connection, you'll need to dial in to and log on to your ISP every time someone on the network wants to go online. At best this makes connecting inconvenient; at worst it may prevent some computers on your network from connecting if your main PC isn't first logged on. And if you try to share a too-slow connection, there simply won't be enough bandwidth available for multiple PCs to comfortably share.

◄ *SEE ALSO 1.4, "Connecting to the Internet"* ►

WORDS TO GO . . . WORDS TO GO . . . WORDS TO GO

A **broadband** Internet connection is a faster connection than dial-up, typically made via cable or DSL technology.

Cable Internet is a broadband technology that enables fast Internet connections.

A **dial-up** Internet connection is made via traditional phone lines and is limited to 56.6Kbps.

Digital subscriber line (DSL) technology uses standard phone lines to create a broadband Internet connection.

An **Internet service provider (ISP)** is a company that connects individual users to the Internet backbone—for a fee.

A **modem** is a piece of equipment used to connect a computer to the Internet by modulating and demodulating an analog signal to and from a digital format.

1.3 CHOOSING AN INTERNET SERVICE PROVIDER

Choosing Between Dial-Up and Broadband

Choosing a Broadband Technology

Price

Not all Internet service providers are created equal. Some provide faster service, some charge a lower price, some offer additional features, and some come with excellent technical support. When it comes time to choose an ISP—or to switch from your existing one—you have to consider a variety of factors and make the best choice for your particular needs.

Choosing Between Dial-Up and Broadband

The first decision you have to make is how you want to connect—via dial-up or broadband? While dial-up providers may offer a slight pricing advantage in some areas, dial-up connections are on the decline. That's because most users need the faster broadband connection to watch videos and listen to music online, download large files and large e-mail attachments (including digital photos), play real-time online games, and browse sophisticated websites.

In fact, many broadband ISPs offer service plans that are no more expensive than those available from most dial-up ISPs. If broadband is available in your area, that is the recommended type of connection to get.

Choosing a Broadband Technology

As you recall, there are two primary types of broadband technology—DSL and cable Internet. Which of these is best for your particular needs? Here are some factors to consider when performing your evaluation.

◄ SEE ALSO 1.2, *"Broadband vs. Dial-Up"* ►

Availability

Not all types of broadband are available in all areas; you may only have access to one type of service where you live. For example, DSL is available only for those homes that are within a set distance from your phone company's central office; if you live too far away, you can't get a DSL connection. You'll need to see what's available before you make a decision.

As to what companies offer service in your area, the general rule of thumb is to contact your cable company for cable Internet and your telephone company for DSL. Other providers may also operate in your area, but these are good places to start.

1.3

WARNING . . .WARNING . . .WARNING

Some rural areas may not have cable service and may be too distant to receive DSL service. While dial-up is always an option in this scenario, you can get faster speeds by going with a satellite-based Internet connection—presuming that you have a clear sightline to the satellite, that is. (That means no trees or buildings in the way.) Satellite Internet connections reach speeds of 1.5 Mbps (faster than dial-up but a little slower than other forms of broadband) and are available from HughesNet (www.hughesnet.com) and WildBlue (www.wildblue.com).

Installation

The easiest type of broadband to install is digital cable; in most cases, you can plug in a cable modem yourself without the need for professional installation. DSL installation is a little more complex, sometimes requiring a visit from your local telephone company. If you're looking for easy installation, ask what's involved before you make your choice.

Speed

The fastest type of connection available in most areas is cable Internet. DSL is typically a little slower—but still much faster than traditional dial-up connections. Some ISPs offer different connection speeds at different prices; so-called high-performance plans may double or even triple the basic connection speed. A high-performance plan may be just the thing if you watch a lot of movies online or download a lot of big music files. You should subscribe to the tier that offers the best compromise between speed and price for your needs.

Price

How much should you pay for your Internet service? It all depends on the type of service and speed offered.

Dial-up ISPs typically offer service for $20 to $30 per month. Broadband service can often be found for anywhere from $30 to $60 per month, depending on the connection speed. Look for introductory specials in which the monthly rate is lower for a period of time; in addition, some cable and phone companies will offer package plans with a discount if you also subscribe to their other services (cable television, landline phone, and so forth).

1.4 CONNECTING TO THE INTERNET

Get the Info

Connect via Dial-Up

Connect via Broadband

Configure Your PC

Make the Connection

To connect your computer to the Internet, either via dial-up or broadband, you need to establish an account with an Internet service provider. You also need some kind of modem, either a dial-up modem or a broadband modem. Most PCs have dial-up modems built in; if you have a broadband account, your ISP will probably supply the broadband modem.

Once you're signed up with your ISP, you then have to connect the modem to your PC and configure your PC for the new connection. Let's take a brief tour through all the steps necessary to get you signed up and connected.

◀ SEE ALSO 1.2, *"Broadband vs. Dial-Up"* ▶

Get the Info

When you sign up with an ISP, both you and the ISP have to provide certain information to each other. You provide your name, address, and credit card number, and your ISP provides a variety of semi-technical information, including the following:

▶ Your desired username and password

▶ Your assigned e-mail address (in the form of *xxx@xxx.xxx*)

▶ The names of the ISP's incoming and outgoing mail servers (which you need to plug into your e-mail program)

▶ Your e-mail POP account name and password

▶ If you have a dial-up account, the phone number to dial in to—typically a local number for your area

For most ISPs, your username, e-mail name, and POP account name (along with the first half of your e-mail address) will be the same name. It's also likely that you will be assigned a single password for both your initial login and POP e-mail access.

Connect via Dial-Up

Since a dial-up connection is made through your normal telephone line, you want to make sure your computer is situated near a phone jack. Connect a phone cable between the phone line and the input connector on your modem; you can then connect a second phone cable between the output of your modem and your telephone, if that phone is in use.

If you have an internal modem, this is all you need to do. If your computer uses an external modem, you'll need to connect the modem to your PC (typically via a USB port on the back of your computer) and then install the modem. Follow the instructions that came with the modem for more details.

Connect via Broadband

One of the noticeable differences between dial-up and broadband is that you don't connect your phone (DSL) or cable line to the standard modem built into your PC. Instead, you use an external DSL or cable modem supplied by your ISP. This modem connects between your PC and the connection source. In the case of a DSL modem, it connects to any phone jack in your house; in the case of a cable modem, it connects to any cable jack. The modem typically connects to your PC via either USB or Ethernet.

You'll probably have the choice of doing the installation yourself or having your ISP do the job for you. Professional installation is nice but not always necessary. In most instances, you can opt to receive the modem via mail and make all the connections yourself. It's really just a matter of connecting the proper cables and running an installation CD; in a perfect world, the installation software configures the necessary network settings within Windows to recognize the new connection, and you're up and ready to surf—typically in less than a half hour.

Configure Your PC

Once you have your modem connected, you need to configure your computer to work with your ISP. If your ISP provides installation software, all you have to do is run this installation program. If your ISP doesn't provide installation software, you'll have to configure your computer manually.

In Windows Vista and Windows 7, you do this by clicking the Start menu and selecting Connect To. When the Connect to a Network dialog box appears, click Set Up a Connection or Network, then follow the onscreen directions from there.

In Windows XP, you set up a dial-up connection using the Network Connection Wizard. You start this wizard by clicking the Network and Internet Connections icon from the Control Panel.

Configuring a Mac running OS X is equally easy. Click the System Preference icon from the dock; when the System Preferences window opens, click Network. Then when the Network window opens, select the type of connection you have and proceed from there.

Make the Connection

When your system is properly connected and configured, it's time to connect to the Internet. If you have a dial-up connection, you typically do this by launching any Internet application, such as Internet Explorer or Windows Mail. When the application launches, Windows automatically dials your ISP and establishes a connection. (Alternately, your ISP may have provided its own connection software; if so, launch that software to establish a dial-up connection.)

Connecting is easier if you have a broadband connection. Unlike a dial-up connection, which requires you to manually connect to your ISP whenever you want to go online, a broadband connection is always on. That is, whenever your broadband modem is turned on and connected to your PC, you are automatically connected to your ISP. Using the Internet is as simple as launching any Internet software such as your web browser or e-mail program. Since you have an "always on" connection, the Internet is always there, waiting for you to use it.

1.5 CREATING USERNAMES AND PASSWORDS

Create Strong Passwords

Keep Your Passwords Personal

Usernames and passwords are everywhere. When you sign up for an account with an Internet service provider, you have to choose a username and password for your account. You also have to choose usernames and passwords for many of the websites that you visit. For that matter, you should also create a username and password for your personal account in Windows itself. All your important accounts need to be password protected.

◀ *SEE ALSO 1.3, "Choosing an Internet Service Provider"* ▶

How do you manage all these usernames and passwords? And how do you make sure your passwords are secure? Given how many passwords a typical user has to deal with on any given day, this is an important topic.

Create Strong Passwords

The stronger the passwords you create, the less likely they are to be guessed or cracked. Computer hackers use special software to "guess" different password combinations; if the software cracks your password, the hacker can gain access to your accounts.

So when you're creating a username and password for an online account or website, you want to create a password that is not easily cracked. The stronger the passwords you create, the safer your personal data will be.

A strong password is one that is not easily guessed. Believe it or not, many users use the password **password** or use other common words that are easily guessed. For this reason, you should not use easily guessed words such as your middle name, your wife's maiden name, or the name of your dog or cat. You should also not use any common identifiers such as your birth date or the last four digits of your Social Security number. It's better to use nonsense words or random combinations of letters and numbers—anything that isn't found in a dictionary. Make the password as nonsensical as you can while still being able to remember it.

To make an even stronger password, increase its length. Remember, eight characters is better than six—and way better than four. You should also use a combination of letters, numbers, and special characters (!@#$%), the better to create nonsensical passwords.

One approach to creating a memorable but unguessable password is to think of a passphrase—a complete sentence or string of words that mean something to you. Then use the first letter of each word to create the password followed by a relevant number. For example, you may think of the passphrase "my dog spot is 3 years old." If you take the first letter of each word, you get the password **mdsi3yo**; add Spot's birth year and you get **mdsi3yo2005**. Not very easy to guess, but not impossible to remember either.

Keep Your Passwords Personal

Most important, you should never share your password with anyone. As blatantly obvious as that sounds, many people feel no compunction about providing others with their passwords, especially if the person asking appears to be in a position of authority. This is a huge security risk; your password is yours and yours alone and should never be shared or compromised.

The practice of gaining access to passwords by gaining the trust of the user is called **social engineering.** It may take the form of a phone call or e-mail from someone purporting to be from your ISP or your company's IT department, asking you to confirm your user ID and password. When you reply, the budding social engineer on the other end of the line now has the information he or she needs to directly access your computer. For this reason, you should *never* give out your password, no matter how official sounding the request.

SEE ALSO 3.5, *"Protecting Against Phishing Scams"*

Similarly, you should never leave your password (or a list of passwords) sitting openly on your desk, either at home or at work. Many security breaches come from strangers spotting users' passwords written on sticky notes in open offices. While posting your password on your computer monitor might make things easy for you, it also makes things easier for password thieves. Don't do it.

WORDS TO GO . . .WORDS TO GO . . .WORDS TO GO

Social engineering is the practice of gaining access to passwords or other private information by gaining the trust of the user.

1.6 SHARING A CONNECTION ON A HOME NETWORK

Sharing with a Wireless Router

Sharing with a Combination Router/Modem

Enabling Wireless Security

If you have a broadband Internet connection and a wireless home network, you can share that Internet connection between all the computers in your household. It's an easy process.

Sharing with a Wireless Router

For most users, the easiest way to share an Internet connection is to use the ISP's broadband modem and your own wireless **router.** Follow these general steps:

1. Connect the appropriate cable between the cable/DSL wall outlet and the broadband modem.

2. Connect an Ethernet cable between your broadband modem and your wireless router. Most routers have a dedicated "modem in" connection, although you can connect the cable to any Ethernet port on your router.

3. Connect an Ethernet cable between the wireless router and your main PC.

4. Configure the wireless router for network use, using the unit's accompanying installation software.

5. Configure each computer on your network for a broadband connection, as described previously.

◀ SEE ALSO 1.4, *"Connecting to the Internet"* ▶

Once you've set everything up, any computer connected to your wireless network should have automatic access to your Internet connection.

Sharing with a Combination Router/Modem

Some broadband ISPs provide subscribers with a combination wireless router/modem. This single piece of equipment serves as both your broadband modem and your wireless network router, which makes connecting things much simpler.

◀ SEE ALSO 1.3, *"Choosing an Internet Service Provider"* ▶

In this setup, you run the cable or DSL cable from the wall outlet to the router/modem. The router/modem doesn't need to be physically connected to any PC; it automatically beams the Internet connection to all your wireless computers—and also manages all data transfer and communications on your home network.

The advantage of this approach, of course, is that you only have one piece of equipment instead of two (separate router and modem). In addition, this device is often provided free (or at a reduced rate) by your cable or DSL company so you don't have to purchase your own wireless router.

Enabling Wireless Security

One of the risks inherent with a wireless Internet connection is having neighbors or other unauthorized users tap into the connection—or, even worse, gain access to the data on your personal computers. You can keep your connection secure from unauthorized access by enabling wireless security on your wireless router.

◖ SEE ALSO 3.1, *"Protecting Against Computer Attack"* ▶

This is done by assigning to your wireless network a fairly complex encryption code called a network key. In order to access your network and your Internet connection, a computer must know the code—which, unless it's officially part of your network, it won't.

There are several ways to assign a network key to your network. Most wireless routers come with configuration utilities that let you easily activate this type of wireless security, typically during the router's installation/setup process. In addition, you can use Windows' built-in wireless security function, which adds the same encryption via the operating system.

There are four primary types of wireless security in use today:

▶ **WPA2.** WPA stands for **WiFi** Protected Access, and the new WPA2 standard offers the strongest level of security available today. With WPA2 (and the older WPA standard), network keys are automatically changed on a regular basis.

▶ **WPA.** This is the older, slightly less secure version of WiFi Protected Access security.

▶ **WEP 128-bit.** WEP stands for Wired Equivalent Privacy. There are two levels of WEP protection, the stronger 128-bit and the weaker 64-bit.

▶ **WEP 64-bit.** This is the weakest level of wireless protection available. If you have an older laptop PC or wireless adapter, you may have to use this level of protection instead of WEP 128-bit or WPA/WPA2.

You should choose the highest level of protection supported by all the equipment on your network—your wireless router, wireless adapters, and notebook PCs. If just one piece of equipment doesn't support a higher level of security, you have to switch to the next highest level; the security level you choose has to fit the lowest common denominator, as defined by the wireless equipment in use. Check the instruction manual for each piece of equipment to determine its top level of wireless security.

So if your wireless router and all your wireless adapters and notebook PCs support WPA or WPA2 encryption, you should switch to that method because it provides the strongest protection. Otherwise, choose either WEP 128-bit (preferred) or WEP 64-bit encryption.

WORDS TO GO . . .WORDS TO GO . . .WORDS TO GO

A **router** is a piece of equipment that connects together all the computers on a network; wireless networks use wireless routers.

WiFi is the 802.11x wireless networking standard used in home and public networks.

1.7 CONNECTING TO A PUBLIC WIFI HOTSPOT

Finding a Hotspot

Make the Connection

If you have a notebook PC, you can connect to the Internet when you're out and about simply by using one of the many available public WiFi **hotspots.** A hotspot is a location that offers either free or paid wireless Internet access. When you connect your notebook PC to a hotspot, you connect to the Internet.

Your notebook PC connects to the access point via WiFi using its built-in wireless adapter, just as it does to your home wireless network. Most hotspots have a 200- to 300-foot range, which is good enough to cover most retail locations—and maybe even extend out into the street a bit.

Finding a Hotspot

There are literally hundreds of thousands, if not millions, of public WiFi hotspots across the United States alone, and at least that many around the rest of the world. That doesn't mean you can stand out in the middle of a street and expect to find WiFi access, however; you still have to know where to look if you want to wirelessly connect.

Probably the easiest place to find a WiFi connection is at your local coffeehouse. Most large coffee chains (such as Starbucks and Caribou Coffee) offer WiFi access, as do many local independent coffeehouses.

Most major U.S. hotel chains today also offer some sort of Internet access to their paying guests. The type of access offered depends on the chain—and, in many cases, the individual location. Access can be free or provided for an additional daily charge—typically $10/day or so. If the access is free, expect to receive an access number or password when you check in. If the access is paid, you can probably put it on your hotel bill; if not, you'll need to provide a credit card number to log on.

If you can't find a WiFi coffeehouse or hotel, you can always stop by your local FedEx Office (formerly FedEx Kinko's) location. Most FedEx Office stores offer Internet-connected PCs for rental as well as wireless Internet access for your notebook.

In addition, many airports and train stations offer some form of WiFi access to their waiting travelers. Airport access varies from airport to airport; some airports offer free access throughout the entire terminal, some offer paid access only, and some offer access only in kiosks or at designated gates or public areas. You also may find WiFi access (typically free) in the club rooms offered by many airlines. When in doubt, turn on your PC and see what's available.

Interestingly, many public locations today are starting to offer free or paid WiFi access. For example, many big convention centers are wired for wireless, meaning you can connect to the Internet when you're attending a trade show, expo, or business conference. Ask your event organizer what type of access (if any) is available.

Another type of public WiFi hotspot is provided by some cities and towns. This type of citywide wireless Internet access can be either paid or free; if free, it's typically advertiser supported. (That means you get a banner ad in your web browser when you log on.)

Still not sure where to find a WiFi hotspot? You can search by location at one of these WiFi directories:

▶ JiWire (www.jiwire.com)

▶ Total Hotspots (www.totalhotspots.com)

▶ WiFi FreeSpot Directory (www.wififreespot.com)

▶ WiFinder (www.wifinder.com)

Make the Connection

Once you've found a public WiFi hotspot, how do you connect and access the Internet? Follow these general steps:

1. Enable your notebook's wireless adapter. Some notebooks have a switch on the front or side or use a particular keyboard key or combination of keys to turn on and off wireless functionality. Read your notebook's instruction manual to find the wireless adapter's on/off mechanism and then turn it on.

2. Select a hotspot. With the internal WiFi adapter working, your notebook automatically detects all wireless access points and routers in the immediate area; you then identify the particular public hotspot to which you want to connect. For example, in Windows Vista, you connect to a WiFi hotspot by opening the Windows Start menu and selecting Connect To; in Windows XP, right-click the network connection icon in the system tray and then select Connect to a Network. When the Connect to a Network window appears, identify and select the desired wireless network and then click Connect. (The Mac OS should automatically recognize a nearby hotspot and ask you if you want to connect.)

3. Set the network location (Windows Vista and Windows 7). The first time you connect to a network with Windows Vista and Windows 7, you're prompted to set a network location. When connecting to a public hotspot, select Public.

4. Log on to the hotspot. Being connected to a hotspot is not the same as obtaining full access; you may have to manually log on to the hotspot to use it. Typically, you do this by opening your web browser and going to your designated home page. The hotspot senses this and intercepts your command, instead displaying its own logon page. At this point, you need to enter any requested information to initiate the connection and start browsing the Internet. If, however, you open your browser and go directly to your normal home page, then no logon is required.

WARNING . . . WARNING . . . WARNING .

Not all hotspots are free. Some public hotspots charge for use by the hour, the day, or the month. If you're accessing a paid hotspot, you'll need to provide a credit card number and select a billing option.

WORDS TO GO . . . WORDS TO GO . . . WORDS TO GO

A **hotspot** is a public location that offers wireless Internet access.

2

SURFING THE WEB

2.1 CHOOSING A WEB BROWSER

Internet Explorer

Mozilla Firefox

Google Chrome

Opera

Safari

The World Wide Web is the most popular part of the Internet. The web is a collection of web pages hosted on websites; each page is linked to other pages via clickable **hyperlinks.**

You access web pages via use of a software program called a **web browser.** All browsers work pretty much the same way; you enter the URL for a web page into the browser's Address bar, then the browser displays that web page. All the content of a web page is displayed in the browser window, including text, graphics, videos, animations, and the like.

◀ SEE ALSO 1.1, "How the Internet Works" ▶

The most popular web browser today is Microsoft's Internet Explorer, but it's not the only browser available. Most browsers have similar features, but some users prefer one over another.

Internet Explorer

Internet Explorer (IE) is the web browser built into the Microsoft Windows operating system. The first version of IE was released in 1995, and it competed with then-popular browsers such as Netscape Navigator and Mosaic. IE eventually beat all competitors to become the most popular web browser available, with more than 70 percent market share.

The most recent version of IE is Internet Explorer 8, which adds new features to previous versions of the browser. IE8 features tabbed browsing so that multiple web pages can be opened in the same browser window. It also offers a pop-up window blocker, protection against phishing sites, and an InPrivate mode that enables private and anonymous browsing of the web.

Internet Explorer 8.

You can download Internet Explorer for free at www.microsoft.com/windows/ Internet-explorer/.

◁ SEE ALSO 2.2, *"Using Internet Explorer"* ▷

Mozilla Firefox

The number-two web browser today is Mozilla Firefox. Many users praise Firefox for its advanced features and speed of operation.

Like Internet Explorer, Firefox offers tabbed browsing and a host of useful security features, including private browsing and a pop-up blocker. Firefox also offers a download manager for safer and more efficient downloading of files and programs from the Internet.

You can download Firefox for free at www.mozilla.com/firefox/.

Mozilla Firefox 3.1.

Google Chrome

The newest competitor in the browser wars is Google, with its Chrome browser. Chrome offers tabbed browsing, private browsing, a pop-up blocker, and speedy operation—especially when compared to Internet Explorer. The browser's streamlined interface drops the typical title bar and search box at the top of the window, freeing up valuable space to display web pages. (You use the address box to enter both URLs and search queries.)

The Chrome browser is specially designed for use with Google's many web-based applications. For example, when you use Chrome to open Google Docs or Google Calendar, the window drops all browser-specific features to appear like a standard application window. In addition, Chrome has Google Gears built in so that Google's web-based applications can be operated when you're not online.

◀ **SEE ALSO 9.2, "Understanding the Google Docs Suite"** ▶

You can download Chrome for free at www.google.com/chrome/.

Google Chrome.

Opera

Opera is an established web browser, currently at version 9.6. Like most browsers today, Opera features tabbed browsing and a pop-up blocker. Opera also offers the web-based Opera Link service, which lets you store and synchronize your bookmarks and history across multiple computers. You can download Opera for free at www.opera.com.

The Opera web browser.

Safari

If you have an Apple Macintosh computer, Apple's Safari web browser is built into the operating system. Safari offers an elegant iTunes-like interface, tabbed browsing, private browsing, and a built-in pop-up blocker. Also useful is Safari's AutoFill feature, which lets you enter personal information into online forms with the click of a button.

Safari is available for both Apple and Windows computers. Download it for free at www.apple.com/safari/.

The Windows version of Apple's Safari web browser.

WORDS TO GO . . .WORDS TO GO . . .WORDS TO GO

A **hyperlink** is a piece of text or a graphic on a web page that, when clicked, links to another page on the web.

A **web browser** is a software program that enables you to access the web and display specific web pages. Popular web browsers include Internet Explorer, Mozilla Firefox, Google Chrome, Opera, and Apple's Safari.

2.2 USING INTERNET EXPLORER

Browser Operations

Tabbed Browsing

Searching from the Browser

Given its status as the most popular web browser today, it's likely that Internet
Explorer is the browser you use. While basic browsing is quite easy, IE includes a
wealth of additional features that many users find valuable.

Browser Operations

All operations are accessed at the top of the browser window. Here you will find
the following:

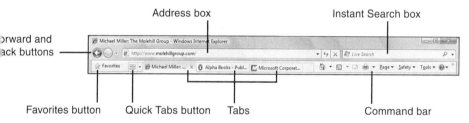

The key parts of the Internet Explorer interface.

> ► **Forward and Back buttons.** Click the Back button to redisplay the last-
> viewed web page. Click the Forward button to move forward again.

> ► **Address box.** Enter the URL of the web page you want to access, then
> press Enter. Click the Refresh button to reload the current web page; click
> the Stop button to halt the current page from loading.

> ► **Instant Search box.** Enter one or more queries to search the web. Click
> the down arrow next to the Instant Search box to select the default search
> engine such as Google or Windows Live Search.

> ► **Favorites button.** Click this button (the one with the star on it) to display
> the Favorites panel. Here you can add the current page to your Favorites
> list, view your favorite sites, view a history of recently visited sites, and
> view RSS feeds for your favorite blogs and news sites.

> ► **Quick Tabs button.** This is the far-left button on the row of tabs when
> you have multiple tabs open. Click it to display a grid of your most-visited
> web pages.

▶ **Tabs.** Each web page can be displayed in its own tab. Click a tab to see that web page, or click the empty tab at the right to enter a new URL.

▶ **Command bar.** This toolbar accesses all the features and operations of the browser. The Home button takes you to your designated home page; the Feeds button displays all RSS feeds on the current page; the Mail button launches your designed e-mail program; the Print button prints the current web page; the Page button displays a menu of operations related to the current web page; the Safety button displays a menu of security-related operations; and the Tools button displays a menu of browsing-related tools and operations.

Tabbed Browsing

Older versions of Internet Explorer feature a single-document interface—that is, each browser window can contain only a single web page. Internet Explorer 8, in contrast, has a multidocument interface, with multiple web pages displayed in a single browser window via the use of tabs, a feature called **tabbed browsing.**

The use of tabs within a single browser window lets you open multiple web pages simultaneously. This is great when you want to keep previous pages open for reference or want to run web-based applications in the background.

To open a web page on a new tab, just click the empty tab to the right of any open tabs and enter a URL into the Address box and press Enter. You can also choose to open a link within a page in a new tab by right-clicking the link and selecting Open in New Tab.

You switch between tabs by clicking a tab with your mouse or by pressing Ctrl+Tab on your keyboard. You can also reorder your tabs by dragging and dropping them into a new position.

You can view the contents of all open tabs with IE's Quick Tabs feature. When you click the Quick Tab icon or press Ctrl+Q, all open web pages are displayed as thumbnails in a single window. Click any thumbnail to open that tab in the full window.

Searching from the Browser

Normally, you search for information by going directly to a search site such as Google or Yahoo! In Internet Explorer, you don't have to visit the search site to perform a search; you can do all your searching from within the browser window by using the Instant Search box.

◀ *SEE ALSO 4.3, "Examining the Top Search Sites"* ▶

The Instant Search box is located next to the Address box at the top right of the browser window. To conduct a search from within the browser, just enter your query into the Instant Search box and press the Enter key on your keyboard. Your query is sent via IE over the Internet to the selected search provider. The search site receives the query, searches its own previously compiled index of web pages, and returns a page of search results, which is displayed in the Internet Explorer window.

By default, IE routes your search to Microsoft's Windows Live Search site. If you prefer to use another search engine, such as Google, you can change this default. Just click the down arrow next to the Instant Search box and select the desired search engine from the list.

SEE ALSO 4.4, "Searching with Google" ▶

If the search site you want isn't in this list, select Find More Providers from the pull-down menu. When the Search Providers web page appears, click the search engine you want to use. You can then return to the Find More Providers list to select this new search engine as your default.

WORDS TO GO . . .WORDS TO GO . . .WORDS TO GO

Tabbed browsing lets you open multiple web pages within a single browser window, each page displayed on its own tab.

2.3 BROWSING WEB PAGES

Internet Explorer, like all browsers, enables you to quickly and easily browse the World Wide Web. You can browse by entering the URL for a given page or by clicking a link to another page.

◀ *SEE ALSO 1.1, "How the Internet Works"* ▷

When you first launch Internet Explorer, it loads your predefined home page. You can return to your home page at any time by clicking the Home icon on the IE Command bar.

To set your home page, start by navigating to the page you wish to use as your home page. Then click the down arrow next to the Home icon and select Add or Remove Home Page. When the Add or Change Home Page dialog box appears, select Use This Webpage as Your Only Home Page and then click Yes. Alternately, you can create a series of tabs that open when you click the Home button.

To navigate to a specific web page, enter that page's URL into the Address box and press Enter. Internet Explorer loads the new page into the current tab. (To load a page into a new tab, first click the New Tab tab and enter the URL on the new tab.)

Most web pages contain links to other web pages. These links are typically underlined text, although images can also contain links. (Your cursor will change shape, to a pointing hand, when you hover over a link.) To jump to a linked page, click the link on the current web page. Internet Explorer now loads the new page into the current tab.

To return to the previous page viewed, click the browser's Back button. (Alternately, you can press the Backspace key on your keyboard.) If you've backed up several pages and want to return to the page you were on last, click the Forward button.

◀ *SEE ALSO 2.6, "Revisiting Your Browsing History"* ▷

2.4 BOOKMARKING FAVORITE PAGES

When you find a web page you like, you can add it to a list of favorite sites within Internet Explorer. This way, you can easily access any of these sites or pages just by selecting them from the list. IE calls this the Favorites list; other browsers call them bookmarks.

To add a page to your Favorites list, navigate to that page and then click the Favorites button. When the Favorites panel appears, click the Add to Favorites button. When the Add a Favorite dialog box appears, confirm the page's name and select the folder where you want to place this link. Then click OK.

You can, at any time, quickly jump to pages saved in your Favorites list. To display your Favorites, click the Favorites button. The Favorites pane now appears; select the Favorites tab.

Click the Favorites button to display the Favorites pane.

Your favorite sites are now displayed. Click any folder in the Favorites pane to display the contents of that folder. Click a favorite page to display that page in the browser window.

2.5 SAVING A WEB PAGE

If you find a web page you like, you can save it on your computer for future reference. There are several ways to do this.

First, you can save the page's URL to your Favorites list, as described previously.
Second, you can save a shortcut to the page on your computer desktop. To do
this in Internet Explorer, navigate to the page you want to save, right-click anywhere in an open area on the page, then select Create Shortcut from the pop-up
menu. When the confirmation dialog box appears, click Yes. IE now creates a
shortcut to this page on your desktop. Double-click this shortcut to launch Internet Explorer and navigate to the page.

◀ *SEE ALSO 2.4, "Bookmarking Favorite Pages"* ▶

The third way to save a web page is to literally save the contents of a page (text
and graphics) on your computer's hard disk. To do this, navigate to the page you
want to save, click the Page button in Internet Explorer, then select Save As.
When the Save Webpage dialog box appears, select where you want to save the
page and then click Save. To open the stored page (within Internet Explorer),
open the Documents folder, navigate to where you saved the page, and then
double-click the file icon.

2.6 REVISITING YOUR BROWSING HISTORY

Internet Explorer has three ways of keeping track of web pages you've recently visited so you can easily revisit them without having to reenter the web page address.

To revisit the last page you visited, click the Back button on the toolbar. You can continue clicking Back to go to the next-most-recent page you visited.

To revisit one of the most recent pages viewed in your current session, click the down arrow next to the Forward button. This drops down a menu containing the last 10 pages you've visited. Click any page on this menu to jump directly to that page.

To revisit pages you've viewed in the past several days, use IE's History feature. You can display your history by clicking the Favorites button to display the Favorites pane. In the new pane, select the History tab. Click a specific page to display that page in the main browser window.

You can sort the sites in the History list by date, site, most visited, or order visited today. You can also search your history list for specific sites by selecting the Search History option.

2.7 BLOCKING POP-UP WINDOWS AND PHISHING SITES

Pop-Up Blocker

SmartScreen Filter

The web is full of minor annoyances and major risks. The former category is typified by unwanted **pop-up windows** that appear when you navigate to certain websites. The latter category is represented by **phishing sites**—bogus websites that try to trick users into entering personal information.

Fortunately, most of today's web browsers include protection against both pop-up windows and phishing sites. We'll examine how Internet Explorer protects against these annoyances and risks.

Pop-Up Blocker

Until a few years ago, unwanted pop-up windows were legion. When you visited certain websites, all of a sudden you'd see a new, typically smaller window displayed on your desktop. This is a pop-up window, so-called because it pops up without you having to do anything; the process is automated via use of special code on the underlying web page.

Pop-up windows are extremely annoying, which is why most web browsers added pop-up blocker technology. With Internet Explorer, the pop-up blocker is enabled by default so that the automatic opening of unwanted pop-up windows is blocked.

When a site tries to open a pop-up window that is blocked by Internet Explorer, a notification appears in the Information bar of the browser window, just above the current web page. If you click the notification, you can choose to temporarily or permanently allow pop-ups from this site. If you ignore the notification, no further pop-ups will be allowed.

In some instances, pop-up windows are necessary. For example, a website might display additional useful information in a pop-up window—but if pop-ups are blocked, you won't see this info. To enable pop-ups from a specific website, click the Tools button and select Pop-up Blocker, Pop-up Blocker Settings. When the Pop-up Blocker Settings dialog box appears, enter the address of the specific website, then click the Add button. This site will now be added to a list of allowed sites for pop-ups.

SmartScreen Filter

One of biggest Internet-related dangers is identity theft, which is typically enabled by providing your personal information to an untrusted third party. One of the most popular scams involves a third party creating what is known as a phishing site, a site that looks like an another official site but in reality exists only to extract information from unsuspecting users.

For example, a site might be designed to look like the PayPal site. You're prompted to provide your personal information, including your name, address, bank account number, and the like. When you do so, that information is fed to the identity thief, who uses it for nefarious purposes.

SEE ALSO 3.5, "Protecting Against Phishing Scams" ▶

To protect you from phishing scams, IE8 incorporates a SmartScreen Filter. (In IE7, this was called the Phishing Filter.) This filter automatically connects to an online service that contains a huge database of suspicious websites and alerts you if you attempt to go to one of these sites.

If you attempt to click a link to a known phishing site, the SmartScreen Filter blocks access to the site, changes the Address bar to red, navigates to a neutral page, and displays a warning message. In other words, if the site is fraudulent, Internet Explorer won't let you go there.

In addition, the SmartScreen Filter helps protect you from sites that *might* be fake. If you attempt to click a link to a site that is not on the list of known fraudulent sites but behaves similarly to such sites, the SmartScreen Filter changes the Address bar to yellow and cautions you of potentially suspicious content. Unless you're sure the site is good, don't click through.

The SmartScreen Filter is enabled by default. You can also have the filter manually check any given website. Just click the Safety button and select SmartScreen Filter, Check This Website; the filter will check the site and display its findings in a new dialog box.

WORDS TO GO . . .WORDS TO GO . . .WORDS TO GO

A **phishing site** is a bogus website that tries to trick users into entering personal information.

A **pop-up window** is a typically unwanted web page in a browser window that opens automatically when a page is viewed. Pop-ups are typically used to display advertisements.

2.8 PRIVATE BROWSING

Managing Cookies

InPrivate Browsing

Even though you might do it in private on your personal computer, browsing the web is not a private affair. Every website you visit is automatically tracked, which makes it easy for interested parties—authorized or not—to recover your browsing activity. If you'd rather others not know what websites you visit, this is a disturbing realization.

Fortunately, there are ways to cover your tracks when you browse the web. **Private browsing** can now be a reality.

Managing Cookies

One way that your web browsing is tracked is via a small file called a **cookie.** Websites create and store cookie files on your computer's hard disk; these files contain information about you and your web activities.

For example, a cookie file for a particular site might contain your username, password, credit card information, and the most recent pages you visited on that site. The cookie file created by a site is accessed by that site each time you visit in the future, and the information is used however the site wishes.

A two-stage process is necessary to use a cookie. First, the website's server creates the cookie file and stores it on your computer, typically without your knowledge or consent. Second, when you next visit the website, the cookie file is uploaded to the site's web server, where the information is read and used accordingly.

Adjust the Privacy Level

If you value your privacy, you can control how cookies are created and stored on your computer. Internet Explorer lets you adjust the browser's privacy level to determine which types of cookies are automatically accepted—or rejected. You do this by clicking the Tools button and selecting Internet Options. When the Internet Options dialog box appears, select the Privacy tab. Adjust the slider to the privacy level you want and then click OK.

Internet Explorer has six levels of cookie management, ranging from accepting all cookies to declining all cookies:

▶ **Accept All Cookies.** Accepts all first-party and third-party cookies.

▶ **Low.** Accepts all first-party cookies but blocks third-party cookies from sites that don't have privacy policies. When IE is closed, automatically deletes third-party cookies from sites that use personal information without your implicit consent.

▶ **Medium.** When IE is closed, automatically deletes first-party cookies from sites that use personal information without your consent. Blocks third-party cookies from sites that don't have privacy policies or from sites that use personal information without your implicit consent.

▶ **Medium-High.** Blocks first-party cookies from sites that use personal information without your implicit consent. Blocks third-party cookies from sites that don't have privacy policies or from sites that use personal information without your *explicit* consent.

▶ **High.** Blocks all cookies from sites that don't have privacy policies or from sites that use personal information without your *explicit* consent.

▶ **Block All Cookies.** Blocks all new cookies. Existing cookies can't be read, even by the sites that created them.

Note that Internet Explorer differentiates between first-party and third-party cookies. A first-party cookie originates from the website you are currently viewing and is typically used to store your preferences regarding that site. A third-party cookie originates from a website different from the one you are currently viewing and is typically used to feed advertisements from separate ad sites to the current website. In general, third-party cookies are less desirable than first-party cookies.

The default setting is Medium, which pretty much blocks all advertising-related cookies and deletes any cookies that contain personal information when you close Internet Explorer. If you'd rather no website store any personal information you haven't explicitly approved, choose the High setting.

Delete All Cookies

Internet Explorer also lets you automatically delete all the cookie files stored on your computer. This is useful if you want to erase all tracks of the websites you've visited; with no cookie files, your employer or spouse won't know your browsing history. To delete all cookie files, click the Safety button and select Delete Browsing History. When the Delete Browsing History dialog box appears, check the Cookies option and click Delete.

By the way, you can also use the Delete Browsing History dialog box to delete your temporary Internet files (cache), browsing history, form data, and any website passwords you've entered.

InPrivate Browsing

If you like the convenience of cookies but don't want a specific browsing session recorded, you can use Internet Explorer 8's new InPrivate Browsing feature to browse completely anonymously. With InPrivate Browsing enabled, no record of the pages you visit are kept via any means, cookies or otherwise. No one need know where you've been on the web.

To enable InPrivate Browsing, click the Safety button on the Command bar and select InPrivate Browsing. This opens a new browser window with the InPrivate logo displayed in the Address bar. When you browse from an InPrivate window, IE stores no data about the web pages you visit; cookies, temporary files, and history are all disabled.

WORDS TO GO . . .WORDS TO GO . . .WORDS TO GO

A **cookie** is a small text file created by a website and stored on your computer; it records information about your site visit.

Private browsing is a mode of browsing in which no record is kept of the sites you visit.

2.9 USING BROWSER ADD-ONS

Toolbars

Other Add-Ons

Internet Explorer, by itself, is a powerful and versatile web browser. The browser, however, can be enhanced by the installation of various **add-ons**—auxiliary programs designed to view specific types of web-based content.

Toolbars

Some of the most popular browser add-ons are toolbars that install above the tabs in the browser window. These toolbars, typically from sites such as Google and Yahoo!, make it easier to use the various features of these sites.

For example, the Google toolbar (available at toolbar.google.com) features a search box and one-click access to Google News and other content. The eBay toolbar (available at pages.ebay.com/ebay_toolbar/) lets you search eBay auctions and view the status of your current bids.

WARNING . . .WARNING . . .WARNING

While toolbars from major websites are legitimate, some toolbars from lesser-known websites are actually a form of spyware, designed to report your browsing activity back to another site on the web. As such, you may need to run an anti-spyware program to completely get rid of these malware toolbars.

SEE ALSO 3.3, "Protecting Against Spyware"

To manage the toolbars installed in Internet Explorer, click the Tools button and select Toolbars. You can then check those toolbars you want displayed or uncheck those you want to disable.

Other Add-Ons

Other add-on programs can be managed from within Internet Explorer. In IE8, you manage all add-ons by clicking the Tools button and selecting Manage Add-Ons. This displays the Manage Add-Ons dialog box, where all add-ons are organized by type—toolbars and extensions, search providers, and accelerators, as well as InPrivate blocking lists and subscriptions. Select a tab to view all available add-ons of that type.

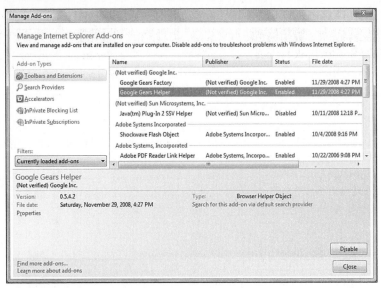

Managing browser add-ons in Internet Explorer 8.

You may need all of the add-ons currently running to view the variety of content currently available on the web—or you may not. For example, you might find that a particular website has installed an add-on to view content on its site, but that add-on is not necessary when visiting other sites. Single-site add-ons of this type can drain resources and cause your browser to run slower than normal.

Many users choose to strip their browsers of all but the most essential add-ons. This is done via the Manage Add-Ons dialog box; just select the add-on to remove and then click the Disable button.

Determining which add-ons to keep and which to disable is mainly a matter of trial and error; there are no universal recommendations. One user might want to disable the Shockwave Flash add-on, used to display animations and videos, while another user might balk at not having any Flash animations display in his browser. The key is whether you frequently visit sites that use a particular add-on; if not, you can speed up your web browsing by disabling that add-on.

If you're unsure of what an add-on does, consult the Manage Add-Ons dialog box. When you select an add-on, information about that program is displayed at the bottom of the dialog box. Click the Properties link in the information pane for even more details.

Table 2.1 presents some of the more common add-ons you may encounter.

TABLE 2.1   COMMON BROWSER ADD-ONS

Add-On	Description
Adobe PDF Reader Link Helper	Lets you view PDF files in the browser window instead of in the separate Acrobat Reader application
Google Gears Factory and Helper	Used to run web-based applications when offline
Java Plug-In SSV Helper	Enables the running of Java-based applications in the browser window
Shockwave Flash Object	Enables the running of Flash-based animations and videos in the browser window

2.9

WORDS TO GO . . . WORDS TO GO . . . WORDS TO GO

A browser **add-on** is a program that runs inside a web browser and is designed to provide additional functionality, typically in the form of viewing specific types of web page content.

3

PROTECTING YOURSELF — AND YOUR FAMILY — ONLINE

3.1 PROTECTING AGAINST COMPUTER ATTACK

Potential Threats

How High Is Your Risk?

Firewall Software

Using the Windows Firewall

Using the Mac OS X Firewall

Firewall Hardware

Anytime you're connected to the Internet, you're at risk for all sorts of malicious behaviors—**computer attacks,** viruses, spyware, identity theft, and the like. That's because connecting to the Internet is a two-way street: Your computer is connected to the global network, and the global network is connected to your computer. That means not only can your computer access other computers on the web, but other computers can also access your computer.

If other users can access your computer, they can also take that opportunity to read your private data, damage your system hardware and software, and even use your system (via remote control) to cause damage to other computers. This risk is even more pronounced if you have an always-on broadband connection; the risk is lower with dial-up connections because you're online for shorter periods of time.

To access your system, the only thing a vandal needs to know is your computer's Internet Protocol (IP) address, which is how all computers on the Internet are identified. Even though *you* might not know this address offhand, it's coded into every packet of data sent from your computer, so it's relatively easy to obtain. An attacker can then use the IP address to directly access your computer and do whatever he or she wants (and is enabled) to do.

◀ *SEE ALSO 1.1, "How the Internet Works"* ▶

Potential Threats

What is a computer attack? By definition, it's any operation executed with the intent to disrupt, deny, degrade, or destroy information on a computer or computer network. This type of attack takes place over the Internet, with the operation executed by a remote computer or a master computer controlling a network of hijacked **zombie computers.**

An attacker typically stumbles onto a computer by conducting a scan for systems that are relatively easy to break into. After infiltrating a system, what kind of damage can the attacker do? It's a long and scary list.

For example, an attacker can steal all the account information on your computer (including passwords) and then share that information with other attackers so they can target your system for future attacks. Not only can an attacker read or copy your data to other computers, he or she can also damage, destroy, or delete that data. In fact, any file on your computer could be wiped from existence—including your application programs and essential operating system files.

3.1

Sometimes, however, an attacker doesn't need to stick around to inflict damage. It takes very little time to download a virus onto your hard disk, programmed to execute at a later date. Most often, this type of virus configures your computer to carry out other attacks—effectively hijacking your computer to do the attacker's bidding. This is often how mass attacks are perpetrated on commercial websites, by an attacker operating hundreds of zombie computers by remote control. The advantage to the attacker, of course, is anonymity; when the attacks are traced, it's your computer that's fingered, not his.

Finally, an attacker can simply crash your system. Even with a broadband connection, your bandwidth is finite. Imagine your computer being bombarded with thousands of tiny messages all at once, and you can see how an attacker can clog your bandwidth and bring your system to its knees. (This is called a **denial-of-service attack** and is more often targeted at large companies and websites than at individual PCs.)

How High Is Your Risk?

In most instances, computer attacks are directed at large computer networks or websites, typically by an individual with a grudge against the organization attacked. Malicious attacks against individual computers are more rare but not unheard of, again especially if the attacker has a grudge against the victim of the attack.

Your risk of attack depends a lot on who you are and what you do. In essence, attackers like to go after large and visible targets. It's a matter of efficiency and effectiveness; why go through all the effort to mount a large attack just to bring down a single home computer? The effort is better spent on a larger target, one that will bring more notoriety to the attacker.

That's not to say, of course, that smaller companies and individuals are completely safe from attack. Some attackers like to infiltrate individual systems and small networks to hijack the computers they use for larger attacks. Do you really want your personal computer turned into a zombie that is used to commit a larger computer crime?

The threat is real, even to individuals. Computer attackers can and do attack household-based personal computers—which means you need to be prepared to defend your system.

Firewall Software

How do you stop a malicious individual from trying to attack your computer or home network? The only surefire solution is to disconnect your computer from the Internet, but that's not very practical for most users. A better solution is to use a **firewall** program to protect your system from attack. A firewall is a piece of software placed between your computer or network and the Internet that blocks unauthorized inbound traffic, thus insulating your system from any potential attack.

A firewall functions like a guard at a door—it lets good visitors in and keeps bad visitors out. In the case of your computer system, good visitors are the normal e-mail communications and web pages you visit; bad visitors are attackers trying to bomb or infiltrate your system.

Most personal firewall software is relatively inexpensive (under $50), is easy to install, and operates in the background whenever you start your computer and connect to the Internet. The best of these programs not only block unauthorized access, but also create a log of all computers that try to attack your system—and alert you of any successful attempts.

The most popular personal firewalls include the following:

- ▶ CA Personal Firewall (www.casecuritystore.com)
- ▶ Comodo Firewall Pro (www.personalfirewall.comodo.com)
- ▶ eConceal Pro (www.mwti.net)
- ▶ InJoy Firewall (www.fx.dk/firewall/)
- ▶ Norman Personal Firewall (www.norman.com)
- ▶ Online-Armor Personal Firewall (www.tallemu.com)
- ▶ Outpost Firewall PRO (www.agnitum.com/products/outpost/)

▶ PC Tools Firewall Plus (www.pctools.com/firewall/)

▶ Sunbelt Personal Firewall (www.sunbelt-software.com/
Home-Home-Office/Sunbelt-Personal-Firewall/)

▶ WebRoot Desktop Firewall (www.webroot.com)

▶ ZoneAlarm Pro (www.zonealarm.com)

Using the Windows Firewall

If you're running Windows Vista or Windows XP, you already have a firewall program installed on your system. The Windows Firewall is activated by default, although you can always check to make sure that it's up and working properly. In Windows Vista, open the Control Panel and select Security, Windows Firewall. When the Windows Firewall window appears, you can turn the firewall on and off, choose to allow particular programs through the firewall, or click Change Settings to configure the firewall's settings.

In Windows XP, open the Control Panel and go to the Windows Security Center. All Windows security settings are visible there, including those for the Windows Firewall.

Using the Mac OS X Firewall

The Apple OS X operating system also includes built-in firewall software to protect your computer from attack. The firewall should be activated to default. To activate it manually, open System Preferences and select Sharing. Next, click Firewall and then click Start. This will launch the firewall program on your computer.

Firewall Hardware

You can also protect your system from attack by using firewall hardware. This is a piece of equipment that sits between your computer or home network and your Internet connection and automatically stops any authorized traffic coming from the Internet.

If your computer is connected to a network, chances are your network router includes a firewall—and it's probably enabled by default. Check your router's instruction manual for more information on configuring the built-in firewall function.

◄ SEE ALSO 1.6, "Sharing a Connection on a Home Network" ▶

A **computer attack** is any operation executed over the Internet with the intent to disrupt, deny, degrade, or destroy information on a computer or computer network.

A **denial-of-service attack** occurs when multiple computers overload a particular computer or web server with thousands of messages at the same time.

A **firewall** is a piece of software or hardware that acts as a barrier between an individual computer or network and the Internet to prevent unwanted outside access.

A **zombie computer** is a computer that has been hijacked by a virus or spyware and used to attack another computer by remote control.

3.2 PROTECTING AGAINST COMPUTER VIRUSES

How Computer Viruses Work

How to Catch a Virus

Symptoms of Virus Infection

Practicing Safe Computing

Anti-Virus Programs

Your computer doesn't have to be physically attacked to suffer damage. Millions of computers each year are infiltrated by malicious software (**malware**)—and one of the most damaging types of malware is the **computer virus.**

A computer virus is a software program designed to do damage to your computer system by deleting files or even taking over your PC to launch attacks on other systems. A virus attacks your computer when you launch an infected software program, launching a "payload" that oftentimes is catastrophic.

Computer viruses represent one of the largest threats to both home and business computer users today; tens of millions of computers are infected by computer viruses every year. It's a simple fact—you must protect your computer against virus infection or risk the consequences.

How Computer Viruses Work

A computer virus is a rogue computer program that injects copies of itself into other programs on your computer system. Many viruses are so-called Trojan horses, hidden in the code of legitimate software programs—programs that have been infected, that is. When the host program is launched, the code for the virus is executed and the virus loads itself into your computer's memory. From there, the virus code searches for other programs on your system that it can infect; if it finds one, it adds its code to the new program, which, now infected, can be used to infect other computers.

Computer viruses can be destructive or simply annoying. Just as you try to protect your own body from biological viruses and find a cure when you become infected, you want to protect your computer from computer viruses and find a cure if your system ever becomes infected.

How to Catch a Virus

Viruses are spread by contact with other computers or data copied from other computers. So whenever you share data with another computer or computer user, you risk exposing your computer to potential viruses.

You can transmit a virus in many ways, including …

> ▶ Opening an infected file attached to an e-mail message or instant message.

> ▶ Launching an infected program file downloaded from the Internet.

> ▶ Sharing a data CD, USB memory drive, or floppy disk that contains an infected file.

> ▶ Sharing over a network a computer file that contains an infected file.

Of all these methods, the most common means of virus infection today is via e-mail—with instant messaging close behind. Whenever you open a file attached to an e-mail message or instant message, you stand a good chance of infecting your computer system with a virus—even if the file was sent by someone you know and trust. That's because many viruses "spoof" the sender's name, thus making you think the file is from a friend or colleague. The bottom line is that no e-mail or instant message attachment is safe unless you were expressly expecting it.

Almost as risky is the act of downloading files from so-called file-sharing sites or peer-to-peer (P2P) networks. Many files on these sites are infected with viruses, making music and video downloading quite dangerous indeed.

◀ *SEE ALSO 7.1, "Finding Music Online"* ▶

Symptoms of Virus Infection

Here's the big question: How do you know whether your computer system has been infected with a virus?

In general, whenever your computer starts acting different from normal, it's possible that you have a virus. For example, you might see strange messages or graphics displayed on your computer screen or find that normally well-behaved programs are acting erratically. You might discover that certain files have gone missing from your hard disk or that your system is acting sluggish—or failing to start at all. You might even find that your friends are receiving e-mails from you that you never sent, or that you're getting returned e-mails from people you've never heard of (a sure sign that your computer has been hijacked to send out reams of spam messages).

If your computer exhibits one or more of these symptoms—especially if you've just downloaded a file from the Internet or received a suspicious e-mail message—the prognosis is not good. Your computer is probably infected.

Practicing Safe Computing

The only surefire way to avoid the threat of computer viruses is to never use the Internet, never share homemade data CDs or USB drives, and never install a new piece of software on your PC. You can, however, be proactive in reducing the chance of downloading a virus from the Internet by following some specific advice, as detailed in the following sections.

Don't Open E-mail Attachments

Most virus infections today are spread via e-mail. The virus is typically encased in a file attached to an e-mail message; when you click to view or open the file, you launch the virus—and your computer is automatically infected.

To that end, the best way to reduce your risk of virus infection is to never open e-mail attachments, especially from people you don't know. But you also shouldn't open attachments from people you *do* know if you aren't expecting them. That's because some viruses can hijack the address book on an infected PC, thus sending out infected e-mails that the owner isn't even aware of. Click on any e-mail attachment and chances are your computer will be infected.

Don't Open Files Sent via Instant Messaging

The previous advice goes for any files sent to you via instant messaging. IM is a growing source of virus infection, if only because users (especially younger ones) are naturally trusting of other users. So don't accept any files sent to you via instant messaging; if a trusted friend really wants to send you a file, ask him or her to e-mail it to you—and then use normal caution before opening it.

◁ *SEE ALSO 13.2, "Instant Messaging"* ▷

Don't Click IM or Chat Links

If someone you don't know sends you a link to another site while you're instant messaging or in a chat room, don't click it! Nine times out of ten, this link either directly downloads a virus file to your PC or takes you to a website that has plenty of infected files to download. In any case, ignore the unsolicited links and you'll be a lot safer.

Don't Execute Files Found in Newsgroups or Message Boards

E-mail and instant messaging aren't the only channels for downloading virus-infected files. You can find plenty of infected files in web message boards, blogs, and Usenet newsgroups. For this reason, resist downloading programs you find in these channels; while many are safe, some are not.

◁ *SEE ALSO 11.5, "Using Usenet Newsgroups"* ▷

Download Programs Only from Reliable Sources

Many sites on the web host infected files. The owners of these sites are just waiting for naïve users to download the files so that their PCs can become infected. For this reason, you should avoid downloading files from sites with which you're not familiar.

Instead, download files only from reliable file archive websites such as Download.com (www.download.com) and Tucows (www.tucows.com). These sites scan all their files for viruses before making them available for downloading. It's the only safe way to download files from the Internet.

◁ *SEE ALSO 5.1, "Searching for Files and Programs Online"* ▷

Display and Check File Extensions

Certain types of files can carry virus infections; certain types of files can't. Consult Table 3.1 to find out which files are potentially dangerous and which aren't.

TABLE 3.1 TYPES OF FILES THAT CAN AND CAN'T CARRY COMPUTER VIRUSES

Safe File Types	Potentially Unsafe File Types
BMP	BAT
GIF	COM
JPG	DOC
MP3	DOT
MPEG	EXE
PDF	INF
QT	JS
TIF	REG
TXT	SCR
WAV	SYS

Safe File Types	Potentially Unsafe File Types
WMA	VB
	VBE
	VBS
	XLS
	XLW
	ZIP

3.2

To guard against the riskier file types, you need to configure Windows to display all file extensions, which you do via the Folder Options applet in the Windows Control Panel. You can then examine the extension of any file before you open it.

To configure the Mac OS X to display file extensions, click the desktop to activate the Finder, then select Finder, Preferences. When the Finder Preferences window appears, click the Advanced tab and check Show All File Extensions.

Anti-Virus Programs

If you're serious about protecting your computer against viruses, it's essential that you install and use an **anti-virus program.** Anti-virus programs vigilantly guard your system for any viruses that might arrive via file download or e-mail attachment, scan all the files on your system for hints of infection, and either clean or delete any files that have been found to be infected.

Most anti-virus programs work in a similar fashion, detecting known viruses and protecting your system against new, unknown viruses. These programs check your system for viruses each time your system is booted and can be configured to check any programs you download from the Internet. They're also used to disinfect your system if it becomes infected with a virus.

The most popular anti-virus programs for the home and small business include the following:

- ▶ AVG Anti-Virus (www.avg.com)
- ▶ CA Anti-Virus (www.casecuritystore.com)
- ▶ ESET NOD32 Anti-Virus (www.eset.com)
- ▶ F-PROT Anti-Virus (www.f-prot.com)
- ▶ F-Secure Anti-Virus (www.f-secure.com)
- ▶ Kaspersky Anti-Virus (www.kaspersky.com)
- ▶ McAfee VirusScan Plus (www.mcafee.com)

- Norman Anti-Virus & Anti-Spyware (www.norman.com)
- Norton Anti-Virus (www.symantec.com)
- Panda Anti-Virus (www.pandasecurity.com)
- Trend Micro Anti-Virus plus Anti-Spyware (www.trendmicro.com)
- Vexira Anti-Virus (www.centralcommand.com)

In addition, Microsoft plans to distribute a free anti-virus program starting in the second half of 2009. Check Microsoft's website (www.microsoft.com) for more information.

WARNING . . .WARNING . . .WARNING

Whichever anti-virus program you choose, you'll need to configure the program to go online periodically and update the virus definition database that the program uses to look for known virus files. Because new viruses are created every week, this file of known viruses must be updated accordingly.

WORDS TO GO . . .WORDS TO GO . . .WORDS TO GO

An **anti-virus program** is a piece of software designed to identity, block, and remove computer viruses.

A **computer virus** is a software program designed to do damage to your computer system.

Malware is a piece of malicious software such as a computer virus or spyware.

3.3 PROTECTING AGAINST SPYWARE

What Spyware Is—and How It Works

How to Become Infected with Spyware

Adware: A Special Kind of Spyware

Do You Have Spyware on Your System?

Anti-Spyware Programs

Similar to computer viruses is the malware called **spyware.** Spyware is a type of program that installs itself on your computer, typically without your knowledge or consent, and then surreptitiously sends information about the way you use your PC to some interested third party.

◄ *SEE ALSO 3.2, "Protecting Against Computer Viruses"* ▣

Having spyware on your system is nasty, almost as bad as being infected with a computer virus. The added load of spyware programs in your system's memory inevitably leads to sluggish performance at the very least. Some spyware programs do more than just slow down your system, instead hijacking your computer and launching pop-up windows and advertisements when you visit certain web pages. If there's spyware on your computer, you definitely want to get rid of it.

What Spyware Is—and How It Works

Spyware and viruses are similar but technically different. Like a Trojan horse virus, spyware typically gets installed in the background when you're installing another program. Unlike a virus, however, spyware doesn't replicate itself. Once it's installed, its job is to spy on your system, not to spread itself to other computers.

Spyware is characterized by the fact that it installs without your permission or with your permission based on misleading information. Once installed, it transmits data from your computer to a third-party computer, again without your knowledge or permission. In other words, spyware is a software program you didn't ask for from someone you don't know that does stuff you have no control over.

It's important to remember that a spyware program is a stealth program. It runs in the background, hidden from view, and monitors your computer and Internet usage. That could mean recording the addresses of each web page you visit, the addresses or contents of each e-mail you send or receive, the contents of all the instant messages you send or receive, or the contents of each chat room you visit. A spyware program can even record every keystroke you type with your computer keyboard—including usernames, passwords, and other personal information.

The information recorded by the spyware is typically saved to a log file. That log file, at a predetermined time, is transmitted (via the Internet) to a central source. That source can then aggregate your information for marketing purposes, use the information to target personalized communications or advertisements, or steal any confidential data for illegal purposes.

How to Become Infected with Spyware

Spyware can get onto your computer in many of the same ways that viruses infect your PC. Typical means of transmission include e-mail attachments, misleading links on websites, and files downloaded from the Internet.

That said, some of the biggest sources of spyware are peer-to-peer music-trading networks. Not legitimate online music stores such as Apple's iTunes Store, but rather rogue file-trading networks such as Blubster, eDonkey, and LimeWire. In many instances, spyware is actually attached to the file-trading software you have to download to use the network; when you install the software, the spyware is also installed.

◄ *SEE ALSO 7.1, "Finding Music Online"* ►

Another way to have spyware installed on your system is to be tricked into doing it. You go to a website, perhaps one mentioned in a spam e-mail message, and click on a link there. What you see next looks like a standard Windows dialog box asking you if you want to scan your system for spyware, or optimize your Internet browsing, or something similar. In reality, the "dialog box" is just a pop-up window designed to look like the real deal, and when you click the Yes button, you're authorizing the installation of spyware on your system. In some instances, clicking No also installs the software, so you're damned if you do and damned if you don't.

Finally, some spyware is installed through known security holes in the Internet Explorer browser. When you navigate to a web page controlled by the software author (again, typically from a link in a spam e-mail message), the page contains hidden code that exploits the browser's weaknesses and automatically downloads the spyware.

Adware: A Special Kind of Spyware

Some spyware, called **adware,** is actually used by advertisers and marketers. Like other types of spyware, adware is typically placed on your PC when you install some other legitimate software, piggybacking on the main installation. Once installed, the adware works like spyware, monitoring your various activities and reporting back to the host advertiser or marketing firm. The host firm can then use the collected data in a marketing-related fashion—totally unbeknownst to you, of course.

For example, adware might monitor your web surfing habits and report to the advertiser which sites you visit. The adware might pop up a window and ask for your demographic data, which it also reports back to the host. The adware might even use your personal data to generate its own targeted banner ads and display those ads on top of the normal banner ads when you visit other websites.

Adware is the type of spyware you most often encounter when you download software from P2P file-sharing networks; the adware is typically bundled as part of the network's client software. The P2P network generates revenue from the adware company, while the adware company generates revenues by serving you personalized ads or by selling the data it collects.

Do You Have Spyware on Your System?

Most spyware infections are recognizable by how they affect the performance of your system. Put simply, spyware tends to slow down operations on most computers—and sometimes worse. Some spyware programs can cause Internet Explorer to freeze or not work properly; others may actually cause your computer to crash. So if your computer is acting slowly or suspiciously, the usual suspect is some sort of spyware infection.

In particular, take notice if your computer exhibits any or all of the following behaviors—all symptomatic of a spyware infection:

> ▶ Your computer runs slow or exhibits other unusual problems, including system freezes and crashes.

> ▶ Your computer has a mind of its own—it sends e-mails to people in your address book without your knowledge or permission, or it shows a lot of hard disk activity or Internet access when you're not actively using it.

> ▶ Your computer's hard disk and/or network activities lights constantly blink or stay lit.

▶ You get a lot of returned or bounced-back e-mails, caused by the spyware program taking control of your e-mail program and using it to mail out loads of spam—without your knowledge or permission.

▶ You find that your web browser's home page has been changed to another site without your approval, or you see a strange new toolbar in your web browser.

▶ When you perform a web search, you end up at some strange site; many spyware developers like to send you to a site of their choosing whenever you perform a search.

▶ You get a lot of unexpected pop-up windows onscreen.

▶ You see one or more strange new sites in the Favorites section of your web browser.

As you can see, many of these symptoms are similar to what you might expect from a computer virus infection. Other symptoms are wholly unique to the world of spyware. In any instance, if your computer exhibits one or more of these symptoms, you need to run an **anti-spyware program.**

Anti-Spyware Programs

Fortunately, several companies offer anti-spyware programs that scan your system for known spyware. These programs work much the same way that anti-virus programs detect and remove computer viruses. Anti-spyware programs are designed to identify any and all spyware programs lurking on your computer and will also uninstall the offending programs and remove their entries from the Windows Registry.

Know, however, that spyware is different enough from a computer virus that most anti-virus programs won't detect spyware—and vice versa. While there are some exceptions (some of the major anti-virus programs have added anti-spyware components), you'll probably need to install an anti-spyware program *in addition to* an anti-virus program.

The most popular anti-spyware programs today include the following:

▶ Ad-Aware (www.lavasoftusa.com)

▶ CounterSpy (www.sunbelt-software.com)

▶ ParetoLogic Anti-Spyware (www.paretologic.com/products/paretologicas/)

▶ Spybot Search & Destroy (www.safer-networking.org)

▶ Spyware Doctor (www.pctools.com/spyware-doctor/)

▶ Webroot Spy Sweeper (www.webroot.com)

▶ Windows Defender (www.microsoft.com/athome/security/spyware/software/)

Most of these are low-cost (under $30) programs, and many of them are free. In addition to these standalone programs, some of the major Internet security suites, such as Norton Internet Security and the McAfee Internet Security Suite, include anti-spyware modules. Many of these companies also offer enterprise versions of their programs specifically designed for use in larger organizations.

Because most anti-spyware programs depend in part on a database of known spyware programs, it's important to keep this database of spyware definitions up-to-date. You'll need to configure your program to update its list of definitions on a regular basis—weekly at least, daily if possible.

WORDS TO GO . . . WORDS TO GO . . . WORDS TO GO

Adware is spyware used by advertisers and marketers.

An **anti-spyware program** is a piece of software designed to identity, block, and remove spyware programs.

Spyware is a type of program that installs itself on your computer and surreptitiously sends information about the way you use your PC to a third party.

3.4 PROTECTING AGAINST IDENTITY THEFT

How Do Identity Thieves Work?

What Happens When Your Identity Is Stolen?

How to Avoid Identity Theft Online

Inspect Your Credit Reports

When someone steals your personal identifying information—whether that be your credit card number, Social Security number, or ATM PIN—that constitutes a crime known as **identity theft.** This phrase is a catch-all term for any crime, no matter how minor, involving the illegal use of your individual identity in any form.

Identity theft can be the result of online negligence (responding to phishing e-mails or being the victim of a computer virus) or real-world theft (having your wallet stolen or credit card statements pilfered from your trash). However it's accomplished, the identity thief obtains one or more of your valuable numbers and then uses those numbers to access things that are yours—typically, your money.

◄ *SEE ALSO 6.3, "Shopping Safely"* ►

That's not to say that all identity theft crimes are financial in nature. Stolen Social Security numbers are often used by illegal immigrants to establish an official presence or obtain work; terrorists have been known to use stolen account and driver's license numbers to create false identities in a new community. In addition, identity theft can be used as a means of blackmail (the victim is forced to pay a ransom to avoid some form of embarrassment or to retrieve his stolen information) or in industrial espionage (to "fake" entrance into secure systems).

How Do Identity Thieves Work?

So how does a thief obtain your personal information? There are any number of ways—both online and offline. Online ID theft is facilitated by the fact that Internet communications travel over a public network; a tech-savvy ID thief can obtain access to your data by any one of several methods.

Phishing Scams

A phishing e-mail is one that purports to be from a real website or institution. The communication looks quite official, often using the official logo of the original firm.

What's fishy about the phishing e-mail is that it asks for some sort of interaction with the recipient, most often directing you to the host website via an embedded link in the e-mail itself. When the recipient clicks the link to go to the referenced website, however, it's not the real website. Instead, the scammer has created a clever forgery of the referenced site; it looks like the original but instead is hosted by the scammer. If the recipient proceeds to enter a password or personal information, that information is passed directly to the ID thief—and then used for various fraudulent activities.

3.4

◯ *SEE ALSO 3.5, "Protecting Against Phishing Scams"* ▶

E-mail Interception

It's possible for a tech-savvy scammer to intercept your private e-mails—including those that contain personal information. This can be done at either end of the communication or at the ISP's incoming or outgoing mail servers.

WiFi Data Sniffing

If you have a notebook PC, you've probably done some work at a public WiFi hotspot. If so, know that every bit of data you receive from the Internet or send via e-mail can be intercepted by thieves using special "sniffer" programs. These programs enable the thief to eavesdrop on all your incoming and outgoing communications, see all the websites you visit, and intercept any form of data you send to those websites. That means if you order something from an online retailer while at a public hotspot, your ordering info (including your credit card number) can be picked off by the WiFi-sniffing thief.

◀ *SEE ALSO 1.7, "Connecting to a Public WiFi Hotspot"* ▢

Surreptitious Spyware

Another way for a tech-savvy ID thief to pilfer your personal data is to install a Trojan horse–type computer virus or spyware program on your computer—without your knowledge, of course. This type of malicious software sits in the background, monitoring everything your computer does. When it finds something interesting, it goes online and transmits that data to the ID thief over the Internet.

WARNING . . .WARNING . . .WARNING

As scary as online ID theft is, data is much more frequently stolen the old-fashioned way—physically in the real world. There is simply more opportunity to steal private data offline than there is online. So make sure you protect all your essential information, whether you're online or not!

What Happens When Your Identity Is Stolen?

So someone gets hold of your credit card number, Social Security number, bank account number, or other personal information. What might the ID thief do with this data?

There's a long list of fraudulent activities an ID thief might engage in. A thief might withdraw some or all of the funds in your checking account or open a new bank account in your name and then write bad checks against that account. He might create (and then pass) counterfeit checks using your name and account number or take out a bank loan in your name, for which you are then responsible for paying. He might make unauthorized purchases against your credit card or open new credit card accounts in your name—and then make purchases that you're responsible for. He may even use your ID to rent an apartment, obtain utility services (such as electricity, gas, or cable television), or establish a new telephone or cell phone account in your name—and then rack up large numbers of expensive long-distance calls.

That's not all. A savvy identity thief can get a new driver's license issued in your name but with his or her picture. He can use your name and Social Security number to obtain government benefits or get a job (popular among illegal immigrants). If captured for any criminal activity, the ID thief can give the police your personal information—which puts your name on police records.

How to Avoid Identity Theft Online

Your first line of defense against identity theft is to become aware of the problem. When you know that ID theft exists and the many ways your information can be appropriated, you're well ahead of your less-informed contemporaries. Knowing what can happen and how makes you more alert—and less likely to fall victim to the most common forms of identity fraud.

Another key defense is deterrence. That means taking steps to safeguard your personal information, both online and in the physical world. There are many things that you can do, including the following:

▶ Password-protect your computer user account.

▶ Password-protect individual files, especially those that contain personal information.

▶ Install anti-virus and anti-spyware programs.

▶ Install a firewall on your PC.

▶ Enter personal information only on secure websites. (Look for the "lock" icon in your browser's status bar.)

▶ Create strong passwords for all your software and web accounts.

◀ *SEE ALSO 1.5, "Creating Usernames and Passwords"* ▷

▶ If you use a notebook computer, take precautions to guard against physical theft—and, if possible, encrypt the data on the notebook's hard drive.

▶ When you dispose of an old computer, wipe all the personal information stored on the hard drive using a data scrambling utility such as Active@ Kill Disk (www.killdisk.com), CBL Data Shredder (www.cbltech.com/ data-recovery/software/data-shredder.html), Eraser (www.heidi.ie/eraser/), Master Shredder (www.intercrypto.com/master-shredder/), Secure Delete (www.secure-delete.net), or WinShredder (www.anti-software.com).

You can further protect against identity theft by practicing safe computing techniques. As noted previously, you should never open computer files sent to you unexpectedly or from strangers, via either e-mail or instant messaging. In addition, never click hyperlinks sent to you via e-mail, even if it's from someone you know; some viruses hijack other users' e-mail programs and replicate themselves via bulk e-mail mailings. Further, don't download programs from websites you don't know and trust—and avoid downloading programs and files from file-sharing websites, which are often rife with embedded spyware.

Inspect Your Credit Reports

Even if you take all these precautions, you can still be the victim of identity theft. To that end, you should request and inspect your credit reports on a regular basis—at least once a year. These reports are generated by the three major credit reporting firms, and they list every piece of past and present credit opened in your name, as well as your bill-paying history.

It pays to inspect these reports for accuracy (mistakes are sometimes made) and to be sure that there are no new accounts that you don't know anything about. An unknown account on your credit report could have been opened by an ID thief.

Federal law requires each of the three nationwide credit reporting companies to provide you with one free copy each year of your credit report, if you request it. To that end, the three companies have created a single service you can use to request all the reports at once. To order a copy of your free reports, you can do the following:

▶ To order over the web, go to www.AnnualCreditReport.com.

▶ To order by phone, call 1-877-322-8228.

▶ To order by mail, write Annual Credit Report Request Service, P.O. Box 105281, Atlanta, GA, 30348-5281.

If you prefer, you can also contact each of the three services directly. The companies' contact information is as follows:

▶ **Equifax,** www.equifax.com, 1-800-685-1111, P.O. Box 740241, Atlanta, GA, 30374-0241

▶ **Experian,** www.experian.com, 1-888-397-3742, P.O. Box 9532, Allen, TX, 75013

▶ **TransUnion,** www.transunion.com, 1-800-916-8800, P.O. Box 6790, Fullerton, CA, 92834-6790

WORDS TO GO . . . WORDS TO GO . . . WORDS TO GO

Identity theft is a crime that involves the illegal use of your individual identity or personal data.

3.5 PROTECTING AGAINST PHISHING SCAMS

How Does Phishing Work?

Guarding Against Phishing Scams

Much identity theft comes from an activity called **phishing.** This is a particular type of scam that extracts valuable information from the victim using a series of fake e-mails and websites.

How Does Phishing Work?

A typical phishing scam starts with an e-mail message. A phishing e-mail is one designed to look like an official e-mail from a legitimate company or website. A savvy phisher uses logos and other information from the targeted institution's actual e-mails or website to give the fake e-mail an authentic look. The e-mail typically informs the recipient of some recent event or activity and asks the individual to confirm an operation or review his information on the firm's website.

Within the e-mail is a link to that website. At first glance, this appears to be a legitimate link. But if you hover your cursor over the link, you'll see that the actual URL is different from the one visible in the text. In other words, clicking the link doesn't take you to where you think you're going but to a completely different web page.

The counterfeit website is an important part of the phishing scam. Like the official-looking e-mail, the web page you land on is designed to look as authentic as possible. However, the page you link to is a spoof web page; if you enter the requested information, that info will be transmitted to the con artist behind the phishing scam, and you're now a victim of identity theft.

◀ SEE ALSO 3.4, *"Protecting Against Identity Theft"* ▶

What institutions are commonly spoofed in phishing e-mails? The name of just about every major corporation and financial institution has been appropriated to deleterious effect, but some of the more common brands used for phishing purposes include Bank of America, Citibank, eBay, Fifth Third Bank, HSBC Bank, NatWest, PayPal, and Wachovia.

Guarding Against Phishing Scams

Phishing scams by their very nature are difficult to guard against. We're used to getting official communications via e-mail from all manner of companies and institutions; e-mail is how corporate America communicates to its customers.

But as phishers continue to impersonate all manner of organizations, our trust in e-mail as a communications medium diminishes. How do we know which e-mails to trust and which to trash?

The first defense against phishing e-mails is awareness. You need to learn what phishing e-mails look like and what institutions are likely to be targets of phishing scams.

Second, you should never click a link in an unsolicited e-mail message. That web link is a dead giveaway that it's a phishing message, as most legitimate organizations will never include such a link in their e-mail communications. Even if you think the message is legitimate, you shouldn't click the link to go to the website. Instead, enter the entity's actual web address into your web browser and go to that site directly—not via the link. If something there needs to be verified, you can do it manually.

WARNING . . .WARNING . . .WARNING

Never click a link in an unsolicited e-mail message—even if the message *looks* official!

You should also take advantage of all the anti-phishing technology available today. For example, if you're running Windows Vista on your computer, it includes a Phishing Filter that works within both Windows Mail and Internet Explorer 7. The Phishing Filter compares all the links in your Windows Mail e-mail messages to an online list of known phishing websites. If the link matches a fraudulent site, Windows Mail displays a warning message at the top of the message. (This same Phishing Filter is also included in Microsoft Outlook 2007, and other web browsers incorporate similar technology.)

If you attempt to click a link to a known phishing site, the Phishing Filter in Internet Explorer blocks access to the site, changes the Address Bar to red, navigates to a neutral page, and displays a warning message. If you attempt to click a link to a site that is not on the list of known fraudulent sites but behaves similarly to such sites, the Microsoft Phishing Filter changes the Address Bar to yellow and cautions you about potentially suspicious content.

3.5

WORDS TO GO . . .WORDS TO GO . . .WORDS TO GO

Phishing is a type of scam that extracts personal information from the victim using a series of fake e-mails and websites.

3.6 SAFE SURFING FOR CHILDREN

Ten Tips for Kid-Safe Surfing

Content-Filtering Software

Kid-Safe Directories

Cyber Bullying

The Internet contains an almost limitless supply of information on its billions of web pages; likewise, the Internet's social networks, blogs, and forums provide an opportunity to communicate and form communities with new friends from all around the globe. But with all this valuable information and interaction comes some degree of offensive content and inappropriate communication—or at least offensive to and inappropriate for the youngest members of your family.

Even if just a small percentage of the Internet is unsuitable for children, that still leaves millions of individual pages and profiles that feature sexual, violent, and hateful content. How do you protect your children from the bad stuff on the web—while still allowing access to all the good stuff?

Ten Tips for Kid-Safe Surfing

The most important thing you can do, as a parent, is to create an environment that encourages *appropriate* use of the Internet and discourages deliberate searching for inappropriate content. Although there are technological tools you can employ to keep inappropriate content away from your children, nothing replaces traditional parental supervision. At the end of the day, you have to take responsibility for your children's online activities. Provide the guidance they need to make the Internet a fun and educational place to visit—and your entire family will be better for it.

Before you let your kids loose on the web, share these tips to ensure a safer surfing experience:

▶ Make sure your children know to never give out any identifying information (home address, school name, telephone number, and so on) or to send their photos to other users online.

▶ Provide your children with online pseudonyms so they don't have to use their real names online.

▶ Don't let your children arrange face-to-face meetings with other computer users without parental permission and supervision. If a meeting is arranged, make the first one in a public place and be sure to accompany your child.

▶ Teach your children that people online may not always be who they seem; just because someone says that she's a 10-year-old girl doesn't necessarily mean that she really is 10 years old or a girl.

▶ Consider making Internet surfing an activity you do together with your younger children—or turn it into a family activity by putting your kids' PC in a public room (like a living room or den) rather than in a private bedroom.

▶ Set reasonable rules and guidelines for your kids' computer use. Consider limiting the number of minutes/hours they can spend online each day.

▶ Monitor your children's Internet activities. Ask them to keep a log of all websites they visit, oversee any chat sessions they participate in, check out any files they download, even consider sharing an e-mail account (especially with younger children) so that you can oversee their messages.

▶ Don't let your children respond to messages that are suggestive, obscene, belligerent, or threatening—or that make them feel uncomfortable in any way. Encourage your children to tell you if they receive any such messages and then report the senders to your ISP.

▶ Install **content-filtering software** on your PC and set up a kid-safe directory or search engine as your browser's start page.

▶ If your children are old enough to be on social networking sites such as MySpace and Facebook, sign up as a friend to their pages—so you can see what they and their friends are doing and saying online. While you're at it, discourage your children from displaying overly personal information and pictures on their personal pages.

◀ SEE ALSO 11.2, "Social Networking—Safely and Sanely" ▶

Teach your children that Internet access is not a right; it should be a privilege earned by your children and kept only when their use of it matches your expectations.

Content-Filtering Software

If you can't trust your children to always click away from inappropriate web content (and you can't—children will always be too curious for their own good), you can choose instead to block access to that inappropriate content. This is done by installing content-filtering software on your kids' PCs.

Content-filtering software blocks access to those sites and pages that contain adult-oriented content, working from either a list of inappropriate sites or a list of inappropriate topics (or both). You can use the software's built-in list of inappropriate sites and content, or you can add your own list of sites and keywords to avoid.

When your child tries to access a blocked site or a page that contains questionable content, access is blocked and a warning message is displayed instead. With content-monitoring software installed on your children's computer, they won't be able to access the really bad stuff on the web.

The most popular filtering programs include the following:

▶ Cyber Sentinel (www.cybersentinel.co.uk)

▶ CyberPatrol (www.cyberpatrol.co.uk)

▶ CYBERsitter (www.cybersitter.com)

▶ FilterPak (www.centipedenetworks.com)

▶ MaxProtect (www.max.com)

▶ Net Nanny (www.netnanny.com)

▶ Netmop (www.netmop.com)

▶ Safe Eyes (www.internetsafety.com)

▶ WiseChoice (www.wisechoice.net)

Prices for these programs run from around $30 to $60. In addition, many of the big Internet security suites (such as those from McAfee and Norton/Symantec) offer built-in content-filtering modules.

Kid-Safe Directories

If you don't want to go to all the trouble of using content-filtering software, you can at least steer your children to some of the safer sites on the web. The best of these sites offer kid-safe searching so that all inappropriate sites are filtered out of the search results.

The most popular kid-safe directory sites and search engines include:

▶ AltaVista—AV Family Filter (www.altavista.com; click the Settings link and then click the Family Filter link)

▶ Ask Kids (www.askkids.com)

▶ Fact Monster (www.factmonster.com)

- ▶ Google SafeSearch (www.google.com; click the Preferences link and then choose a SafeSearch Filtering option)

- ▶ KidsClick! (www.kidsclick.org)

- ▶ Live Search SafeSearch (www.live.com; click the Options link, then choose a SafeSearch filtering option)

- ▶ KOL: Kids Online (kids.aol.com)

- ▶ Yahoo! Kids (kids.yahoo.com)

3.6

Finally, know that these kid-safe sites are good to use as the start page for your children's web browser. They are true launching pads to guaranteed safe content on the web.

Cyber Bullying

There is one particular form of online abuse that your children need to be aware of. **Cyber bullying** is, as the name implies, bullying carried out online, and it's on the rise. Bullies used to limit their tormenting behavior to the schoolyard or playground, but now they can send harassing messages via e-mail and instant messaging and can prey on their victims in Internet chat rooms and social networking sites.

Understanding Cyber Bullying

Cyber bullying is just like normal bullying except it takes place on the Internet. It's just as serious as physical bullying; youths have committed suicide after being victims of cyber bullying incidents.

Cyber bullying can include any or all of the following:

- ▶ Harassing instant messages or text messages via cell phone

- ▶ Harassing comments on blogs

- ▶ Stealing passwords to log on to sites posing as your child

- ▶ Creating "hate" websites that put down your child

- ▶ Sending embarrassing pictures (real or fake) via e-mail or cell phones

- ▶ Harassing a child in online games and virtual worlds

- ▶ Leaving hateful comments on a child's blog or MySpace/Facebook page

Whatever the behavior, cyber bullying is a real threat. According to the National Crime Prevention Center, 40 percent of all teenagers with Internet access have reported being bullied online within the past 12 months. And only

10 percent of those victims told their parents about the incident—so just because you don't know doesn't mean it isn't happening!

Defending Against Cyber Bullies

One of the advantages of monitoring your children's Internet activities is that you're more likely to become aware of any potential cyber bullying. If you suspect your child is a victim of a cyber bully, the first thing to do is contact authorities at your child's school. A call from the teacher or principal can be surprisingly effective in stopping this sort of behavior.

You may also want to confront the bully's parents, just as you would those of a normal schoolyard bully. In some instances, especially with older youths, having your child confront the bully himself might be advisable. (That said, your child shouldn't respond to the bully's online messages; the contact should be in person, along the lines of "Leave me alone, stop harassing me.")

Along these lines, the National Crime Prevention Council offers the following five tips to prevent cyber bullying:

- ▶ Do not give out personal information online, whether in instant message profiles, chat rooms, blogs, or personal websites.
- ▶ Never tell anyone your password, even friends.
- ▶ If someone sends a mean or threatening message, don't respond. Save it or print it out and show it to an adult.
- ▶ Never open e-mails, read text messages or instant messages, or accept friend requests from someone you don't know or from someone you know is a bully.
- ▶ Help peers who are harassed online by not joining in.

Beyond these efforts, you can change your child's online ID, have your child start visiting different sites, and in general try to defuse the situation before a more explosive—and potentially physical—conflict occurs.

WORDS TO GO . . . WORDS TO GO . . . WORDS TO GO

Content-filtering software blocks access to websites and web pages that contain inappropriate content.
Cyber bullying is bullying behavior carried out online.

4

SEARCHING THE WEB

4.1 HOW SEARCH ENGINES AND DIRECTORIES WORK

Web Directories

Search Engines

Conducting a Search

With billions and billions of pages on the web, finding the precise information you want is a daunting challenge. This is why search sites, such as Google and Yahoo!, are consistently among the most popular sites on the web. You use these search engines and directories to find the websites and pages that you want.

◀ *SEE ALSO 1.1, "How the Internet Works"* ▶

Web Directories

One approach to organizing the web is to physically look at all web pages and organize them into a **web directory.** In a directory, web pages are organized by human editors into a variety of easy-to-browse categories. A directory doesn't search the web—in fact, a directory only catalogs a very small part of the web. But a directory is very organized and very easy to use.

Directories—such as the original Yahoo! directory—were, in the early days of the web, the most popular way to find sites and information. In fact, there are still some very popular directories today, including Best of the Web (www.botw. org) and the Open Directory (www.dmoz.org). But directories are hindered by their manual nature; no group of editors can work fast enough to catalog anything but a small percentage of all existing websites. For this reason, web directories have suffered in comparison with today's most popular way of organizing the web—via search engine index.

Search Engines

It's important to note that a directory is *not* a search engine. A **search engine** is not powered by human hands as a directory is; instead, a search engine uses a special type of software program (called a **spider** or crawler) to roam the web automatically, feeding what it finds back to a massive bank of computers. These computers hold **search indexes** of the web—in some cases entire web pages are indexed; in other cases only the titles and important words on a page are indexed. (Different search engines operate differently.)

A search index is essentially a huge database containing tens of billions of entries—much larger than even the largest human-edited directory. It's the quantity of results that attracts the majority of web searchers, although the best search engines (from Google, Yahoo!, and Microsoft) also return high-quality results in terms of relevance and accuracy.

Conducting a Search

Almost every search site on the web contains two basic components—a search box and a search button. You enter your query—one or more **keywords** that describe what you're looking for—into the search box and then click the search button (or press the Enter key) to start the search.

◁ SEE ALSO 4.2, *"Constructing an Effective Query"* ▷

A typical search of this type takes less than half a second to complete. That's because all the searching takes place on the search engine site's own web servers. While you might think you're searching the web, you're actually searching a huge index of websites stored on the search site's servers. That index was created previously, over a period of time, from the results garnered by the search engine's spider software. Because you are only searching a server, not the entire web, your searches are completed in the blink of an eye.

The results of your search are displayed on a series of search results pages. Each page typically contains links to and information about 10 or so web pages that match your query, with the best matches listed first. Click the link next to a result to access the matching page.

WORDS TO GO . . . *WORDS TO GO . . . WORDS TO GO*

You enter **keywords** into a search engine's search box to create a query.

A **search engine** scours the web to create an index of web pages that can then be searched by users.

A **search index** is the database of web pages assembled by search engines.

Spider software is used by search engines to crawl the web.

A **web directory** is a collection of websites collected and organized by human editors.

4.2 CONSTRUCTING AN EFFECTIVE QUERY

Keywords

Wildcards and Word Stemming

Exact Phrases

How you construct your search query determines how relevant the results will be. The more effective your query, the better targeted the results.

◀ SEE ALSO 4.1, *"How Search Engines and Directories Work"* ▶

Keywords

When constructing a query, it's important to focus on the keywords you use because the search sites look for these words when they process your query. Your keywords are compared to the web pages the search site knows about—the more keywords found on a web page, the better the match.

You should choose keywords that best describe the information you're looking for, using as many keywords as you need. Don't be afraid of using too many keywords; in fact, using too *few* keywords is a common fault of many novice searchers. The more words you use, the better idea the search engine has of what you're looking for.

For example, if you're looking for pages about red 1967 Corvette convertibles, you shouldn't use the single keyword **corvette.** Instead, use all four of the descriptive words to construct the query **red 1967 corvette convertible.** The results will be much more targeted.

Note that with most search engines, keywords are not case-sensitive; it doesn't matter whether you type **corvette, Corvette,** or **CORVETTE.** In addition, it seldom matters in what order you list your keywords. Just make sure to separate each keyword with a space.

Wildcards and Word Stemming

If you're not sure which form of a word to use, some search sites—but, notably, not Google—let you use the asterisk character (*) as a **wildcard.** A wildcard matches any character or group of characters in a word from its specific position in the word to the end of that word. For example, if you're not sure whether you want to search for automobile, automotive, or autos, enter **auto*** to return all three words (as well as automatic, autocratic, and any other word that starts with "auto").

◯ *SEE ALSO 4.4, "Searching with Google"* ▶

As noted, Google doesn't let you use wildcard characters in its queries. Instead, Google uses **word stemming** technology, which automatically searches for all forms of a word—plural, past tense, and so on—without any direction on your part.

4.2

Exact Phrases

Normally, a multiple-word query searches for web pages that include all the words in the query in any order. To search for an exact phrase, you must enclose the phrase in quotation marks.

For example, to search for Ralph Jones, *don't* enter **ralph jones;** this returns any page about guys named Ralph and guys named Jones. Instead, enter **"ralph jones"** with quotation marks around the two keywords. Putting the phrase between quotation marks returns results only about people named Ralph Jones.

WORDS TO GO . . .WORDS TO GO . . .WORDS TO GO

A **wildcard** matches any character or group of characters in a word, and is used to substitute for unknown or missing characters in keywords.

Word stemming technology automatically searches for all forms of a word, with no wildcards necessary.

4.3 EXAMINING THE TOP SEARCH SITES

Google

Yahoo!

Windows Live Search

Other Search Sites

What are the top search sites today? It's a short but powerful list.

Google

The number-one search engine, in terms of searches and users, is Google (www.google.com). In any given month, Google is responsible for 55 percent to 65 percent of all the web searches made in the United States; its market share is even higher in other countries (approaching 90 percent in the United Kingdom, for example).

Google's popularity is a result of its speed, ease of use, and quality results. Those results, in turn, come from its large search index, which is more than six billion pages in size. That's a bigger index than any other search engine today.

The uncluttered Google search page.

The Google home page is known for its uncluttered, easy-to-use interface. The page is dominated by the large search box, with only a few text links to additional searches and services.

Google's search results pages, however, include lots of information in the form of **universal search results.** In the past, Google's default search results linked solely to websites; if you wanted to find other types of content, such as video or images, you had to perform separate searches. With universal search, however, Google mixes all types of content into its search results pages. You may do a search and see a row of images at the top of the search results page or have a video viewing window pop up in the middle of the search results.

In addition to its wide-based web search results, Google also provides a variety of specialty searches, including Google Image Search (images.google.com), Google Book Search (books.google.com), Google Scholar (scholar.google.com), and the hand-edited Google Directory (directory.google.com). Google also offers a variety of other web-based services, including Google Maps (maps.google.com), Google Docs (docs.google.com), Google Calendar (calendar.google.com), YouTube (www.youtube.com), and Blogger (www.blogger.com).

🖸 SEE ALSO 4.4, *"Searching with Google"* ▶

Yahoo!

4.3

Yahoo! (www.yahoo.com) is one of the oldest search sites on the web, number two in traffic only to Google. Originally a human-edited directory, Yahoo! now functions as a full-featured search engine, indexing billions of pages.

Yahoo!'s portal-like home page.

Unlike Google's austere interface, the Yahoo! home page offers a variety of information and services in addition to the standard search box. This makes the Yahoo! home page more like a portal than a search site, attracting many people who use Yahoo! as their browser's home page.

Windows Live Search

The number-three search site today is Windows Live Search (www.live.com) from Microsoft. Like Google, Live Search offers a simple search page, uncluttered with other content.

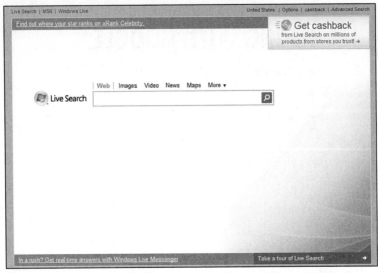

Microsoft's Windows Live Search.

Interestingly, Microsoft is willing to reward people for using their search service. Microsoft's cashback program provides cash rebates to users who purchase products while searching with Live Search.

Other Search Sites

Google, Yahoo!, and Microsoft are the Big Three of searching today, but several other search engines and directories also provide excellent results:

▶ AlltheWeb (www.alltheweb.com)

▶ AltaVista (www.altavista.com)

▶ AOL Search (search.aol.com)

▶ Ask.com (www.ask.com)

▶ HotBot (www.hotbot.com)

▶ LookSmart (search.looksmart.com)

▶ Open Directory (www.dmoz.org)

WORDS TO GO . . . *WORDS TO GO . . .WORDS TO GO*

Universal search results display all matching media for a search query, not just web pages.

4.4 SEARCHING WITH GOOGLE

Entering a Query

Search Results

AND and OR Searches

Including Stop Words

Excluding Unwanted Words

Search Operators

Advanced Search

4.4

Google is the Internet's most popular search engine and for good reason. From the spartan nature of Google's home page to the easy-to-navigate results pages, a Google search is so effortless that just about anyone can do it without undue effort or instruction.

Entering a Query

Google's home page is almost shocking in its simplicity. Unlike what you find with Yahoo! and some other web search portals, Google's home page has no category listings, no news headlines, no stock tickers, no weather reports, and no blatant advertisements. All you see is the Google logo, the search box, two search buttons (Google Search and I'm Feeling Lucky), and some links to additional search services. It's clean, it's simple, and it's fast.

Initiating a basic search is as easy as entering your query, consisting of one or more keywords, into the search box and then clicking the Google Search button. That's all there is to it—just enter your query, click the Google Search button, and wait for the search results page to display.

◀ SEE ALSO 4.2, "Constructing an Effective Query" ▶

Alternately, you can enter your query and then click the I'm Feeling Lucky button. When you click this button, you skip the standard search results page and go directly to the page that is the number-one match to your query.

Search Results

After you click the Google Search button, Google searches its index for all the web pages that match your query and then displays the results on a search results page.

A Google search results page.

Parts of the Search Results Page

The key parts of the search results page include the following:

▶ **Statistics bar.** This bar displays how many results were returned for your query and how long it took to display those results. In many cases, this bar also includes a link to a definition of the keyword.

▶ **Specialized searches.** Located on the left side of the Statistics bar, click one of these links to narrow your query to a specific type of search. The available searches depend on what you're searching for; for example, you may be able to click to perform an image search or a book search.

▶ **OneBox specialized results.** On some searches, Google will display a short list of specialized search results—images, news stories, maps, and the like. These are displayed near the top of the main search results.

▶ **Related searches.** At the bottom of most search results pages, you'll see a list of "searches related to" your current search. Click any of these links to perform a similar search.

▶ **Sponsored links.** These are links paid for by Google's advertisers, typically positioned to the right of (and sometimes above) the main search results.

▶ **Show Options.** Click this link to filter your search results by type, time (how recent), and other factors.

WARNING . . .WARNING . . .WARNING . .

Don't confuse Google's "sponsored links" with legitimate search results.
These sponsored links are actually paid advertisements that may have only
indirect relevance to your query.

Parts of a Search Result

Each individual search result includes key information about the linked-to web
page, including the following:

- ▶ **Page title.** This is the title of the page and a clickable link; click it to view
  the linked-to page.

- ▶ **Page excerpt.** Below the page title is a short excerpt from the associated
  web page. This may be the first few sentences of text on the page, a summary of page contents, or something similar.

- ▶ **URL.** This is the full web address of the selected web page. It is not a
  clickable link; you have to click the page title to jump to the page.

- ▶ **Size.** The size (in kilobytes) of the selected page.

- ▶ **Cached.** Click this link to see the version of the page stored on Google's
  document servers, useful if the information you want has changed or if the
  website is currently down. Note that the cached page may be slightly older
  than the current version of the page.

- ▶ **Similar pages.** These are pages that Google thinks have a lot in common
  with the listed page.

- ▶ **Other relevant pages.** In some instances, other relevant pages from the
  same site are listed (and indented) beneath the primary page listing.

AND and OR Searches

Most users enter a keyword or two into Google's search box, click the Search
button, and are satisfied with the results. This is a rather brute-force method of
searching, however, and typically it generates too many unrelated results.

To generate fewer and better results, you have to refine your query. To do this, it
helps to know a little about how Google queries work.

The first thing to know is that Google automatically assumes the word "and"
between all the words in your query. That is, if you enter two words, Google
assumes you're looking for pages that include both of those words—word one *and*
word two. It doesn't return pages that include only one of the words.

For this reason, you don't have to include the **AND** operator between two words in a query. If you're searching for pages about both dogs and cats, for example, you don't have to enter **dogs AND cats.** Instead, you can enter just **dogs cats** as your query; Google assumes the "and" and automatically includes it in its internal index search.

However, if you want to search for pages that include one word or another word but not necessarily both, you must use the **OR** operator between the two keywords. For example, to search for pages that talk about either dogs or cats but not necessarily both, use the query **dogs OR cats.** (The **OR** operator must be used in all uppercase.)

Including Stop Words

Google automatically ignores many small, common words in your queries. These are called **stop words** and include "and," "the," "where," "how," "what," "or" (in all lowercase), and other similar words—along with numeric digits and single letters (such as "a").

You can override the stop word exclusion by telling Google that it *must* include specific words in the query. You do this with the + operator in front of the otherwise excluded word. For example, to include the word "how" in your query, you'd enter **+how.** Be sure to include a space before the + sign but not after it.

Excluding Unwanted Words

Sometimes you want to refine your results by excluding pages that contain a specific word. To exclude words from your search, use the – operator; any word in your query preceded by – is automatically excluded from the search results. Remember to always include a space before the – and none after.

For example, if you search for **bass,** you could get pages about a male singer and/or a fish. If you want to search for bass singers only, enter a query that looks like this: **bass –fish.**

Search Operators

The previous sections described just a few of the **search operators** you can use within the search box to refine your Google queries. There are many more search operators available, as described in Table 4.1.

TABLE 4.1   GOOGLE SEARCH OPERATORS

Operator	Description
..	Searches within a range of numbers in the form *number1..number2*
–	Excludes pages that contain the specified word from the search results
" "	Searches for the complete phrase in the form *"word 1 word 2"*
()	Used to group keywords in a query
~	Searches for synonyms of the specified keyword
+	Includes the specified stop word in the query
allinanchor:	Restricts search to the anchor text (link text) of web pages; used with multiple keywords
allintext:	Restricts search to the body text of web pages; used with multiple keywords
allintitle:	Restricts search to the titles of web pages; used with multiple keywords
allinurl:	Restricts search to the URLs of web pages; used with multiple keywords
bphonebook:	Displays business phone book listings
define:	Displays definitions of the specified word or phrase
filetype:	Finds documents with the specified extension
inanchor:	Restricts search to the anchor text (link text) of web pages; used with a single keyword
info:	Displays ownership and other information about the web page in question
intext:	Restricts query to the body text of web pages; used with a single keyword
intitle:	Restricts search to the titles of web pages; used with a single keyword
inurl:	Restricts search to the URLs of web pages; used with a single keyword
link:	Finds pages that link to the specified URL
OR	Searches for pages that contain one or another keyword but not necessarily both
phonebook:	Displays phone book listings—addresses and phone numbers—for the specified name
related:	Displays web pages that are similar to the specified URL
rphonebook:	Displays residential phone book listings

continues

TABLE 4.1   GOOGLE SEARCH OPERATORS   *(continued)*

Operator	Description
safesearch:	Enables Google's SafeSearch content filtering for the current search
site:	Restricts search to a particular domain or website
stocks:	Displays the current stock price for the specified stock symbol
weather:	Displays the current weather conditions and forecast for the specified location

For example, if you want to confine your search to words that appear in the page's title only, you'd use the **intitle:** operator like this:

> **intitle:keyword**

Some of these operators are used not to refine a search but to display defined information. For example, to display the current price of a given stock or security, you use the **stocks:** operator like this:

> **stocks:symbol**

Advanced Search

For many users, an easier way to refine their searches is by using Google's Advanced Search page. The Advanced Search page contains a number of options you can use to fine-tune your searches without having to learn the search operators previously discussed.

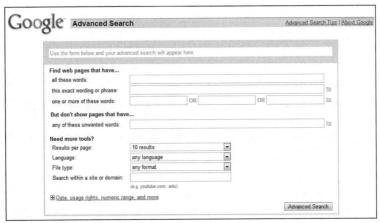

Google's Advanced Search page.

To access the Advanced Search page, click the Advanced Search link on any Google page. Table 4.2 describes the options available on this page.

TABLE 4.2   GOOGLE'S ADVANCED SEARCH OPTIONS

Option	Description
Find web pages that have *all these words*	Google's default search mode (assumed AND operator)
Find web pages that have *this exact wording or phrase*	Searches for the exact phrase (same as " " search)
Find web pages that have *one or more of these words*	Searches for either one word or another (same as OR operator)
But don't show pages that have *any of these unwanted words*	Excludes words from search (same as – operator)
Results per page	Selects how many listings are displayed on the search results page
Language	Searches for pages written in a specific language
File type	Limits search to specific file types
Search within a site or domain	Restricts the search to a specific website or domain

Even more parameters are available if you click the Date, Usage Rights, Numeric Range, and More link. This expands the page to include options for Date (how recent you want the pages to be), Usage Rights (whether a page is free to use or share), Where Your Keywords Show Up (restricts the search to certain areas of a page), Region (narrows the search to a given country), Numeric Range (searches for a range of numbers), and SafeSearch (filters out adult content).

WORDS TO GO . . . WORDS TO GO . . . WORDS TO GO

Search operators enable users to fine-tune their queries within the search box.

Stop words are small words, such as "and" or "the," that are automatically removed from a search query.

4.5 RESEARCHING WITH WIKIPEDIA

How Wikipedia Works

Searching Wikipedia

Contributing to Wikipedia

Issues

When you use Google or Yahoo! to search the web, you're getting unfiltered information from a variety of websites. If you prefer more concise and edited information, check out Wikipedia (www.wikipedia.org).

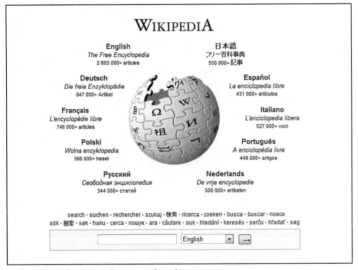

Wikipedia—the free online encyclopedia.

How Wikipedia Works

Wikipedia is a giant online encyclopedia—with a twist. Unlike a traditional encyclopedia, Wikipedia's content is created solely by the site's users, resulting in the world's largest online collaboration. The Wikipedia site is used by people of all types, from students writing school papers to professional researchers to curious individuals. It is fast becoming the primary information site on the web, behind only Google in terms of individual searches.

At present, Wikipedia hosts more than 2.7 million English-language articles, with at least that many articles available in more than 250 different languages.

The articles are written and revised by tens of thousands of individual contributors. These users volunteer their time and knowledge at no charge for the good of the Wikipedia project.

Searching Wikipedia

Searching for information on Wikipedia is similar to using a traditional search engine. Just enter your query into the search box on Wikipedia's home page and then click the right-arrow button. If an article directly matches your query, Wikipedia displays that article. If a number of articles might match your query, Wikipedia displays the list of articles, organized by type or topic. Click the article name to display the specific article.

For example, if you search Wikipedia for **robert kennedy,** it displays the article on Robert F. Kennedy. If instead you search only for **kennedy,** it displays a disambiguation page with sections for matching people, places, transportation, schools and colleges, places named after President John F. Kennedy, and other articles.

Reading an Article

Each Wikipedia article is organized into a summary and subsidiary sections. Longer articles have a table of contents located beneath the summary. Key information is sometimes presented in a sidebar at the top right of the article.

A typical Wikipedia article.

Throughout the article, blue hypertext links to related articles in the Wikipedia database. The sources for key facts within the article are footnoted; the footnotes appear at the bottom of the article. Additional references and information about the topic also appear at the bottom of the page.

Viewing an Article's History

Since Wikipedia articles are continually updated by users, it is sometimes useful to view the history of an article's updates. To do so, click the History tab; this displays a list of edits and who made those edits. You can also use the History tab to read previous versions of an article.

Discussing an Article

Some articles feature discussions from users that can sometimes provide additional insight. Click the Discussion tab to read and participate in ongoing discussions.

Contributing to Wikipedia

Anyone can contribute to Wikipedia. You don't have to possess specialized qualifications, just an adequate knowledge of the subject chosen. Articles submitted are then edited by other users, who can insert additional information or revise the information previously submitted. In this fashion, information in the Wikipedia is constantly improved and updated.

Editing an Article

To edit an existing article, navigate to that article and click the Edit This Page tab. This displays the underlying HTML code for the article. You apply your edits directly to the HTML code and then enter a summary of your edits into the Edit Summary box. When you're finished, click the Save Page button; your changes will be immediately visible.

WARNING . . . WARNING . . . WARNING

Know that other users will quickly read and vet your edits. If you enter incorrect information, expect your edits to either be changed or deleted.

Creating a New Article

You can also propose and create new articles for Wikipedia for topics that are not yet covered. First, search for the topic you want to write about; if an article appears, you don't have to create a new one. If no article appears, Wikipedia tells you that no article title matches your search. Click the Create the Page link and an editing page for the new article appears. Enter your content into the editing box and click the Save Page button when done. This places your newly written article on the Wikipedia site.

Note that you must have a (free) Wikipedia account and be signed in to create an article. You don't need an account to edit an article.

Issues

Given that there is no central authority managing Wikipedia content, some experts dismiss the usefulness of the site. Issues with Wikipedia fall into two general camps: accuracy and depth of coverage.

4.5

WARNING . . .WARNING . . .WARNING

It is best to view Wikipedia content as a starting point rather than the final word. When you're writing a scholarly or professional paper, you should not use Wikipedia as your sole source but rather as a guide to additional sources. In addition, it's always a good idea to check the footnotes and other references in a Wikipedia article to confirm the source of information presented; the most accurate articles are well sourced.

Accuracy

If anyone can write or edit an article, how are you to know if the information he or she submits is accurate? While the Wikipedia community is self-policing (and the information generally accurate), misleading or just plain wrong information can seep into the site. It is possible for mistakes to creep into Wikipedia's content and not be discovered by the base of contributing users—and for those mistakes to be reflected in papers and reports written with Wikipedia as the sole source.

Depth of Coverage

Because Wikipedia users suggest the content, it's likely that some popular culture topics are covered in more depth than topics of a more intellectual bent. This is solely a function of which and how many contributors are interested and expert in a given topic. As such, you can't depend on Wikipedia to always provide adequate content.

4.6 FINDING NEWS AND OTHER INFORMATION ONLINE

News

Sports

Weather

Financial Information

Medical Information

The Internet is a great place to find all manner of information. While a search engine is a good place to start, it's easier to find much specialized information on specialized websites.

News

The Internet is a great place to find both news headlines and in-depth analysis. Most news-related websites are updated in real time, so you're always getting the latest news—on your computer screen, when you want it.

Some of the biggest, most popular news sites on the web are run by the major broadcast and cable news networks or by the major national newspapers. You can turn to these sites to get the latest headlines and—in many cases—live audio and video feeds. These major news sites include the following:

- ▶ **ABC News** (abcnews.go.com)
- ▶ **BBC News** (news.bbc.co.uk)
- ▶ **CBS News** (www.cbsnews.com)
- ▶ **CNN** (www.cnn.com)
- ▶ **Fox News** (www.foxnews.com)
- ▶ **MSNBC** (www.msnbc.com)
- ▶ *The New York Times* (www.nytimes.com)
- ▶ *USA Today* (www.usatoday.com)

Current news headlines on the CNN website.

In addition, you can find a quick overview of the latest headlines at Google News (news.google.com). This site offers the top headlines from a variety of news sources; click any headline to read the complete story.

Sports

The web is also a great resource for sports fans of all shapes and sizes. Whether you're a fan or a participant, there's at least one site somewhere on the web that focuses on your particular sport.

The best sports sites resemble the best news sites—they're actually portals to all sorts of content and services, including up-to-the-minute scores, postgame recaps, in-depth reporting, and much more. If you're looking for sports information online, one of these portals is the place to start:

- ▶ **CBS Sports** (www.cbssports.com)
- ▶ **ESPN.com** (espn.go.com)
- ▶ **FOXSports** (www.foxsports.com)
- ▶ **NBC Sports** (nbcsports.msnbc.com)
- ▶ **SI.com—Sports Illustrated** (sportsillustrated.cnn.com)
- ▶ **SportingNews.com** (www.sportingnews.com)

Weather

When you're interested in the latest weather forecast, know that most of the major news portals and local websites offer some variety of weather-related services. There are also a number of dedicated weather sites on the web, all of which offer local and national forecasts, weather radar, satellite maps, and more. These dedicated weather sites include the following:

▶ **AccuWeather.com** (www.accuweather.com)

▶ **Intellicast.com** (www.intellicast.com)

▶ **Weather Underground** (www.wunderground.com)

▶ **Weather.com** (www.weather.com)

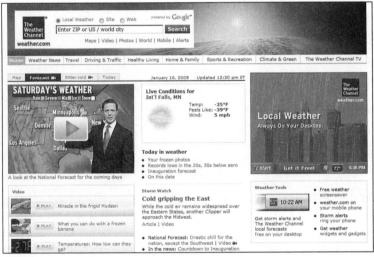

Forecasts and conditions on The Weather Channel's Weather.com *website.*

Financial Information

The Internet is a great place to find up-to-the-minute information about stocks and other securities. Several sites and services specialize in providing real-time (or slightly delayed) stock quotes, most of which are totally free. These sites include the following:

▶ **CNN/Money** (money.cnn.com)

▶ **Google Finance** (finance.google.com)

▶ **MarketWatch** (www.marketwatch.com)

▶ **The Motley Fool** (www.fool.com)

▶ **MSN Money** (moneycentral.msn.com)

▶ **Yahoo! Finance** (finance.yahoo.com)

Medical Information

When you're looking for useful health-related information, you don't have to wait for your next doctor's appointment. A number of websites offer detailed information about illnesses, diseases, and medicines. Many of these sites focus on preventive medicine and wellness, and almost all help you match symptoms with likely illnesses and treatments. Indeed, some of these sites provide access to the same medical databases used by most physicians.

Here are some of the top medical sites on the web:

▶ **KidsHealth** (www.kidshealth.org)

▶ **MDchoice.com** (www.mdchoice.com)

▶ **MedicineNet** (www.medicinenet.com)

▶ **National Library of Medicine** (www.nlm.nih.gov)

▶ **WebMD** (www.webmd.com)

WARNING . . .WARNING . . .WARNING . . .

Information found on these websites cannot take the place of advice from your personal physician.

You can also use the web to search for a new or specialist physician in your area. Two of the best physician search sites are AMA DoctorFinder (webapps.ama-assn. org/doctorfinder/) and DoctorDirectory.com (www.doctordirectory.com).

5

WORKING WITH PROGRAMS AND FILES

5.1 Searching for Files and Programs Online

5.2 Downloading Files

5.3 Using Online Backup and Storage

5.1 SEARCHING FOR FILES AND PROGRAMS ONLINE

Finding Music and Video Files

Finding Software Programs

The Internet is a huge repository for all sorts of computer files, from music and video files to full-featured software programs and utilities. There are literally millions of these files available *somewhere* on the Internet—if you know where to find them.

Finding Music and Video Files

If you want to **download** music, movies, or TV shows, the best places to look are commercial media download sites such as Apple's iTunes Store (www.apple.com/itunes/) or Amazon Video on Demand (www.amazon.com). These sites typically charge a small fee to download a music track or video file, but you're guaranteed a high-quality download free of any computer viruses or spyware.

◀ *SEE ALSO 7.1, "Finding Music Online"* ▶

WARNING . . .WARNING . . .WARNING . . .

If you download files from less-recognized websites, you might be at risk of downloading a file infected with a computer virus. This is particularly true of so-called peer-to-peer file-sharing networks such as BitTorrent and LimeWire that host files uploaded by other users—and thus not checked for virus or spyware infection.

Finding Software Programs

Finding software programs to download is equally easy. In fact, many of the programs you find online are available free; these programs are called **freeware.** Other programs can be downloaded for no charge, but they require you to pay a token amount to receive full functionality or documentation; these programs are called **shareware.** (Both types of programs are in contrast to the software you buy in boxes at your local computer retailer; that is called **commercial software.**)

Where can you find programs and utilities to download? The best places to look are websites dedicated to this type of file downloading, called **file archives.** These sites typically store a huge variety of freeware and shareware programs and utilities, and they are easy to browse or search for specific types of software.

Some of the most popular file archives on the Internet include:

▶ Download.com (www.download.com)

▶ Jumbo (www.jumbo.com)

▶ SnapFiles (www.snapfiles.com)

▶ Tucows (www.tucows.com)

▶ ZDNet Downloads (downloads.zdnet.com)

CNET's Download.com file archive.

There are several good reasons to download from one of these well-established sites. First, they all have huge collections of programs. The more files a site has available, the more likely it is you'll find what you're looking for. Second, they all make the download process relatively easy, typically just one or two clicks of your mouse. Third, all these sites check their files for viruses and spyware before offering them to the public. In other words, these sites make downloading safe and easy.

◉ *SEE ALSO 5.2, "Downloading Files"* ▶

Commercial software is those computer programs you have to purchase.

Downloading a file copies that file from a site on the Internet to your computer. (In contrast, uploading a file copies that file from your computer to a site on the Internet.)

A **file archive** is a website that offers prescreened software programs for downloading.

Freeware is the category of computer program available completely for free.

Shareware is the category of computer program that you can download for free but are encouraged to support with your financial donation.

5.2 DOWNLOADING FILES

The Download Process

Downloading from a File Archive Website

Downloading Files from Any Web Page

Downloading files to your computer is easy enough that anyone can do it—no prior technical expertise is necessary. Just make sure you take necessary precautions to protect against accidentally installing computer viruses and spyware, and then the download is typically a one- or two-click affair.

WARNING . . .WARNING . . .WARNING 5.2

Before you download a file or program to your PC, make sure you have both anti-virus and anti-spyware software installed and functional on your computer. This will protect against downloading files infected with either computer viruses or spyware.

◄ SEE ALSO 3.2, *"Protecting Against Computer Viruses"* ▷

◄ SEE ALSO 3.3, *"Protecting Against Spyware"* ▷

The Download Process

The download process differs a bit from site to site, but in general you need to do the following:

1. Make sure you have anti-virus and anti-spyware software installed on your PC, and make sure these programs are configured to scan all files downloaded.

2. Create a special download folder on your computer's hard drive—typically in the Documents or My Documents folder.

3. Find and download the file you want.

4. If the file was compressed (with a ZIP extension), decompress the file using a file extraction utility. Windows has such a utility built in; just use Windows Explorer to navigate to the file, right-click the file icon, and select Extract All.

5. If the file you downloaded was a software program, you'll need to install the software. Installation instructions are usually included somewhere on the download information page or in a readme file included with the file download. In most cases, installation involves running a file named **setup.exe** or **install.exe;** after the setup program launches, follow the onscreen instructions to complete the installation.

6. Delete the compressed file you originally downloaded.

Downloading from a File Archive Website

As noted previously, the safest and easiest way to find and download files is to use a file archive website such as Download.com or Tucows. Downloading a file from any of these archives is typically easy.

◀ *SEE ALSO 5.1, "Searching for Files and Programs Online"* ▶

Once you locate the file you want, you're prompted to click a specific link or button to begin the download. Some sites will begin the download automatically; other sites will prompt Windows to display a dialog box asking if you want to save or open the file (you want to save it) and where you want to save it. Follow the onscreen instructions to begin the download.

Click the Download Now link to download a file from the Tucows file archive.

Downloading Files from Any Web Page

You don't necessarily have to go to a software archive to find files to download. Many web pages feature files to download or links to downloadable files. For example, most computer manufacturers feature drivers and other utilities you can download from their sites to keep your PC in optimal running condition.

If a website features files for downloading, doing so is typically similar to down-loading files from a file archive. Just click the appropriate button or link to initiate the download.

If a web page contains a link to a file (of any type), you can download that file directly from the link—without actually jumping to the file. In Windows, just right-click the link to the file and select Save Target As from the pop-up menu. When prompted, select a location for the file and then click Save to start the download.

5.2

5.3 USING ONLINE BACKUP AND STORAGE

Online File Storage

Online Backup Services

The Internet is not only a good place to download files, but it's also great for uploading files. In this instance, we're talking about uploading your own files to the Internet for storage or backup.

Online File Storage

Online file storage enables you to upload and store your documents, music tracks, and other files on the Internet. You upload files from your computer to a web-based storage service, and then you can access your files from any location using any computer. You can also authorize other users to access your files—great for group collaborations.

This type of online file storage is sometimes called cloud storage, and it's part of a new movement toward **cloud computing.** In cloud computing, files and programs are hosted not on a single personal computer or network but in a "cloud" of multiple computers that is accessed via the Internet.

Online file storage is not typically free. Most services charge by either the amount of storage space used or the amount of bandwidth used to upload and download the files.

Advantages of Online File Storage

Both individuals and large enterprises are turning to online file storage to host their important documents and files. There are three primary benefits to this type of file storage:

▶ **Universal access.** With PC-based storage, you have to somehow transfer files from one computer or device to another when you change locations. That might mean copying files to a USB travel drive or e-mailing files from one computer to another. With online file storage, you can access your files from any computer wherever you may be. Since the files are stored on the web, it doesn't matter if you're using your home or work computer—or whether you're in the office or on the road. They're the same files wherever you are.

▶ **Reliability.** If you've ever had a hard disk fail, you know how important it is to have access to backup data. Fortunately, online storage space can be used as a giant online backup drive; it's easy enough to mirror your existing data servers online. In addition, most services duplicate your data on multiple servers, so even if they have a failure your data isn't lost.

▶ **Scalability.** If you've ever run out of space on your computer's hard disk, you know how important it can be to have just a little more space. When you rent online storage space, it's easy to "flip a switch" and immediately increase your storage space if you all of a sudden have larger storage needs. You don't have to buy the extra hardware (such as a new external hard disk) required to house the extra data.

Disadvantages of Online File Storage

Of course, there is some risk associated with using online storage services—especially if you rely on them as your principal means of storage. Here are the most important issues:

▶ **Reliability.** While online storage services may be more reliable than storing data on your own system, they're not necessarily completely reliable. What do you do if your service provider has technical problems and either goes offline (which means you can't access your data) or actually loses stored data? If an online storage service doesn't have adequate infrastructure or doesn't maintain multiple backups, your data could be at risk.

▶ **Security.** Although all online storage providers tout how secure their systems are, there still exists the possibility that high-tech thieves could break into the system and view or steal your sensitive data. For large companies especially, it's almost always less safe to store your data elsewhere rather than somewhere you have physical control over it.

▶ **Access problems.** Since you're accessing your data over an Internet connection, you're in big trouble if that connection goes down—either on your end or with your cloud storage provider. The connection doesn't even have to go completely down to cause problems; slow connections can make it problematic to access your own data.

WARNING . . .WARNING . . .WARNING

If your data is vital to you, don't rely exclusively on online file storage. Whatever you store online should also be stored somewhere more accessible for safety's sake.

Online File Storage Services

Where online can you store your valuable data? The following are some of the most popular online file storage services:

- Box (www.box.net)
- Egnyte (www.egnyte.com)
- ElephantDrive (www.elephantdrive.com)
- Microsoft Office Live Workspace (workspace.office.live.com), for Microsoft Office documents only
- myDataBus (www.mydatabus.com)
- steekR (www.steekr.com)
- Windows Live SkyDrive (skydrive.live.com)

Online Backup Services

While you may or may not want to entrust all your documents to an online storage service, there is value in storing backup copies of your valuable data online. Obviously, you should be backing up your data on a regular basis anyway; when you use an online backup service, you back up your files to a service over the Internet rather than to a physical hard disk located in your home or office.

The primary advantage of using an online backup service is that your backup data is located in a different location than your main data. With traditional hard disk backup, if your house burns down, you can lose both your original and backup data. With online backup, your key files are safely stored offsite.

Most online backup services require that you install a program on your computer to automate the backup process. Backups typically take place once a day or once a week, per your schedule, in the background or overnight when you're not using your computer. Pricing is based on your specific backup storage needs and can range from $5 to $50 per month, depending on the amount of data stored.

The following are some of the most popular online backup services:

- Backup.com (www.backup.com)
- Carbonite (www.carbonite.com)
- IBackup (www.ibackup.com)
- iDrive (www.idrive.com)

▶ Mozy (www.mozy.com)

▶ SOS Online Backup (www.sosonlinebackup.com)

Naturally, you can also use many of the online file storage services previously discussed for online backup.

WORDS TO GO . . .WORDS TO GO . . .WORDS TO GO

With **cloud computing,** computer files and programs are hosted not on an individual computer but rather on a "cloud" of computers accessed via the Internet.

5.3

6

SHOPPING AND BANKING ONLINE

6.1 MAKING AN ONLINE PURCHASE

Find a Product

Examine the Product

Order the Product

Check Out

Confirm Your Order

If you've never shopped online before, you're probably wondering just what to expect. Shopping on the web is actually quite easy; all you need is your computer—and a credit card.

No matter which online retailer you shop at, the process is pretty much the same. You proceed through a multiple-step process, which we'll examine next.

◄ *SEE ALSO 6.3, "Shopping Safely"* ►

Find a Product

The first step in online shopping is the actual shopping. That means finding the site where you want to shop and then either browsing through different product categories or using the site's search feature to find a specific product.

Browsing product categories online is similar to browsing through the departments of a retail store. You typically click a link to access a major product category and then click further links to view subcategories within the main category. For example, the main category might be Clothing; the subcategories might be Men's, Women's, and Children's clothing. If you click the Men's link, you might see a list of further subcategories: outerwear, shirts, pants, and the like. Just keep clicking until you reach the type of item that you're looking for.

Searching for products is often a faster way to find what you're looking for if you have something specific in mind. For example, if you're looking for a men's silk jacket, you can enter the words **men's silk jacket** into the site's search box and get a list of specific items that match those criteria. The only problem with searching is that you might not know exactly what it is you're looking for; if this describes your situation, you're probably better off browsing. But if you *do* know what you want—and you don't want to deal with lots of irrelevant items—then searching is the faster option.

Examine the Product

Whether you browse or search, you'll probably end up looking at a list of different products on a web page. These listings typically feature one- or two-line descriptions of each item—in most cases, not near enough information for you to make an informed purchase.

The thing to do now is to click the link for the item you're particularly interested in. This should display a dedicated product page complete with a picture and full description of the item. This is where you can read more about the item you selected. Some product pages include different views of the item, pictures of the item in different colors, links to additional information, and maybe even a list of optional accessories that go along with the item.

If you like what you see, you can proceed to the ordering stage of the process. If you want to look at other items, just click your browser's Back button to return to the larger product listing.

Order the Product

6.1

Somewhere on each product description page should be a button labeled Purchase or Buy Now or something similar. This is how you make the actual purchase: by clicking the Buy Now button. You don't order the product just by looking at the product description; you have to manually click that Purchase button to place your order.

When you click the Purchase or Buy Now button, that particular item is added to your **shopping cart.** This is a virtual shopping cart that functions just like a real-world shopping cart; each item you choose to purchase is added to this cart.

After you've ordered a product and placed it in your shopping cart, you can choose to shop for other products on that site or proceed to the site's checkout. It's important to note that when you place an item in your shopping cart, you haven't actually completed the purchase yet. You can keep shopping (and adding more items to your shopping cart) as long as you want.

You can even decide to abandon your shopping cart and not purchase anything at this time. All you have to do is leave the website, and you won't be charged for anything. It's the equivalent of leaving your shopping cart at a real-world retailer and walking out the front door; you don't actually buy anything until you walk through the checkout line.

Check Out

To finalize your purchase, you have to visit the store's checkout. This is like the checkout line at a traditional retail store; you take your virtual shopping cart through the checkout, get your purchases totaled, and then pay for what you're buying.

The checkout at an online retailer typically consists of one or more web pages with forms you have to fill out. If you've visited the retailer before, the site might remember some of your personal information from your previous visit. Otherwise, you'll have to enter your name, address, and phone number, as well as the address you want to ship the merchandise to (if that's different from your billing address). You'll also have to pay for the merchandise, typically by entering a credit card number.

◁ *SEE ALSO 6.5, "Using PayPal"* ▷

The checkout page provides one last opportunity for you to change your order. You can delete items you decide not to buy or change quantities on any item. At some merchants, you can even opt to have your items gift-wrapped and sent to someone as a gift. All these options should be somewhere in the checkout section.

You might also have the option of selecting different types of shipping for your order. Many merchants offer both regular and expedited shipping—the latter for an additional charge.

Another option at some retailers is to group all items together for a reduced shipping cost or to ship items individually as they become available. Grouping items together is attractive cost-wise, but you can get burned if one of the items is out-of-stock or not yet available; you could end up waiting weeks or months for those items that could have been shipped immediately.

Confirm Your Order

After you've entered all the appropriate information, you're asked to place your order. This typically means clicking a button that says Place Your Order or something similar. You might even see a second screen asking you whether you *really* want to place your order, just in case you had second thoughts.

After your order has been placed, you'll see a confirmation screen, typically displaying your order number. Write down this number or print out this page; you'll refer to this number in case you ever need to contact customer service. Most online merchants will also send you a confirmation message via e-mail containing this same information.

That's all there is to it. You shop, you examine the product, you place an order, you proceed to checkout, and then you confirm your purchase. Then all you have to do is wait for the order to ship!

WORDS TO GO . . .WORDS TO GO . . .WORDS TO GO

A virtual **shopping cart** holds the items you purchase at an online store.

6.1

6.2 COMPARISON SHOPPING

How Comparison Shopping Sites Work

Comparing Prices

Comparing Comparison Shopping Sites

More than 85 percent of all Internet users have shopped online. Online shoppers can purchase just about anything on the Internet, from books and DVDs to designer clothing and airline tickets.

But how do you find the best bargains on the web? While you *could* visit the sites of dozens of different online retailers in search of the lowest prices, that's a very time-consuming process. A better approach is to use a single site to do the comparison shopping for you.

These so-called **comparison shopping sites** compile product listings from thousands of different online retailers. You search the comparison shopping site for a type of product or a specific model number, and the site returns a list of retailers that sell that product, complete with each retailer's current price. Choose the merchant that offers what you want at the price you want, and you're ready to buy!

How Comparison Shopping Sites Work

You may be under the understandable impression that a comparison shopping site scours the web for prices from a wide variety of online retailers, much the way an online search engine scours the web for web pages. But that's a false impression.

Instead, these sites build their price/product databases from product links submitted and paid for by participating online retailers. That's right, most price comparison sites charge retailers to be included in their listings; that's how the sites make money.

There's one exception to this operating model: Google Product Search. Google doesn't accept any paid listings; instead, it crawls the web for product and price information just as it does for other types of information. As such, Google Product Search often includes different information in its search results than do the other comparison shopping sites.

Comparing Prices

To use a comparison shopping site, you first have to narrow down the list of items you're looking for. While you can search for something as generic as a "blue shirt" or "DVD player," the likely results will be too broad to be useful. You get better results when you narrow your search to a particular brand or model.

Most sites let you either browse or search for items. Use whichever method you prefer until you see a page for the specific item you're looking for. At that point, click the "compare prices" link or button, and the site will return a list of merchants that sell that item. Next to each merchant's name will be the merchant's current price on that item. You can normally choose to sort results by price (lowest to highest), merchant name, or merchant rating.

Comparison shopping at Shopping.com

Many comparison shopping sites let customers rate or review the merchants from which they purchase. You probably want to restrict your purchases to merchants with the highest ratings.

WARNING . . .WARNING . . .WARNING

You should avoid lower-rated merchants. These merchants receive lower ratings when they don't ship products in a timely fashion, don't offer quality products, or have poor customer service.

🔘 *SEE ALSO 6.3, "Shopping Safely"* ▶

When you find a product at the price you want, you can click through to view that product on the merchant's own website. At that point, you can make your purchase if you like or return to the comparison shopping site to shop some more.

WARNING . . .WARNING . . .WARNING . . .

The lowest price shown on a price comparison site isn't always the best deal. Make sure you compare the *total* cost—including shipping and handling—rather than just the product price.

Comparing Comparison Shopping Sites

The best of these comparison shopping sites offer more than just pricing information. These full-service sites let you sort and filter their search results in a number of different ways and often include customer reviews of both the products and the merchants who sell those products. Some even let you perform side-by-side comparisons of multiple products, which is great if you haven't yet made up your mind as to what you want to buy.

The most popular (and useful) of these price comparison sites include the following:

▶ BizRate (www.bizrate.com)

▶ Google Product Search (www.google.com/products/)

◀ *SEE ALSO 4.4, "Searching with Google"* ▷

   ▶ Live Search cashback (search.live.com/cashback/)

   ▶ mySimon (www.mysimon.com)

   ▶ NexTag (www.nextag.com)

   ▶ PriceGrabber (www.pricegrabber.com)

   ▶ Pricewatch (www.pricewatch.com)

   ▶ Shopping.com (www.shopping.com)

   ▶ Shopzilla (www.shopzilla.com)

   ▶ Yahoo! Shopping (shopping.yahoo.com)

WORDS TO GO . . .WORDS TO GO . . .WORDS TO GO

A **comparison shopping site** compares prices from thousands of different online merchants.

6.3 SHOPPING SAFELY

Key Features for Safe Shopping

The Best Way to Pay

Shopping online is every bit as safe as shopping at a traditional bricks-and-mortar retailer. The best online retailers are just as reputable as traditional retailers, offering safe payment, fast shipping, and responsive service.

Key Features for Safe Shopping

The key is to make sure you're shopping at a reputable online retailer. For the best and safest shopping experience, make sure the retailer offers the following features:

▶ Payment by major credit card or an online payment service such as PayPal or Google Checkout. (Not being able to accept credit cards is the sign of either a very small or fly-by-night merchant.)

6.3

▶ A **secure server** that encrypts your credit card information—and keeps online thieves from stealing your credit card numbers. (You'll know that you're using a secure site when the little lock icon appears in the lower-right corner of your web browser.)

▶ Good contact information—e-mail address, street address, phone number, fax number, and so on. (You want to be able to physically contact the retailer if something goes wrong.)

▶ A stated returns policy and satisfaction guarantee. (You want to be assured that you'll be taken care of if you don't like whatever you ordered.)

▶ A stated privacy policy that protects your personal information. (You don't want the online retailer sharing your e-mail address and purchasing information with other merchants—and potential spammers.)

▶ Information *before you finalize your order* that tells you whether the item is in stock and how long it will take to ship. (More feedback is better.)

The Best Way to Pay

Without question, the safest way to pay for your online orders is with a credit card. That's because credit card purchases are protected by the Fair Credit Billing Act, which gives you the right to dispute certain charges and limits your liability for unauthorized transactions to $50. In other words, if you don't receive what you ordered, you're out a maximum of $50; the credit card company absorbs the rest of the loss.

In addition, some card issuers offer a supplemental guarantee that says you're not responsible for *any* unauthorized charges made online. Make sure that you read your card's statement of terms to determine the company's exact liability policy.

Note that credit card payment can be handled directly on the merchant's website or via an online payment service, such as PayPal or Google Checkout. These services function as credit card processors, enabling merchants of all sizes to accept credit card payments. For your purposes, PayPal and Google Checkout are every bit as safe as entering your credit card number at a merchant's website.

◀ *SEE ALSO 6.5, "Using PayPal"* ▶

WORDS TO GO . . .WORDS TO GO . . .WORDS TO GO

A **secure server** encrypts your credit card information and provides a safe online shopping experience.

6.4 BIDDING AND BUYING ON EBAY

How eBay Auctions Work

eBay Bidding, Step by Step

Sniping to Win

Buy It Now

Bidding Safely

6.4

Some of the best bargains on the web come from other consumers, just like you, selling items on eBay (www.ebay.com). eBay is the web's largest online market-place, facilitating transactions between people and businesses who have things to sell and those who want to buy those things.

Most of the transactions on eBay are in the form of **online auctions.** An online auction is, quite simply, a web-based version of a traditional auction. You find an item you'd like to own and then place a bid on the item. Other users also place bids, and at the end of the auction—typically a seven-day period—the highest bidder wins.

Not every transaction on eBay is an auction transaction, however. eBay also serves up a fair number of fixed-price sales through their **Buy It Now** feature and through merchants who run their own eBay Stores. With more than 36 million items listed for sale on any given day, you're bound to find something you want to buy. eBay has it all, from vintage collectibles and used clothing to the latest music, movies, and electronics.

How eBay Auctions Work

While fixed-price sales are becoming more common, the majority of eBay sales still take place in the online auction format. An online auction is like a tradi-tional real-world auction in which potential buyers bid up the price of an item one bid at a time. On eBay, anyone can bid on items; all you need is a computer, access to the Internet, and an eBay account. (You can sign up for your free account by clicking the Register button on eBay's home page.)

Listing

The auction process begins when the seller creates a listing for an item and lists the item on the auction site. In the item listing, the seller specifies the length of the auction (1, 3, 5, 7, or 10 days) and the minimum bid he or she will accept for that item. The seller is charged a small listing fee to create the auction listing.

◀ *SEE ALSO 6.6, "Selling Items on eBay"* ▶

A potential buyer then browses or searches for a particular item. eBay's search results pages list all items that match a search query; the buyer clicks an item to view the complete listing page for that item. This listing page typically includes a description of the item, one or more product photos, and details about payment and shipping. (Shipping charges are typically over and above the item's final bid price.)

Also included on the listing page is the starting or current bid price for the item. Any bids made by the buyer must be at or above this price.

Bidding

While a bidder *could* make a bid equal to the current minimum bid, this approach requires a lot of work on the part of the bidder. If, say, you bid the current minimum price of $5 on an item, as soon as another bidder bids $5.01, you'd have to log back on and make another, slightly higher bid—$5.02 to continue this example. Then another bidder bids $5.03, you log back on and bid $5.04, and you see how the work just multiplies.

This is why eBay employs special bidding software that automates the bidding process—and minimizes the number of physical bids you have to place. This software acts as your bidding "proxy," making just the right bids for you to remain on top of the bids placed.

The way the **proxy bidding** works, you place a single bid that specifies the maximum amount you're willing to pay for an item. This amount has to be equal to or greater than the current starting or minimum bid. eBay's built-in bidding software then automatically places a bid *less than* the full amount authorized, just high enough to best the current bid. If other bidders bid the price higher, the proxy bidding software steps back in and increases your bid, up to but not exceeding the maximum amount you specified.

For example, the current bid on an item might be $25. A buyer is willing to pay up to $40 for the item and enters a maximum bid of $40. eBay's proxy software places a bid for the new bidder in the amount of $26—higher than the current bid but less than the specified maximum bid. If there are no other bids, this bidder will win the auction with a $26 bid. Other potential buyers, however, can place additional bids; unless their maximum bids are more than the current bidder's

$40 maximum, they are informed (by e-mail) that they have been outbid—and the first bidder's current bid is automatically raised to match the new bids (up to the specified maximum bid price).

Winning—and Paying

At the conclusion of an auction, eBay informs the high bidder of his or her winning bid. The buyer pays for the item (by credit card via PayPal), and the seller then ships the merchandise directly to the buyer.

Concurrent with the close of the auction, eBay bills the seller for a small percentage of the final bid price. This final value fee (FVF) is directly billed to the seller's credit card.

eBay Bidding, Step by Step

Now that you know the general mechanics of how an online auction works, let's look at the bidding process in more detail. Bidding in an online auction is kind of like shopping at an online retailer—except that you don't make a direct purchase. Instead, you make a bid—and you only get to purchase the item at the end of the auction if your bid was the highest bid made.

6.4

Here's how it works:

1. You look for items using eBay's search function (via the search box on eBay's home page) or by browsing through the product categories.

2. When you find an item you're interested in, take a moment to examine all the details. A typical item listing includes a photo of the item, a brief product description, shipping and payment information, and instructions on how to place a bid.

A typical eBay item listing page.

3. Now it's time to place your bid, which you do by clicking the Place Bid button. (If there is no Place Bid button, the item is being sold at a fixed price and not for auction.) Remember, you're not buying the item at this point; you're just telling eBay how much you're willing to pay. Your bid must be at or above the current bid amount. You should determine the maximum amount you'd be willing to pay for that item and bid that amount—regardless of what the current bid level is.

4. eBay uses automatic proxy bidding software to automatically handle the bidding process from here. You bid the maximum amount you're willing to pay, and eBay's proxy software enters the minimum bid necessary—without revealing your maximum bid amount. Your bid will be automatically raised (to no more than your maximum amount) when other users bid.

5. The auction proceeds. Most auctions run for 7 days, although sellers have the option of running 1-, 3-, 5-, 7-, and 10-day auctions.

6. If you're the high bidder at the end of the auction, eBay informs you (via e-mail) that you're the winner.

7. You pay for the item using your credit card via the PayPal service.

8. The seller ships the item to you.

◀ *SEE ALSO 6.5, "Using PayPal"* ▶

It's important to note that even though you've been using the services of the eBay site, the ultimate transaction is between you and the individual seller. You pay PayPal, PayPal then pays the seller, and the seller ships the item directly to you. You don't pay any fees to eBay or PayPal; all those fees are paid by the seller.

Sniping to Win

Savvy sellers know that the best way to ensure an auction victory is to use a technique called **sniping.** With sniping, you don't place your bid until the very end of the auction; placing an early bid only announces your intent and serves to drive up the price of the item.

Instead, you wait until the literal last seconds of the auction to place your bid. At that point—with a half-minute or less to go—you bid your maximum bid amount. By the time your bid is registered, your competing bidders have no time to respond to your bid by raising theirs. Assuming that your bid is higher than their previous maximum bids, you win the auction.

Sniping requires restraint over the course of the auction, split-second timing at auction's end, and a mastery of the eBay process. You can also use third-party sniping services such as Auction Sniper (www.auctionsniper.com) and EZ sniper (www.ezsniper.com) to automate the sniping process.

Buy It Now

An increasing number of eBay listings are not auction listings. Today, many items are listed at a fixed price or with eBay's Buy It Now (BIN) option.

When you see a Buy It Now button *without* a corresponding Place Bid button, you're looking at a straight fixed-price listing. The item is listed for a fixed price; if you want to buy it, you pay the price listing with no bidding involved. Just click the Buy It Now button to purchase and pay for the item.

When you see a Buy It Now button along with a Place Bid button, you're looking at an auction that has a fixed-price option. In this type of auction, the item is sold (and the auction ended) when you click the Buy It Now button. However, a potential buyer can opt to enter an auction bid instead, in the hopes of getting the item for a lower price than the Buy It Now price. If you want the item now for the price listed, click the Buy It Now button to make your purchase.

Bidding Safely

When you're bidding for and buying items on eBay, you're in "buyer beware" territory. You agree to buy an item, almost sight unseen, from someone about whom you know practically nothing. You make your payment and hope you get the item you want shipped in return. Because in most cases you're buying from an individual and not a large company, it's understandable to be nervous about this type of arrangement.

For this reason, eBay has enacted various processes to protect its buyers from fraudulent sellers. These range from simple seller feedback to a more comprehensive buyer protection plan.

Checking Feedback

The first line of defense against eBay fraud is to intelligently choose the people you deal with. The most effective way to do this is via eBay's Feedback system.

Next to every seller's name on each product listing page is a number and percentage, which represents that seller's Feedback rating. You should always check this rating before you bid. If the number is high with an overwhelmingly positive percentage, you can feel safer than if the seller has a lot of negative feedback. For even better protection, click the seller's name in the item listing to view his or her Member Profile, where you can read individual feedback comments. Be smart and avoid those sellers who have a history of delivering less than what was promised.

Avoid sellers with a low feedback number or a percentage below 90 percent or so. These are signs of dissatisfied prior customers—and poor service.

Buyer Protection Plan

What do you do if you follow all this advice and still end up receiving unacceptable merchandise—or no merchandise at all? Fortunately, eBay—via its PayPal service—offers a buyer protection plan for any auction transaction gone bad.

To qualify for PayPal Buyer Protection, your transaction must meet all of these requirements:

- ▶ You used PayPal to pay for the item.
- ▶ You paid in a single payment. (Items purchased with PayPal's multiple-payment plan are not eligible for protection.)
- ▶ You open a dispute within 45 days of the date you sent the payment.
- ▶ The item itself is eligible for the buyer protection plan; look for the PayPal Buyer Protection logo in the item listing.

If you have a legitimate claim, PayPal protects you for the full purchase price, including the original shipping costs. To file a claim, click the Resolution Center link at the bottom of any eBay page. Fortunately, the vast majority of eBay sellers are extremely honest, so you may never have to take advantage of this program. Still, it's good to know that you have protection if you need it.

The **Buy It Now** option lets you purchase fixed-price items on eBay.

An **online auction,** such as those on the eBay site, lets interested buyers bid up the price of an item for sale via the Internet.

Proxy bidding software automates the bidding process for online auctions; you specify the highest amount you're willing to pay, and the software bids the minimum amount necessary to win the auction.

Sniping lets you win an auction by placing a literal last-second bid.

6.5 USING PAYPAL

Accepting PayPal Payments

When you win an item on eBay, you have to pay for that item. Paying via credit card is preferred, but most individual sellers aren't big enough to qualify for their own merchant credit card accounts. Instead, you'll find that most sellers accept credit card payments via PayPal, an online payment service (owned by eBay) that serves as a middleman between buyers and sellers.

PayPal accepts payments by American Express, Discover, MasterCard, and Visa. Although it's primarily a U.S.-based service, it also accepts payments to almost 200 countries around the globe.

Paying via PayPal is simple; you make your payment via credit card the same way you would if you were shopping at any large online merchant. When you supply PayPal with your credit card information, PayPal handles all the credit card paperwork and then deposits funds in the seller's bank account. As noted previously, PayPal even gives protection against fraudulent sales via the PayPal Buyer Protection plan.

6.5

◄ SEE ALSO 6.4, *"Bidding and Buying on eBay"* ▷

From your standpoint as a buyer, using PayPal is transparent—you don't pay any additional fees to use the PayPal service (outside of your normal credit card fees, of course). When you receive the end-of-auction notification that you're the winning bidder, or if you purchase an item via the Buy It Now option, just click the Pay Now button. This displays a purchase review page on the PayPal site. Make sure that all the transaction details are correct and then scroll to the bottom of the page, select a payment method, and conclude the purchase.

Of course, PayPal isn't just for credit card payments. You can make PayPal payments from your debit card, via a checking account withdrawal, or via withdrawal of standing funds in your PayPal account. Just choose the payment method you prefer when prompted.

Accepting PayPal Payments

If you're selling items on eBay, accepting credit card payments is a necessity. (eBay requires it, as a matter of fact.) Assuming that you're too small to qualify for a merchant credit card account from your local bank or financial organization, the best approach is to use PayPal to accept those credit card payments.

◀ *SEE ALSO 6.6, "Selling Items on eBay"* ▶

You sign up for your seller's account (it's free) at the PayPal website (www.paypal.com). This activates PayPal payments for all your eBay item listings. When a buyer uses his or her credit card to pay via PayPal, PayPal charges the credit card and then notifies you (via e-mail) that you've been paid. Upon this notification, you ship the item, access your account on the PayPal site, and instruct PayPal to either cut you a check or transfer the funds into your bank account.

Signing Up

You can sign up for a PayPal seller's account before you create your first eBay listing or when you've been paid for your first sold item. If you choose to wait to sign up, make sure you choose PayPal as an accepted payment method when you're creating your eBay auction listing; when a buyer chooses to pay via PayPal, you'll be prompted at that time to sign up for your PayPal account.

You can choose from three types of PayPal accounts:

▶ **Personal account.** Good for eBay buyers but not good enough for sellers. This type of account does not let you receive credit card payments.

▶ **Premier account.** The best approach for most sellers. This type of account lets you accept both credit card and non-credit card payments.

▶ **Business account.** Necessary only if you're receiving a high volume of payments. With this type of account, you can do business under a corporate or group name and use multiple logins.

Paying for PayPal

There is no charge to create a PayPal account—although there are fees for actually using the service as a seller. The way PayPal works is that the buyer doesn't pay any fees; it's the seller who is assessed a fee based on the amount of money transferred.

This last point is important. PayPal charges fees based on the total amount of money paid, *not* on the selling price of the item. That means that if a $10 item has a $5 shipping and handling cost, the buyer pays PayPal a total of $15—and PayPal bases its fee on that $15 payment.

For most eBay sellers, PayPal charges 2.9 percent of the final transaction price. This fee is lower if you do a higher volume of sales, as detailed in Table 6.1.

**TABLE 6.1   PAYPAL U.S. TRANSACTION FEES
(AS OF FEBRUARY 2009)**

Monthly Sales	Transaction Fee
$0–$3,000.00	2.9%
$3,000.01–$10,000.00	2.5%
$10,000.01–$100,000.00	2.2%
>$100,000.00	1.9%

PayPal also charges a flat $0.30 per transaction regardless of your sales volume. All fees are deducted from your account with every transaction.

Let's work through a typical transaction. Assume you've sold an item on eBay for $50 plus a $10 shipping and handling charge. The buyer pays PayPal the total amount of $60. PayPal then deducts its 2.9 percent of the $60 ($1.74) plus the $0.30 transaction fee for total fees of $2.04. Those fees are deducted from the $60 paid, which leaves you with $57.96.

6.5

Collecting PayPal Payments

When a buyer makes a PayPal payment, those funds are immediately transferred to your PayPal account, and an e-mail notification of the payment is sent to you. In most cases, this e-mail will include all the information you need to link to a specific auction and ship the item to the buyer.

When you sign in to the PayPal site, select the My Account tab and the Overview tab within that. This displays an overview of your recent PayPal activity, including payments made by buyers into your account. Click any item to view more detail about the activity.

In most cases, the buyers' payments come into your account free and clear, ready to be withdrawn from your checking account. The exception to this is an eCheck payment, in which a buyer pays PayPal from his or her personal checking account. Because PayPal has to wait until the "electronic check" clears to receive its funds, you can't be paid until then either. PayPal will send you an e-mail when an electronic payment clears.

Withdrawing PayPal Funds

You can let your funds build up in your PayPal account, or you can choose (at any time) to withdraw all or part of your funds. You have the option of approving an electronic withdrawal directly to your checking account (for which there's no charge; this takes three to four business days) or requesting a check for the designated amount (at a $1.50 charge; this takes one to two weeks). Just click the Withdraw tab (from the Overview tab) and click the appropriate text link.

6.6 SELLING ITEMS ON EBAY

eBay Fees

Creating a New Listing

Managing the Auction Process

As you've learned, eBay is a good place to buy things. It's also a good place to sell things—if you have things to sell.

◀ *SEE ALSO 6.4, "Bidding and Buying on eBay"* ▶

eBay lets you sell almost any type of item, with a few understandable exceptions such as firearms, alcohol, and the like. You don't have to be a big business to sell on eBay; most sellers are individuals like yourself. You can sell both new, still-packaged items and used items you have lying around your garage or attic.

6.6

Selling on eBay is as simple as creating an item listing and waiting for the bids to come in. You can accept payments via PayPal, which makes it easy for buyers to pay you via credit card. When the auction ends, eBay notifies you and provides the buyer's shipping information; all you have to do then is pack and ship the item in a timely fashion.

eBay Fees

As a seller, you have to pay eBay to sell on its marketplace. eBay charges two types of fees. A **listing fee** is paid when you first create an item listing and is based on the item's starting bid price or fixed price. A **final value fee** (FVF) is charged when you sell an item and is based on the item's final selling price. (In addition, you have to pay PayPal fees if the buyer pays via PayPal.)

eBay's listing fees (also called insertion fees) vary by type of product, asking price, and whether you're selling via auction or at a fixed price. You can find a list of current fees online at pages.ebay.com/help/sell/fees.html.

In most cases, it's cheaper to list an item at a fixed price rather than for auction, as fixed-price listings cost either $0.15 or $0.35 regardless of the asking price. That is not the case with auction listings, where fees range from $0.10 to $4.00 per listing, depending on the item's starting price.

eBay's final value fees also vary by the type of product, the type of listing, and the final selling price. Expect to pay anywhere from 6 to 15 percent of the final selling price; these fees are also listed at pages.ebay.com/help/sell/fees.html.

You'll also have to pay a fee if you accept payment by credit card using eBay's PayPal service. For most users, PayPal charges 2.9 percent of the total transaction price (including shipping/handling charges), plus 30¢ per transaction.

Creating a New Listing

Creating an auction listing is as simple as filling out a few forms on the eBay site. You'll need to prepare a little in advance, however; in particular, you'll want to shoot one or more digital photos of the item, which you can then upload into your item listing.

In addition, if you haven't yet registered for an eBay seller account, do so now. You'll need to provide eBay with your credit card and checking account number for verification and billing purposes.

With these preliminaries out of the way, follow these steps to create a new item listing:

1. Click the Sell button on eBay's home page.

2. When the next page appears, enter a short description of your item, which eBay will use to suggest a product category. Once you've entered this description, click the Start Selling button.

3. eBay now displays the Create Your Listing page. In the first section of this page, select a product category for your listing.

4. Enter a title for your item. Your title can be up to 55 characters long and should include model number, color, size, and other important information about what you're selling.

5. Depending on the type of item you're selling, eBay may now prompt you to enter additional data so that it can provide some prefilled information about the item in the listing. You may be prompted for a brand, model number, title, UPC number, ISBN, or some similar information. Enter what information you know.

6. Now that you've selected an item and category, it's time to add one or more pictures to your item listing. The first photo you upload is free; additional photos cost $0.15 each. Click the Add Pictures button; this displays the Add Pictures pop-up window. Follow the onscreen instructions to browse your hard drive for photos to upload.

7. Enter a detailed description of what you're selling. Provide as much information as you feel is appropriate and then format the text as you like.

8. If you're selling an item via online auction, click the Online Auction tab and enter the item's starting price and the length of the auction. If you're offering the Buy It Now option, enter that price as well. If you're selling an item at a fixed price, click the Fixed Price tab and enter the item's price.

9. Select how you want to be paid. For most sellers, this is as simple as checking the PayPal option and entering your PayPal e-mail address.

10. Just below the price and length section is where you tell buyers how you'll ship the item and for how much. Enter the appropriate details. (If you're not sure how much to charge for shipping, click the Research Rates link to use eBay's Shipping Calculator.)

11. If you offer a returns policy or want to block certain types of buyers (such as ones with low or negative feedback), enter this information now.

12. At the very bottom of the Create Your Listing page, eBay tells you how much this listing will cost based on the starting price and options you've selected. If you're okay with this, click the Continue button.

13. eBay now displays a Review Your Listing page. The top of this page details the fees due, the middle of the page previews your complete item listing, and the bottom of the page previews how your listing will look in eBay's search results. If you like what you see, click the List Your Item button at the bottom of the page.

eBay now displays the Congratulations page, which confirms your listing and presents you with important details about your auction—including your item listing's URL. When you see this page, you're done. Your completed listing should appear immediately on the eBay website—although it might take a few hours to be listed in the appropriate category listings.

Managing the Auction Process

Once you've created your item listing, all you have to do now is sit back and wait for the auction to progress.

When the auction is over or when a buyer purchases a fixed-price item, eBay notifies you (via e-mail) and provides the buyer's shipping information. Most buyers will pay via credit card (using the PayPal service) as soon as the auction is over by clicking the Pay Now link in the end-of-auction notice they receive. If the high bidder doesn't pay immediately, e-mail him an invoice containing the final bid price and the shipping and handling charges.

Then after you've been paid, pack the item and ship it out using the shipping service you specified in your item listing. That's it—you've just completed a successful eBay auction!

WORDS TO GO . . .WORDS TO GO . . .WORDS TO GO

An eBay **final value fee** (FVF) is charged when an item sells, and it is based on the item's selling price.

An eBay **listing fee** is charged when you list an item for sale, and it is based on the item's starting bid price or fixed price.

6.7 USING CRAIGSLIST

Browsing and Buying

Listing an Item for Sale

Making the Sale

eBay is a great way to sell items that are small and easily shipped from one end of the country to another. But if you want to buy or sell something larger and harder to ship, such as a piece of furniture or exercise equipment, it's better to stick to a local marketplace for that item.

◀ *SEE ALSO 6.4, "Bidding and Buying on eBay"* ▶

The best place to sell local items is via craigslist (www.craigslist.org), a network of local **online classifieds.** On craigslist, you pick your local site and then create a classified ad for what you're selling; potential buyers browse the ads, contact the seller, and pay for and pick up the items locally.

Unlike eBay's online auctions, items on craigslist are typically listed at a fixed cost; there is no bidding process. As with traditional print-based classified ads, some sellers might accept lower prices or may list an item at a fixed price "or best offer." All negotiations are between the seller and the buyer. Most sales are paid for with cash.

WARNING . . .WARNING . . .WARNING . .

craigslist doesn't offer the buyer and seller protection plans that you find on eBay. If a buyer pays with a bad check, there's not much the seller can do about it; if a seller gets an item home and finds out it doesn't work as promised, *caveat emptor.*

Browsing and Buying

To use craigslist, you first have to navigate to your specific local site. You do this by going to the national craigslist home page and then clicking your city or state from the list. You then see links to all the product and service categories offered by craigslist in your area.

Listings on a local craigslist site.

Categories available mirror those in a typical newspaper classifieds section, ranging from Housing and Jobs to Personals and Services. As you might suspect, most items offered for sale are in the For Sale category. Within the For Sale category, you'll find additional subcategories such as Computers, Furniture, Musical Instruments, Electronics, Tools, and the like. Click through to a given subcategory to view the ads within that category.

A typical craigslist ad includes a title, a description of the item being sold, and one or more pictures of the item. Some ads include the seller's phone number, but most don't. Instead, you contact the seller by clicking the e-mail link included in the ad.

If you're interested in the item, contact the seller and express your interest. You can then arrange a time to view the item; if you like what you see, you can pay for it then and take it with you.

WARNING . . .WARNING . . .WARNING

Not all local craigslist sites have a large number of listings. In most big cities, such as New York and San Francisco, craigslist is a vibrant marketplace. If you're in some smaller cities and towns, however, you may find fewer listings—and, if you're selling, far fewer potential buyers.

The craigslist site is also popular for people seeking housing, people seeking jobs, and people seeking people (in the form of personals ads). In short, if it's local, you can probably find it on craigslist!

Listing an Item for Sale

Listing an item for sale on craigslist is similar to listing a fixed-price item on eBay. The differences are more in what you *don't* have to do; there are fewer "blanks" to fill in.

The other big difference between eBay and craigslist is that craigslist is absolutely free. The site charges nothing to list an item and charges no final value or commission fees. This makes craigslist quite attractive to sellers; you can list anything you want and don't have to pay if it doesn't sell.

WARNING . . .WARNING . . .WARNING . . .

While the vast majority of craigslist ads are free, not all are. In particular, craigslist charges for job listings in some major cities as well as brokered apartment listings in New York City.

6.7

To list an item for sale on the craigslist site, follow these steps:

1. Navigate to the home page for your local craigslist community and then click the Post to Classifieds link on the left side of the page.

2. When the next page appears, click the category in which you want to list—probably the For Sale category.

3. You're now prompted to select an appropriate subcategory. Do so.

4. You now see the listing creation page. Here you enter information into the appropriate fields: Price, Specific Location, Posting Title, Posting Description, Your E-mail Address, Reply To (to have craigslist "anonymize" your e-mail address), Add/Edit Images, and Permissions. After you've entered all the necessary information, click the Continue button.

5. This displays a preview of your listing; if you like what you see, click Continue. (If you don't like what you see, click the Edit button and make some changes.) Your listing will appear on the craigslist site within the next 15 minutes or so.

Making the Sale

When someone replies to your listing, craigslist forwards you that message via e-mail. You can then reply to the potential buyer directly; in most instances, that means arranging a time for that person to come to your house to either view or purchase the item of interest.

Unlike eBay, where you have to ship the item to the buyer, craigslist buyers more often than not pick up the items they purchase. That means you have to be at home for the buyer to visit, and you have to be comfortable with strangers visiting. You also have to be prepared to help the buyer load up whatever it is you're selling into his or her vehicle for the trip home—which can be a major issue if you're selling big stuff and you're a small person.

WARNING . . .WARNING . . .WARNING

If you're not comfortable with strangers visiting your house, arrange to meet at a neutral location if you're selling something portable. If you're selling a larger item, make sure another family member or friend is home when the buyer is supposed to visit.

As to payment, the vast majority of craigslist purchases are made with cash. You may want to keep some spare cash on hand to make change in case the buyer pays with larger bills.

For higher-priced items, you may want to accept payment via cashier's check or money order. Just be sure that the check or money order is made out for the exact amount of the purchase; you don't want to give back cash as change for a money order purchase.

WARNING . . .WARNING . . .WARNING

Under no circumstances should you accept payment via personal check. It's far too easy for a shady buyer to write you a check and take off with the merchandise, only for you to discover a few days later that the check bounced. If you *must* accept a personal check, hold on to the merchandise for a full 10 working days to make sure the check clears; it's probably easier for all involved for the buyer to just get the cash.

WORDS TO GO . . .WORDS TO GO . . .WORDS TO GO

Online classifieds are the web-based version of traditional print classified ads, connecting local buyers and sellers.

6.8 BANKING ONLINE

Different Approaches

Web-Based Banking

Software-Based Banking

You don't have to stand in line at your local bank anymore. Online banking lets you perform some or all of your normal banking tasks with your personal computer over the Internet. No longer do you have to drive all the way to the nearest teller window to transfer funds, find out account balances, and pay your bills. Instead, all these activities and more can be done online—although you'll still need to visit the bank (or an ATM) to make deposits and withdrawals.

The advantages of online banking, however, may come at a cost. Some banks charge either a monthly or per-transaction fee to access their online banking features; others, however, offer online banking for free. If you anticipate doing a lot of online banking, it pays to shop around for the best deal.

6.8

Online banking has become ubiquitous in the twenty-first century. Chances are good that your current bank offers some kind of online banking; check your bank's website or call your local branch to verify what services are available.

Different Approaches

There are two basic approaches to online banking. **Web-based banking** enables you to use your web browser to access your bank's website, while **software-based banking** lets you use Quicken or Microsoft Money financial management software to electronically access your bank, perform specified activities, and download your latest account information. Some banks offer both web-based and software-based services; others offer only web-based banking. (If you use Quicken or Microsoft Money, make sure your bank interfaces with your financial management program.)

Each approach has its benefits, as you'll see. But which should you use?

If you're just getting started and want the easiest possible approach, go with web-based banking. If you're comfortable with more advanced financial management, however—and if your bank interfaces with Quicken or Microsoft Money—you may prefer the cross-account management capabilities of a financial management program.

Web-Based Banking

The primary benefit of web-based banking is that anyone can do it; you don't need to purchase and learn any particular software program to do your banking. Second, you can access a bank's web page from any PC connected to the web, so you can do your banking when you're away from home; the same can't be said for software programs that are installed on specific machines. Third, setting up your account at a web-based bank is relatively easy compared to all the information-entering you have to do with Quicken or Microsoft Money. On a website, once you enter your account number or username and password, your account should be ready to access. Finally, all your financial information is stored on the bank's website, so if your computer crashes, your data won't be lost.

Software-Based Banking

There are also several benefits to software-based banking with Quicken or Microsoft Money. First, you can do a lot of your work offline without hogging your Internet connection; you need only log on to upload your instructions and download your recent transactions. Second, you can use your financial management program to handle *all* your personal finances from multiple accounts and multiple banks. With web-based banking, you have to access different websites for each of your bank and credit card accounts .

WORDS TO GO . . . WORDS TO GO . . . WORDS TO GO

Software-based banking enables you to access and manage your bank accounts via a financial management software program such as Quicken or Microsoft Money.

Web-based banking enables you to access and manage your bank account from any web browser.

7

MUSIC, PICTURES, AND VIDEOS

7.1 FINDING MUSIC ONLINE

Digital Audio Formats

Digital Rights Management

Online Music Stores

File-Sharing Networks

The Internet is a great place to find, download, and listen to music of all types and styles. You can listen to streaming music "live" or download tracks to listen to on your PC, iPod, or other portable music player. It's a great way to beef up your music player—without buying a single physical CD.

◀ *SEE ALSO 7.3, "Listening to Internet Radio"* ▶

Digital Audio Formats

Before you start downloading music, it's important to understand the various audio file formats available today. There are many different ways to make a digital recording, and different online music stores (and portable music players) use different file formats.

There are two types of audio files: compressed and uncompressed. **Uncompressed audio** files reproduce the exact file contained on a compact disc; these files are very large but have excellent sound quality. **Compressed audio** files remove bits and pieces of the original music to create a smaller file (that's easier to store and download from the Internet) but with reduced audio fidelity.

Most music files you find online are compressed files, as uncompressed files are simply too large to download efficiently. That said, some types of compressed files sound better than others. Here's a quick overview of the most popular compressed audio file formats found on the web:

▶ **MP3**   The MP3 format (file extension .MP3) is the oldest and most universal compressed audio format. Almost every music player program and portable music player, including the Apple iPod, is MP3 compatible.

▶ **AAC**   The AAC format (file extension .AAC or .M4A) is Apple's proprietary format and is used by both iTunes and the iPod. AAC-format files are typically a little larger than MP3 files but have higher-quality sound.

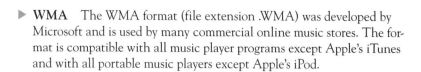

▶ **WMA**   The WMA format (file extension .WMA) was developed by Microsoft and is used by many commercial online music stores. The format is compatible with all music player programs except Apple's iTunes and with all portable music players except Apple's iPod.

When you're downloading music, you probably don't have a choice of formats; you have to take the music in the format in which it's offered. Practically, that means if you have an iPod and use the iTunes store, you'll get your music in AAC format. If you have any other type of player (such as the Microsoft Zune or Creative Zen) and get your music from any other online music store (such as Amazon or Napster), you'll get your music in either MP3 or WMA format.

When you're copying files from your CD to your PC, however, you have your choice of format. For compatibility with all portable music players (including the iPod), use the MP3 format. If you have an iPod and only want to play your files on other iPods, you can use the better-sounding AAC format. Or, if you have a non-Apple player and never want to play your music on an iPod, you can use the equally good-sounding WMA format.

Another factor that affects sound quality, no matter the file format, is the **bitrate** at which a recording was made. Tracks recorded at a higher bitrate retain more of the original audio information and sound better. Tracks recorded at a lower bitrate sacrifice sound quality but result in smaller-sized files.

7.1

Digital Rights Management

Until quite recently, most music you downloaded from online music stores was encoded with **digital rights management** (DRM) technology. DRM was designed to protect copyright owners from unlawful distribution, copying, and sharing of their music. If a track you downloaded is protected with DRM, you're limited as to how you can copy and listen to that song.

DRM works by encoding the audio file in a type of wrapper file format. This wrapper file includes a user key, which is used to decode and play the track—under specified conditions. For example, a DRM license might dictate how many different PCs or portable music players the track can be copied to, whether it can be burned to CD, and so on. If you try to use the song in a way not permitted by the license, the DRM protection keeps it from playing.

DRM technology can be applied to audio files in the AAC and WMA formats; it cannot be applied to MP3 files. This is why most online music stores encoded their music as either AAC or WMA formats—to facilitate DRM.

Recently, however, the trend has been away from DRM to selling DRM-free tracks, most often in the MP3 format. (Apple iTunes is an exception to this, selling its DRM-free tracks in its own AAC format.) The benefit to DRM-free music is that once you purchase it, you can use it however you wish. You can play it on any number of PCs or portable music players and burn it onto an unlimited number of custom CDs. It's a much more listener-friendly solution, which is why many online music stores are now offering DRM-free music.

Online Music Stores

One of the great things about digital music is that you can listen to just the songs you want. You're not forced to purchase an entire album; you can download that one song you really like and ignore the rest. Even better, you can take songs you like from different artists and create your own playlists; it's like being your own DJ or record producer.

Where do you go to download your favorite songs? You have a lot of choices, but the easiest is to shop at an online music store. These are websites that offer millions of individual songs from your favorite artists, all completely legal. You pay about a dollar per song and download the music files directly to your computer's hard disk. From there you can copy your downloaded music to your portable music player or burn downloaded tracks to a custom music CD.

WARNING . . .WARNING . . .WARNING

Downloading music can be difficult on a slow dial-up Internet connection due to the large file sizes involved. When you're downloading music, it's best to have a high-speed broadband connection.

When you're shopping for songs to download, here are some of the most popular online music stores:

- ▶ Amazon MP3 Downloads (www.amazon.com)
- ▶ Dada (www.dada.net)
- ▶ eMusic (www.emusic.com)
- ▶ HDGiants (www.hdgiants.com)
- ▶ iMesh (www.imesh.com)
- ▶ iTunes Store (www.apple.com/itunes/store/)
- ▶ MP3.com (www.mp3.com)

- Napster (www.napster.com)

- PassAlong (www.passalong.com)

- Puretracks (www.puretracks.com)

- Rhapsody (www.rhapsody.com)

- Wal-Mart Music Downloads (mp3.walmart.com)

SEE ALSO 7.2, "Downloading Music from the iTunes Store" ▶

File-Sharing Networks

Some Internet music doesn't come from any website—it comes from other users. Over the past couple decades, the web has seen a profusion of **file-sharing networks,** where you can swap music files with your fellow computer users. You connect your computer (via the Internet) to the network, which already has thousands of other users connected. When you find a song you want, you transfer it directly from the other computer to yours.

Of course, file sharing works in both directions. When you register with one of these services, other users can download digital audio files from *your* computer as long as you're connected to the Internet.

7.1

File-Sharing Software

Most file-sharing networks require you to download a copy of their software and then run that software whenever you want to download. You use their software to search for the songs you want; the software then generates a list of users who have that file stored on their computers. You select which computer you want to connect to, and then the software automatically downloads the file from that computer to yours.

The most popular of these file-sharing services include:

- Blubster (www.blubster.com)

- FrostWire (www.frostwire.com)

- LimeWire (www.limewire.com)

- MP3 Rocket (www.mp3rocket.com)

In addition, BitTorrent (www.bittorrent.com) is a file-sharing program used for downloading both music and video files. Many people use BitTorrent to find and download their favorite songs—and their favorite television shows.

Issues

There are several downsides to swapping music over a file-sharing network—and they're serious enough to keep many users away.

First, and most important, if you're downloading copyrighted songs (which you probably are), it's illegal. The Recording Industry Association of America has kept itself quite busy filing lawsuits against file sharers—regular users including college students and little old ladies. The RIAA invariably wins these lawsuits, so if you don't want to risk getting sued, you shouldn't use a file-sharing network.

Second, when you install some file-sharing programs, you also install spyware. These spyware programs can track everything you do on your computer and feed that information back to some marketing service. If you don't like spyware inhabiting your PC, stay away.

◄ SEE ALSO 3.3, *"Protecting Against Spyware"* ▷

Finally, many file-sharing networks are rife with computer viruses. You might think that you're downloading an audio file but instead find yourself loading the latest computer virus onto your hard disk. These file-sharing networks don't have any oversight (unlike paid sites), so you never know what you're actually downloading. Unless you're extremely diligent about using anti-virus software and checking every file you access, download at your own risk.

◄ SEE ALSO 3.2, *"Protecting Against Computer Viruses"* ▷

Know that these risks are unique to file-sharing networks. If you download from a reputable online music store, such as the iTunes Store or Amazon MP3 Downloads, you don't face any of these issues. Files downloaded from commercial online music stores are legal and free from spyware and viruses. If you want a guaranteed safe downloading experience, stick with one of the commercial sites—and stay clear of the file-sharing networks.

The **bitrate** of an audio recording affects the resulting sound quality; the higher the bitrate, the better the sound.

Compressed audio results in smaller files that can be comfortably downloaded but with some sacrifice in sound quality. The most popular compressed audio formats are AAC, MP3, and WMA.

Digital rights management (DRM) is a technology used to prevent unauthorized use of copyrighted music and video files.

File-sharing networks let you download music and video files uploaded by other users; these sites often have illegal copies of music and movies available.

Uncompressed audio reproduces exactly what you hear on a CD—but results in files too large to be downloaded from the Internet.

7.1

7.2 DOWNLOADING MUSIC FROM THE ITUNES STORE

Finding and Downloading Music

Playing Music

Syncing Music to Your iPod

The most popular online music store today is Apple's iTunes Store. The iTunes Store (www.apple.com/itunes/store/) offers millions of songs for downloading, priced from $0.69 to $1.29 each; movies, TV shows, podcasts, and other media are also available.

◀ *SEE ALSO 7.1, "Finding Music Online"* ▷

◀ *SEE ALSO 10.6, "Understanding Podcasts"* ▷

All songs available in the iTunes Store are in Apple's proprietary AAC file format, which means that they won't play in most third-party music player programs or on most non-Apple portable music players. But you can use Apple's iTunes software to play the files and (of course) play all downloaded songs on your Apple iPod.

As of early 2009, most tracks in the iTunes Store were being offered without DRM encoding. Prior to this, all iTunes tracks had DRM encoding. These DRM-free tracks are dubbed iTunes Plus tracks and are available in better-sounding, higher-bitrate versions.

Finding and Downloading Music

To use the iTunes Store, you first have to download the iTunes software. To download the software, go to the iTunes Store home page and click the Free Download button.

Once the iTunes software is up and running on your computer, you access the iTunes Store by clicking the iTunes Store icon in the program's Source pane on the left side of the window. The iTunes Store home page displays featured music and videos and includes links to key parts of the store.

There are several different ways to find music in the iTunes Store. To browse by genre, click the Genres button next to the Music link in the iTunes Store pane.

New music is displayed in the Music tab of the New and Noteworthy pane in the middle of the page. In addition, you can use the Search iTunes Store box at the top of the page to search for specific songs or artists.

The iTunes Store in the iTunes program.

7.2

Once you see the results of your search or browsing, click the Buy Song button to purchase a particular song. After you confirm your purchase, the song will be downloaded automatically to your PC and added to your iTunes Library. You can listen to your downloaded music in the iTunes music player or transfer the music to your iPod.

Playing Music

You use the iTunes software to play the music you've downloaded on your computer. To play a track, go to the Library section of the Source pane and select Music. This displays all the songs you have stored on your computer.

You can click the View buttons at the top of the iTunes window to display your music in several different ways: List, Grid, or Cover Flow, which lets you "flip" through all the album covers for your digital music. Within a view, click the Albums, Artists, Genres, or Composers buttons to sort your music appropriately.

To view all the songs for a given album, click an album cover. To play an individual song, double-click the title in the song list—or select the song and click the Play button in the transport controls. To play an entire album, double-click the album cover.

Syncing Music to Your iPod

Any time you connect your iPod to your PC, the music in your iTunes library is automatically synced to your iPod. Connecting the iPod to your PC is as simple as connecting the cable that comes with your iPod to a USB port on your computer. When the iPod is connected, your PC automatically launches the iTunes software and downloads any new songs and playlists you've added since the last time you connected. You can then listen to your newest downloads on your iPod.

7.3 LISTENING TO INTERNET RADIO

Playing Internet Radio

Finding Internet Radio Stations

Downloadable music isn't the only music available on the Internet. Many real-world radio stations, as well as numerous web-only stations, broadcast over the Internet using a technology called **streaming audio.**

◄ *SEE ALSO 7.1, "Finding Music Online"* ▷

Streaming audio is different from downloading an audio file. When you download a file, you can't start playing that file until it is completely downloaded to your PC. With streaming audio, however, playback can start before an entire file is downloaded. This also enables live broadcasts—both of traditional radio stations and made-for-the-web stations—to be sent from the broadcast site to your PC.

Another difference is that streaming audio doesn't save any files on your computer, so listening to it is more of a "live" experience; you can't go back and listen to it again. In contrast, when you download an audio file to your computer, you can listen to that file whenever you want and however many times you want.

7.3

Playing Internet Radio

Internet radio can be listened to from within many music player programs. For example, the iTunes music player has a Radio function that facilitates finding and listening to a variety of Internet radio stations. In addition, many Internet radio sites feature built-in streaming software or direct you to sites where you can download the appropriate music player software.

WARNING . . .WARNING . . .WARNING

Although you can listen to Internet radio over a traditional dial-up connection, you'll hear better-quality sound over a broadband connection. Streaming audio over dial-up frequently results in unwanted stopping and starting as the audio is streamed over the slow dial-up connection.

Finding Internet Radio Stations

When you're looking for Internet radio broadcasts (of which there are thousands daily), you need a good directory of available programming. The following sites offer links to either traditional radio simulcasts or original Internet radio programming:

- ▶ AOL Radio (music.aol.com/radioguide/bb/)
- ▶ Jango (www.jango.com)
- ▶ LAUNCHcast (music.yahoo.com/launchcast/)
- ▶ Live365 (www.live365.com)
- ▶ Mike's Radio World (www.mikesradioworld.com)
- ▶ Pandora (www.pandora.com)
- ▶ RadioTower.com (www.radiotower.com)
- ▶ SHOUTcast (yp.shoutcast.com)
- ▶ XM Radio Online (xmro.xmradio.com)

WORDS TO GO . . .WORDS TO GO . . .WORDS TO GO

Streaming audio lets you listen to music in real time without first downloading the complete file to your computer.

7.4 SEARCHING FOR IMAGES ONLINE

Google Image Search

Photo Sharing Sites

The Internet is also a great source for finding digital photos and other images. You can download the images you find to your computer to use as desktop wallpaper or just store the images for future viewing.

WARNING . . .WARNING . . .WARNING . . .

Commercial use of copyrighted images is prohibited. This means you can use photos you find on the web for your own personal use but not for any commercial web page or document.

Google Image Search

One of the best ways to find photos and other images online is to use Google Image Search (images.google.com). Google's image index is the largest on the web.

7.4

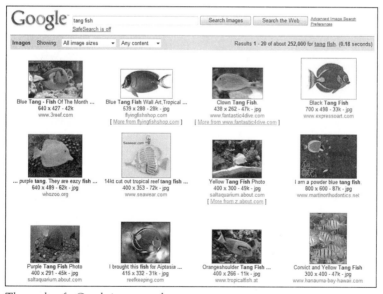

The results of a Google image search.

◀ **SEE ALSO 4.4, "Searching with Google"** ▶

Basic Searching

Using Google Image Search is as easy as entering your query and clicking the Search Images button. Google returns a search results page with matching images displayed in a grid of thumbnail pictures.

You can fine-tune your search results by using the filters at the top of the search results page. Click the first list to filter by image size (Small to Extra Large); click the second list to filter by content type (Any content, News content, Faces, Clip art, Line drawings, or Photo content).

For each thumbnail image, Google lists an image caption, the size of the image (in both pixels and kilobytes), the file type, and the host website. To view any image, all you have to do is click the thumbnail.

Viewing Images

When you click a thumbnail image on the search results page, the original page is displayed in a frame at the bottom of the next page. At the top of the page is the Google Images frame, which includes the image thumbnail, information about the image, and a few important links:

▶ To view the host page without the Google frame, click the Remove Frame link.

▶ To view the picture full size, click the See Full Size Image link.

▶ To return to your search results, click the Back to Image Results link.

Photo Sharing Sites

Another place to find photos on the web is the many photo-sharing websites. These sites let users post their photos for other users to view and, in many cases, download.

◀ *SEE ALSO 7.5, "Sharing Digital Photos Online"* ▶

Of all these sites, far and away the most popular among hobbyist and professional photographers is Flickr (www.flickr.com). Flickr is a more public site than some other photo sharing sites, which tend to be repositories for private photos shared with friends and family. In contrast, Flickr lets photographers share their work with all of the site's users.

Flickr works by creating a home page for each photographer. On this page, the photographer's photos are grouped into "sets," typically organized by topic. From here you can click a photo to view it full screen or choose to view all photos as an onscreen slideshow.

To download a photo from Flickr, click the All Sizes icon above the photo. When the next page appears, click the Download the Large Size link; when prompted, opt to save the photo as a file on your hard disk.

7.4

7.5 SHARING DIGITAL PHOTOS ONLINE

E-mailing Digital Photos

Photo Sharing Sites

Printing Photos Online

Before the advent of the Internet and digital photography, if you wanted to share your photos with friends and family, you had to have extra prints made and then hand them out or mail them off. This approach is not only time-consuming, it's also costly; you have to pay for each extra print you make.

In today's age of digital photography, you can still make photo prints. But now you can share your photos digitally online with anyone who has an Internet connection—it's easier, faster, and cheaper than sharing photographic prints.

E-mailing Digital Photos

Perhaps the easiest way to share your digital photos is to e-mail them. No special software or services are required; all you have to do is attach your photos to an e-mail message you create in your regular e-mail program and then send that message to as many recipients as you like.

◀ *SEE ALSO 12.7, "Working With File Attachments"* ▶

Attaching Photos

Since a digital photo is just another type of computer file, the process of attaching a photo to an e-mail message is the same as attaching any file. Create a new message in your e-mail program, click the attachments button, and then select those photos you want to attach. Click the Send button and your message is sent on its way, complete with the photos you selected.

Resizing Photo Attachments

As easy as this process is, there is one issue you need to be aware of before you start e-mailing your photos far and wide. The issue is the size of the photo files you e-mail.

If you're e-mailing photos pretty much as they were shot with your camera, you're probably e-mailing some very large files. This can be a problem if you or your recipients are using a slow dial-up Internet connection; the larger the attached files, the longer it takes to send or receive an e-mail message. In addition, some ISPs have trouble handling messages that are too large; you want to avoid messages more than 1 MB or 2 MB in size.

For this reason, you may want to resize your photos before you e-mail them. If your recipients will only be viewing your photos on their computer screens, you should make your photos no larger than the typical screen—no more than 800 pixels wide by 600 pixels tall.

You can use any photo editing program, such as Adobe Photoshop Elements or Google's Picasa, to resize your pictures. For that matter, some e-mail programs can be configured to automatically resize large photos when they're attached. In Windows Vista, the Windows Photo Gallery application includes an E-mail button that, when clicked, lets you select a size for the picture you want to send.

WARNING . . .WARNING . . .WARNING

If your recipients will be printing the photos you send, you probably don't want to resize them. A photo resized to 800×600 pixels doesn't have enough picture resolution to create a detailed print. You'll want to keep your photos at their original size if they're going to be printed; any resizing will result in fuzzy prints.

7.5

Photo Sharing Sites

If you're sharing your photos with large numbers of people, an even better solution is to post your pictures on a photo sharing website. These sites let you store your photos in online photo albums, which can then be viewed by any number of visitors via their web browsers—for free. These sites also offer photo printing services, and some also sell photo-related merchandise such as picture T-shirts, calendars, mugs, and the like. Most of these sites are free to use; they make their money by selling prints and other merchandise.

Using a Photo Sharing Site

To use a photo sharing site, you start by signing up for a free account. Once your account is created, you choose which photos on your PC you want to share. Once the photos are selected, the site automatically uploads them from your PC to the website. You then organize the photos into photo albums, each of which has its own unique URL. You can then e-mail the URL to your friends and family; when they access the photo site, they view your photos on their computer screens. If they like what they see, they can order their own photo prints (which they pay for, not you).

Choosing a Photo Sharing Site

The most popular of these photo sharing sites include:

- ▶ dotPhoto (www.dotphoto.com)
- ▶ DropShots (www.dropshots.com)
- ▶ Flickr (www.flickr.com)
- ▶ Fotki (www.fotki.com)
- ▶ FotoTime (www.fototime.com)
- ▶ Kodak Gallery (www.kodakgallery.com)
- ▶ PhotoWorks (www.photoworks.com)
- ▶ Picasa Web Albums (picasaweb.google.com)
- ▶ PictureTrail (www.picturetrail.com)
- ▶ Shutterfly (www.shutterfly.com)
- ▶ Snapfish (www.snapfish.com)
- ▶ Webshots (www.webshots.com)
- ▶ Winkflash (www.winkflash.com)

Printing Photos Online

Most photo sharing websites also offer photo printing services. Once you've uploaded your photos, all you have to do is select the photos you want to print and then click the appropriate button.

You'll probably have the option of choosing different sizes of prints. Most sites offer a selection of 4"×6", 5"×7", 8"×10", 11"×14", 16"×20", 20"×30", and wallet-sized prints in either matte or glossy finish. Choose the size and quantity you want for each print and then enter your payment and shipping information.

Most sites ship within a day or two of receiving your order; add shipping time, and you should receive your prints in less than a week. Shipping is typically via the U.S. Postal Service or a similar shipping service.

Other sites, such as those for Wal-Mart and Walgreens, offer photo prints that you can pick up in your local stores. Upload your prints as normal from your computer but then opt for local pickup. Your files are sent to your nearest location and printed there.

7.6 WATCHING VIDEOS ON YOUTUBE

Finding Videos

Viewing Videos

Sharing Videos

Music and photos aren't the only forms of media you can find on the Internet. One of the fastest-growing uses of the Internet is watching videos—both commercial videos (movies and TV shows) and homemade videos from other users.

The biggest video site on the web is YouTube (www.youtube.com). YouTube is a true video-sharing community, where you can view videos uploaded by other users—and share your own videos as well. The most popular YouTube videos quickly become **viral videos,** getting passed around from e-mail to e-mail and linked to other sites and blogs on the web.

SEE ALSO 7.7, "Uploading YouTube Videos" ▶

Finding Videos

7.6

How do you find videos to watch on the YouTube site? Most new users start out by browsing for interesting videos. Browsing is perhaps the best way to discover new videos; you can click through the categories until you find something you like.

WARNING . . .WARNING . . .WARNING

While YouTube has strict content policies and a self-policing community, there are no parental controls on the site—so it's viewer beware!

Browsing YouTube is a simple matter of clicking a link—and then another link, and then another link, and then another link. The more you click, the more you discover.

When you're not sure what you want to watch, browsing YouTube is probably the way to go. If you have a particular type of video in mind, however, searching is a better approach.

To search for a video, simply enter your query into the search box found at the top of every YouTube page. YouTube now returns a list of videos that best match your search criteria. If you see a video you want to watch, click the thumbnail for that video.

Viewing Videos

Viewing YouTube videos is a relatively self-contained experience. All YouTube videos play on their own video viewing page in your web browser. No additional software is necessary, save for the Adobe Flash Player plug-in for your browser. (You can download the Flash Player from www.adobe.com/products/flashplayer/.)

When you click the title or thumbnail of any video on a search or browse page, a page for that video is displayed. The main part of this page is the video player, which plays the video you've just selected. Playback starts automatically, although you can pause and restart it at any time using the transport controls underneath the video player.

Watching a YouTube video.

WARNING . . . WARNING . . . WARNING

Some large videos or videos played over a slow Internet connection may pause periodically after playback has started. This is due to the playback getting ahead of the streaming video download. If you find a video stopping and starting, just click the Play/Pause button to pause playback until more of the video has downloaded.

Many videos are available in high-quality or high-definition versions. To view the higher-quality version, just click the Watch in High Quality or Watch in HD link underneath the video player. In addition, you can view the video full screen by clicking the Full Screen button on the lower-right side of the video player; press Esc to exit full-screen mode.

Sharing Videos

Videos become viral when they're shared among hundreds and thousands of users—and the easiest way to share a YouTube video is via e-mail. YouTube lets you send an e-mail to your friends that contains a link to the video you like. When a friend receives this e-mail, he or she can click the link in the message to go to YouTube and play the video.

When you want to share a video, go to that video's page, click the More Share Options link underneath the video player. When the Share tab expands, scroll to the Send This Video section.

Enter the e-mail addresses of the intended recipients into the To box (separate multiple addresses with commas) or select one or more recipients from your contacts list. Enter a personal message if you want and then click the Send button. In a few minutes your recipients will receive the message, complete with a link to the selected video.

7.6

To view the video, all a recipient has to do is click the video thumbnail or link in the message. This opens a web browser, accesses the YouTube site, and starts playing the video you shared.

7.7 UPLOADING YOUTUBE VIDEOS

Recording a YouTube Video

Uploading Videos from a Camcorder

Uploading Videos from a Webcam

YouTube isn't just for viewing other people's videos; you can also upload your own videos to the YouTube site. How you do this depends on what type of video you're uploading.

◀ SEE ALSO 7.6, *"Watching Videos on YouTube"* ▶

Recording a YouTube Video

Most videos shown on YouTube are recorded with standard consumer-grade camcorders. You don't need fancy professional equipment; just use your camcorder to shoot the video and then edit what you shoot using any video editing program.

Before you upload a video to YouTube, you have to make sure the video meets YouTube's requirements. Here are the file specs you need to meet:

- ▶ MPEG-4 format video with either the DivX or XviD codecs
- ▶ MP3 format audio
- ▶ 640×480 pixel resolution for standard definition, standard aspect ratio playback; 1280×720 pixel resolution for widescreen high-definition playback
- ▶ Frame rate of 30 frames per second (FPS)
- ▶ Length of 10 minutes or less
- ▶ File size of 100 MB or less

A quick word about resolution: YouTube's standard video playback window is just 320 pixels wide by 240 pixels tall, which is much lower quality than standard definition television. YouTube, however, encourages the uploading of what it calls high-quality videos, which play back at 640×480 resolution. As such, 640×480 should be the lowest quality you use for your videos; this also happens to be the default quality resolution found on most standard definition camcorders.

In addition, YouTube is now enabling the playback of true **high definition** (HD) videos at a widescreen resolution of 1280×720 pixels. If you have a new HD camcorder, you can upload your videos in full resolution for playback on the YouTube site.

In addition, Windows Movie Maker is a video editing program included free with Microsoft Windows, and iMovie is a similar program included free with Apple Macintosh computers. Both of these programs are more than adequate for basic YouTube video editing.

Uploading Videos from a Camcorder

Assuming you've recorded your camcorder video in a YouTube-approved format (or edited your video file as such), uploading to YouTube is easy. You start by clicking the Upload button at the top-right corner of any YouTube page. When the Video File Upload page appears, click the Browse button to locate the video file on your hard drive and then click the Upload Video button.

When the next page appears, enter a title and description for your video and then select a video category. Opt to share your video with others (that is, create a public video) and then click the Save Changes button.

YouTube now begins to upload the file you specified. Know, however, that it can take several minutes to upload a large video, especially over a slow Internet connection. There's also additional processing time involved after the upload is complete, while YouTube converts the uploaded video to its own format and adds it to the YouTube database.

When the video upload finishes, YouTube displays the Upload Complete page. To view your video, click the My Videos link on any YouTube page and then click the thumbnail for your new video.

Uploading Videos from a Webcam

If you have a webcam video camera connected to your computer, you have two ways of uploading webcam videos to YouTube.

First, you can save your webcam videos as you do normally and then upload those videos via YouTube's normal video upload process. Or, if you like, you can upload videos as you shoot them "live" from your webcam. This second method of uploading webcam videos utilizes YouTube's Quick Capture feature. Here's how it works.

7.7

WARNING . . .WARNING . . .WARNING . . .

When you use Quick Capture to upload "live" webcam videos to YouTube, you don't have the opportunity to edit those videos; whatever you record is what gets shown on YouTube, warts and all.

With your webcam connected and running, click the Upload button on any YouTube page. When the Video File Upload page appears, click the Quick Capture button at the top right of the page.

This displays the Quick Capture page. Pull down the list boxes above the video window to select your webcam video and audio options. You should now see the picture from your webcam in the video window; click the Record button to start recording.

When you're finished with the recording, click the Stop button. At this point, you have the option of clicking Cancel to delete your recording, Preview to view a preview of the video you just recorded, or Save to save your video to the YouTube site. When you click Save, YouTube automatically uploads the video to the site and displays a page where you enter the video's title, description, and other information. Click the Save Changes button, and your video will be available for viewing in a few minutes.

WORDS TO GO . . .WORDS TO GO . . .WORDS TO GO

High definition (HD) video reproduces widescreen videos at a minimum resolution of 1280×720 pixels—the same resolution used for HDTV broadcasts.

7.8 WATCHING TV SHOWS AND MOVIES ONLINE

TV Shows Online

Video on Other Websites

Movies Online

YouTube isn't the only website where you can watch videos online. There are many sites that offer both amateur and commercial videos—including the latest TV shows and movies.

WARNING . . .WARNING . . .WARNING

Whether you're streaming or downloading videos, you must have a fast broadband connection for acceptable performance. Watching video on a dial-up connection most often results in poor performance.

TV Shows Online

Many viewers are now getting their TV fix on their own schedule by watching their favorite shows on their computer over the Internet. There are many sites that offer full shows for either real-time streaming or downloading; these sites include the following:

- ▶ ABC.com (abc.go.com)
- ▶ AOL Video (video.aol.com)
- ▶ CBS.com (www.cbs.com)
- ▶ Comedy Central (www.comedycentral.com)
- ▶ Fancast (www.fancast.com)
- ▶ FOX (www.fox.com)
- ▶ Hulu (www.hulu.com)
- ▶ Joost (www.joost.com)
- ▶ NBC.com (www.nbc.com)
- ▶ TV Land (www.tvland.com)

- ► TV.com (www.tv.com)
- ► tvDuck (www.tvduck.com)
- ► Veoh (www.veoh.com)

For example, you can go to the NBC.com website to view full episodes of their top prime-time shows. Missed this week's episode of *Heroes* or *The Office?* They're available online for free.

Video on Other Websites

Many non-video-specific websites offer videos as part of their site content. For example, the CBS News site (www.cbsnews.com) features all sorts of videos on its home page; you can watch the previous evening's broadcast of the CBS Evening News along with special web-only newscasts. All you have to do is select the video you want to watch and then click the Play button on the embedded video player; there's no separate software to launch.

Movies Online

Other sites offer full-length movies for watching via real-time streaming or for downloading to your PC. The most popular sites for viewing or downloading current and classic movies include the following:

- ► Amazon Video on Demand (www.amazon.com)
- ► Blockbuster (www.blockbuster.com/download/)
- ► CinemaNow (www.cinemanow.com)
- ► iTunes Store (www.apple.com/itunes/store/)
- ► Netflix (www.netflix.com)

◄ SEE ALSO 7.2, *"Downloading Music from the iTunes Store"* ▶

Whereas most TV viewing sites are free, these movies sites typically charge for each movie view. Some sites let you "rent" the movie for a limited period of time for fees in the $1 to $5 range, while others let you purchase the download for unlimited viewing for fees in the $10 to $20 range.

In addition, if you're a Netflix subscriber, you can download select movies directly from the Netflix website to your computer. Go to www.netflix.com for more information.

8

MAPS AND DIRECTIONS

8.1 UNDERSTANDING ONLINE MAPPING

In the old days, if you needed a map or driving directions, you'd pull out a printed atlas or head over to your local AAA branch. Today, however, you can generate maps online of virtually any location by using an online mapping site.

There are several major map-making sites you can use, all of which also generate turn-by-turn driving directions when you input your starting and ending addresses. The default maps are typically street-type maps, although some sites can also overlay satellite images onto the normal map view. Some sites even display live traffic conditions and street-level photographs!

The following sites are the most popular mapping sites on the web today:

▶ Expedia Maps (maps.expedia.com)

▶ Google Maps (maps.google.com)

▶ MapQuest (www.mapquest.com)

▶ Rand McNally (www.randmcnally.com)

▶ Windows Live Search Maps (maps.live.com)

▶ Yahoo! Maps (maps.yahoo.com)

◀ *SEE ALSO 8.2, "Mapping a Location with Google Maps"* ▶

All of these online mapping sites are free and let you print out the maps you generate to take with you when driving.

8.2 MAPPING A LOCATION WITH GOOGLE MAPS

Searching for Maps

Navigating a Google Map

Displaying Satellite Images

Displaying Terrain Maps

Displaying Street View Photos

Displaying Live Traffic Conditions

Sharing Maps

One of the most popular online mapping sites today is Google Maps (maps. google.com), which offers a ton of useful mapping services all packed into an easy-to-use interface. Like other online mapping sites, Google Maps lets you generate maps for any given address or location; you can also click and drag the maps to view adjacent sections, overlay the map info on satellite images of the given area, view local traffic conditions, display nearby businesses as a series of pushpins on the map, and have Google Maps plot driving directions to and from one location to any other location.

◄ *SEE ALSO 8.1, "Understanding Online Mapping"* ▷

8.2

Searching for Maps

Unlike other map sites, Google Maps doesn't present any complicated forms to fill out to generate a map. To display a map of a given location, all you have to do is enter information about that location into the top-of-page search box. When you click the Search button, a map of that location is displayed on the page.

Searching by Address

The most obvious way to display a map of a given location is to enter the location's street address or general location. There are a number of ways you can enter an address or a location, as detailed in Table 8.1. (And, as with all search queries, capitalization isn't necessary.)

TABLE 8.1   GOOGLE MAPS ADDRESS FORMATS

Address Format	Example
City, state	san diego, ca
Zip	92101
Address, city, state	802 5th avenue, san diego, ca
Address, city, zip	802 5th avenue, san diego, 92101
Street intersection, city, state	5th ave and f street, san diego, ca
Street intersection, zip	5th ave and f street, 92101
Latitude, longitude	32.723, –117.155
Airport code	SAN
Subway station, country (in the United Kingdom and Japan only)	paddington, uk

Remember to put a comma after each part of the address. In most instances, you don't need to spell out words like "east," "street," or "drive." Common abbreviations are okay, and you don't need to put a period after the abbreviation. In addition, you can substitute the symbol "&" for the word "and."

For many major cities, Google Maps also accepts just the city name. For example, entering **miami** gives you a map of Miami, Florida; entering **san francisco** displays a map of the California city. If, on the other hand, you enter a city name that's fairly common (such as **greentown,** which appears in Indiana, Ohio, and several other states), Google will either display a map of the largest city with that name or provide a list of cities or matching businesses for you to choose from. Likewise, you can't enter just a state name or abbreviation. Although Google recognizes most cities, it doesn't recognize states or countries.

If you want to enter latitude and longitude, you have two options. First, you can enter latitude and longitude as decimal degrees, using the – sign to express west longitude or south latitude. Second, you can use N, S, E, and W designations. What you *can't* do is express latitude and longitude using degrees-minutes-seconds (such as 28 24' 23.4"); Google doesn't recognize the ' and " syntax.

WARNING . . .WARNING . . .WARNING

If Google doesn't recognize an address you entered (such as when an address could be on either an "east" or a "west" street, or the same address for a "drive" and a "lane"), Google will display a list of possible addresses. Assuming you can identify the correct address from this list, click the link to display the map of that location.

Searching by Landmark

Sometimes you don't need to know the exact address to generate a Google map. Google has hard-coded many landmarks and institutions into its map database so that you only have to enter the name of the landmark or location into the search box. For example, entering **hoover dam** generates a map of the Hoover Dam.

Displaying Street Maps from a Google Web Search

You don't have to go to the Google Maps page to display a Google map. When you enter a street address, city, and state (or zip code) into the standard Google web search box, the OneBox at the top of the search results page displays a small map of the address. You can click the link to see the full Google Maps page or use the Start Address box to generate a page of driving directions to the address.

◀ *SEE ALSO 4.4, "Searching with Google"* ▶

Navigating a Google Map

When you map an address, Google displays a map of that address on the right side of the browser window. The address itself is listed in the Search Results pane on the left side of the window (along with pictures of that address, if available), and information about the address is displayed as a balloon overlaid on the main map.

8.2

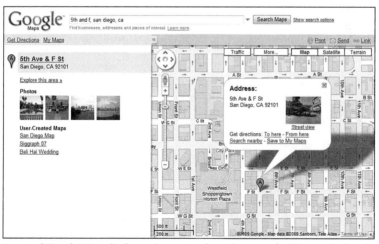

A typical Google Maps display; information about the mapped address is displayed in a text balloon.

To display the map the full width of your browser window, click the arrow on the top-left corner above the map. This hides the entire left-hand panel and expands the map to fill the space.

You can use the balloon info to set this address as your default location in Google Maps, to generate driving directions to or from this address, to initiate a search for nearby businesses, or to save this map in Google's My Maps.

Once you have a Google map displayed onscreen, you navigate around the map using the navigation controls at the top left of the map. To pan in any direction, click the arrow buttons on the top navigation control. To zoom in and out of the map, drag the slider control up or down. To drag the map in any direction, position the cursor anywhere on the map, click and hold the mouse button, and then drag the map around. To center the map on a new location, position the cursor over that location and then double-click the mouse.

The closer you zoom in on a map, the more detail is displayed. You won't see specific road information until you're fairly zoomed in; even then, major roads are displayed first, and then minor roads are displayed on more extreme zoom levels.

Displaying Satellite Images

By default, Google Maps displays a standard map of any location you enter. But that's not the only way you can view a location. Google Maps also incorporates satellite images, which let you get a bird's eye view on the actual location. It's like having access to your very own spy satellite!

WARNING . . .WARNING . . .WARNING

Google's satellite images aren't always as current as its map data, meaning you could be looking at an image that was taken months or even years ago. (Google doesn't say how current any of its satellite images are.)

To display the satellite image of a location, click the Satellite button at the top of the map. You can use the standard navigation and zoom controls to pan around and zoom into or out of the satellite image.

WARNING . . .WARNING . . .WARNING

If you zoom in too far on a satellite map, you may reach the limits of the satellite imagery, as not all locations have super-high-resolution satellite photos. When you zoom in too far, you'll see a screen with the repeated message, "We are sorry, but we don't have imagery at this zoom level for this region."

Displaying Terrain Maps

If you want to view the different types of terrain (woods, fields, lakes, and so on) in a given location, Google Maps offers a special color-coded terrain view. To switch to terrain view, click the Terrain button.

Displaying Street View Photos

Google Maps now offers ground-level photos of many urban and suburban locations. When you're viewing a map of many cities and towns, you'll see a **Street View** icon, which looks like a little yellow person, on top of the navigational controls. Drag the icon onto a given street and Google displays a panoramic photo of that location.

WARNING . . .WARNING . . .WARNING

If Street View is not available for a given location, the Street View button will not be present.

Use your mouse to pan left or right around the photo, or you can drag within the photo to move up or down the street. You can also use the navigation controls in the upper left of the photo to pan around and zoom in and out of the photo.

Displaying Live Traffic Conditions

8.2

You can also use Google Maps to view live traffic conditions in many major cities. To display this traffic data, just call up a map and then click the Traffic button.

When viewing traffic conditions, major roads appear as green (smoothly flowing traffic), yellow (busy), or red (congested). Road construction is indicated by a separate icon, as are road closures.

Sharing Maps

Once you've created a map of a given location, Google lets you save and share that map. There are several ways to do so.

Linking to a Specific Map

The key to saving or sharing any map you've created is that Google assigns every possible map its own unique URL. When you know the URL, you can share it with others—or save it to your computer desktop.

To link to a map, create the map and then click the Link link. Google now displays the URL for this map in a separate dialog box. Highlight the link in the

Paste Link in E-mail or IM box, right-click your mouse, and select Copy from the pop-up menu. To paste this link into an e-mail message or text document, position your cursor in the message, right-click your mouse, and select Paste from the pop-up menu.

E-mailing a Map

There's an even easier way to e-mail a map to friends and family—or to yourself so you'll have a link to the map as a message in your inbox. Start by creating a map and then click the Send link. This opens a new Send dialog box. The link to the map is displayed in the text of the message; enter the recipient's e-mail address and your own e-mail address and then click the Send button.

Google now sends the message via its Gmail service, although no Gmail account is required to send the message. The recipient needs only to click the link in the message to view your map.

Printing a Map

Google also lets you print a hard copy of any map you create. This is as easy as clicking the Print link above the map; nothing more is necessary.

WORDS TO GO . . .WORDS TO GO . . .WORDS TO GO

Google Maps' **Street View** displays street-level photos of select locations.

8.3 GENERATING DRIVING DIRECTIONS

Generating Turn-by-Turn Directions

Generating Multiple-Stop Directions

Changing Your Route

Printing Your Directions

Google Maps does more than just display maps; it can also generate driving directions from one location to another. It's a simple matter of entering two locations and letting Google get you from point A to point B (and even to points C and D).

◀ *SEE ALSO 8.2, "Mapping a Location with Google Maps"* ▶

Generating Turn-by-Turn Directions

To generate driving directions, click the Get Directions link; the left-hand pane now expands to include two search boxes. Enter your starting location into the first box (A) and your ending location into the second box (B).

Assuming you're driving to your destination, select By Car from the pull-down list. (If you're walking to a destination within a major city, select Walking from the list instead.) Click the Get Directions button and Google displays step-by-step driving directions on the left side of the page; an overview map of your entire route is displayed on the right.

8.3

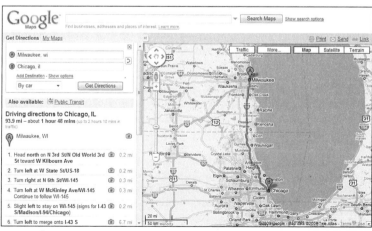

Driving directions generated with Google Maps.

To view street-level photos of each turn (where available), click the photo icon next to that particular step in the Directions panel. This helps you get an idea of what to expect when you travel.

Generating Multiple-Stop Directions

Google also lets you generate directions for a multiple-stop trip—that is, directions to one location, then to another, then to another if you wish.

To create multiple-stop directions, start by generating directions from the starting point to your first stop. Then click the Add Destination link; this extends the Directions panel to include a third address box (C). Enter your second stop into this box and then click the Add Destination button; directions from the first stop to the second stop will now be generated. Keep clicking the Add a Destination link to create more complex trips and directions.

Changing Your Route

If you don't like the directions Google suggests or would rather take a slightly different route to your destination, Google lets you change your driving directions—by dragging the route on the map.

Start by generating your driving directions as normal and then locate that part of your route that you want to change. Click and hold the left mouse button on that part of the route, then drag the route to a different location. The route readjusts to include the changes you've made.

Printing Your Directions

If you want to take your directions with you on your trip (and you probably do), you can easily print them on your computer's printer. All you have to do is click the Print link; this makes a hard-copy printout of the directions page, map and all.

8.4 USING GOOGLE EARTH

Different Versions

Navigating Google Earth

Searching for Locations

Configuring View Options

Saving and Printing a View

Displaying Driving Directions

Displaying and Using Layers

Displaying Places of Interest

Creating Custom Placemarks

Google Maps is a web-based mapping service. **Google Earth,** on the other hand, is a software program that lets you create, view, and save high-resolution, three-dimensional fly-bys of any location on the planet. It's kind of like Google Maps on steroids.

◀ *SEE ALSO 8.2, "Mapping a Location with Google Maps"* ▷

Different Versions

8.4

Before you use Google Earth, you have to download the software to your PC, which you do from earth.google.com. Google offers four different versions of Google Earth:

- ▶ **Google Earth (basic),** the version for most users that lets you perform a variety of general mapping functions. This version is a free download.

- ▶ **Google Earth Plus,** which can be purchased for $20. This version includes all the features of the basic version but adds support for select GPS devices, the ability to import spreadsheet data, a variety of drawing tools for annotation purposes, and high-resolution printing.

- ▶ **Google Earth Pro,** which is designed for professional and commercial use. This version, which costs $400, includes all the features of Google Earth Plus, augmented with multiple terabytes of detailed aerial and satellite images from cities around the world, the ability to import custom data and blueprints, and the use of a variety of add-on modules.

> ▶ **Google Earth Enterprise,** which offers a variety of onsite deployment solutions for large organizations, including Google Earth Fusion (integrates custom data), Google Earth Server, and Google Earth EC (Enterprise Client). Contact Google for custom pricing.

The basic (free) version is ideal for most individuals. If you want to interface Google Earth with a GPS unit, however, the additional cost of the Google Earth Plus may be worth it.

Navigating Google Earth

When you first launch Google Earth, you see a large view of the planet Earth as well as surrounding navigation and display controls. The major parts of the screen include three panes (Search, Places, and Layers), the main view display, and the navigation controls. You can hide or display certain parts of the interface by checking them on or off in the View menu.

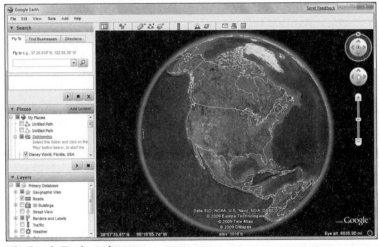

The Google Earth window.

You start your journey through Google Earth from the 3D view of the globe. You can zoom in on any location on the planet—and navigate from place to place around the planet—using the program's navigation controls.

Google Earth includes three navigation controls, all located at the top right of the map. The Look control is at the top (with the Rotate ring around it), the Move control is in the middle, and the Zoom control is at the bottom. Click the appropriate control with your mouse to complete the desired task, as follows:

▶ Click and drag the top Look control to move around from a single vantage point, as if you're turning your head.

▶ Drag the Rotate control (the outer ring of the Look control) to rotate the view. Rotating clockwise moves north to the right; rotating counterclockwise moves north to the left.

▶ Double-click the North button (the N at the "top" of the Rotate control) to return north to the straight-up position.

▶ Click or click and drag the middle Move control to move your position from one point to another.

▶ Click the bottom Zoom In (+) and Zoom Out (–) buttons (or use the corresponding slider control) to zoom in to or out of the map.

Both the Look and Move controls work like a joystick—that is, you can use your mouse to click and hold each control and then drag your mouse to move or look in the designated direction.

Searching for Locations

You don't have to zoom and pan to a specific location. Instead, Google Earth lets you search for places just as you do in Google Maps and then zooms directly in to the desired location.

To search for a location, select the Fly To tab in the Search pane and then enter the location in the search box. When you click the Search button, Google Earth zooms in to the location you entered.

As with Google Maps, Google Earth lets you search using a variety of entry formats. Table 8.2 details the different ways to search for a location.

TABLE 8.2 GOOGLE EARTH SEARCH FORMATS

Format	Example
Location	Disney World
Country	France
City country	paris france
City, state	minneapolis, mn
Zip	60515
Number street, city, state	1500 opus place, downers grove, il
Number street, city, zip	1500 opus place, downers grove, 60515
Cross street, city, state	42nd and broadway, new york, ny
Latitude, longitude (in decimal)	37.7, –122.2
Latitude, longitude (in DMS format)	37 25'19.07"N, 122 05'06.24"W

Google Earth also lets you search for businesses by using the Find Businesses tab in the Search pane. You can search within the current view or within any city, state, or country you enter. Items that match your query are pinpointed in the view pane.

Configuring View Options

When you zoom in to a location, you see incredible detail—more than possible with Google Maps. In fact, Google Earth is quite versatile in terms of what you see onscreen; there are many viewing options available.

View Preferences

Most of Google Earth's view options are set by selecting Tools, Options to display the Options dialog box. From within the Options dialog box, select the 3D View tab to adjust the settings detailed in Table 8.3.

TABLE 8.3   GOOGLE EARTH VIEW SETTINGS

Setting	Description
Texture Colors	Sets the color depth of the display; True Color (32 bit) displays a more realistic view.
Anistropic Filtering	This is a texture mapping technology that produces a smoother-looking image, especially around the horizon (when viewing a tilted angle). You should turn this on only if your graphics card has at least 32 MB memory.
Labels/Icon Size	Determines the default size for labels and icons in the viewer.
Graphics Mode	Google Earth is a graphics-intensive application. If your PC has a high-powered graphics card, it can run in the better-looking Direct X mode. If, however, your PC has a less-powerful graphics card (as do many notebook PCs), you can run Google Earth in the less-demanding OpenGL mode. (Safe mode is used only when you're experiencing display problems.)
Show Lat/Lon	Displays latitude and longitude as degrees, minutes, and seconds; degrees only; or using the universal transverse Mercator (for professional mapsters).
Show Elevation	Displays elevations in either feet and miles or meters and kilometers.
Fonts	Determines which fonts are used to display labels in the viewer.

Setting	Description
Terrain Quality	Enables you to select a higher-quality terrain display (takes longer to draw) or a lower-quality one (runs faster on most PCs).
Elevation Exaggeration	Choosing a higher number exaggerates the height of tall objects (terrain and buildings) in the viewer.
Overview Map	Selects the size of the overview map as well as the degree of zoom relation.

Full-Screen Mode

By default, the Google Earth viewer appears in a window within the Google Earth window. To display the viewer full screen, press the F11 key or select View, Full Screen. To return to the standard mode, press F11 again.

Latitude/Longitude Grid

To overlay a latitude/longitude grid on any Google Earth view, press Ctrl+L or select View, Grid. This grid tilts along with the overall view tilt.

Overview Map

Google Earth can display an Overview map on top of its normal map; this shows you where you are in the viewer in relation to the rest of the world. To display the Overview map, press Ctrl+M or select View, Overview Map. You can double-click anywhere in the Overview map to navigate to that location.

Saving and Printing a View

You can save any image displayed in the Google Earth viewer by selecting File, Save, Save Image. You can also print the current image in the viewer by selecting File, Print.

WARNING . . .WARNING . . .WARNING

The free version of Google Earth prints images only at screen resolution. The $20 Google Earth Plus prints images at a much higher resolution—about 2,400 pixels, according to Google.

Displaying Driving Directions

You can also use Google Earth to map driving directions, just as you can with Google Maps. The big difference in using Google Earth for this purpose is that your directions are mapped in a 3D view, so you can get more of a bird's-eye view of where you'll be driving.

◀ SEE ALSO 8.3, *"Generating Driving Directions"* ▶

Getting Directions

The easiest way to generate driving directions is to select the Directions tab in the Search pane and then enter your starting (From) and ending (To) addresses. When you click the Search button, your route is mapped onscreen with each turn placemarked on the map. You can zoom in to, rotate, pan, and tilt the map as you like, as well as zoom in to any specific direction by double-clicking that placemark.

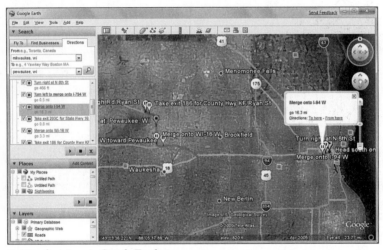

Driving directions in Google Earth.

Touring Your Route

Once you have your route displayed onscreen, you can use Google Earth's tour feature to "fly" the complete route in the viewer. Just select the Route item at the end of the directions listing, click the Play button. You now get a turn-by-turn 3D ride through your entire route.

Printing and Saving Directions

To print step-by-step directions for your route, click the Printable View link in the directions listing. This will open a Google Maps web page in a new browser window, with the directions displayed in that window. From this window, click the Print link to print the directions.

To save your route for future use, select File, Save, Save Place As. Confirm or enter a new filename for your trip and then click the Save button.

Displaying and Using Layers

One of the things that makes Google Earth so useful is its capability to overlay other data on top of its maps. This data is added in the form of **layers.** Available layers are enabled via the Layers pane, where they're organized in folders. Double-click a folder to see and activate specific layers within the major layer category.

Google Earth offers many different types of layers. Layers are available to display roads, geographic features, lodging, attractions, and the like. When you enable a layer, these features are displayed on the map; if you disable the layer, these features disappear.

Displaying Places of Interest

Many of the layers available in Google Earth contain what are known as **places of interest** (POIs). These are specific locations overlaid on a map, such as ATMs, restaurants, gas stations, and the like.

When you click a POI, Google Earth displays an information box for that item. Within this info box is information about this location as well as links to additional information.

Right-click a POI and you get a pop-up menu that lets you copy or save this location as well as generate driving directions. Saving the POI puts it in your My Places folder in the Places pane, so you can return to it at any time. Alternatively, you can copy the POI and then paste it into a specific subfolder in the My Places folder.

Creating Custom Placemarks

The My Places folder is a folder where you can store any item for future use. You can store preexisting POIs, as just discussed, or store custom **placemarks** that you create yourself.

To mark any place on any Google Earth map as a placemark, click the Add Placemark button on the toolbar navigation panel (or select Add, Placemark). A new, blank placemark is now placed on the map. If the placemark is not in the correct location, use your mouse to drag it around the map as necessary.

Also appearing at this time is a New Placemark dialog box. Enter a new name for the placemark, along with any descriptive text you'd like. You can also click the appropriate tabs to change the style or color of the placemark as well as additional attributes. When you're done making your selections, click the OK button.

WORDS TO GO . . .WORDS TO GO . . .WORDS TO GO

Google Earth is Google's 3D mapping software.

A **layer** consists of specific data or points of interest overlaid on a Google Earth map.

Places of interest (POIs) are specific locations, such as restaurants or hotels, overlaid on a map.

A **placemark** is a place of interest on a map that you create yourself.

9

USING WEB-BASED APPLICATIONS

9.1 USING GOOGLE CALENDAR

Creating Calendars

Viewing Your Calendar

Working With Events

Sharing Your Calendar

Google Calendar (calendar.google.com) is a calendar and scheduling application with a difference. Unlike calendar software, which is installed on and runs from your PC's hard disk, Google Calendar is a **web-based application.** It isn't installed on your computer; you access it over the Internet using your PC's web browser.

◀ *SEE ALSO 9.6, "Other Web-Based Applications"* ▶

Like all calendar applications, Google Calendar lets you schedule and keep track of appointments via an onscreen calendar. You enter your appointments directly into the calendar, which you can display in daily, weekly, or monthly view. You can also view your weekly agenda on a single page.

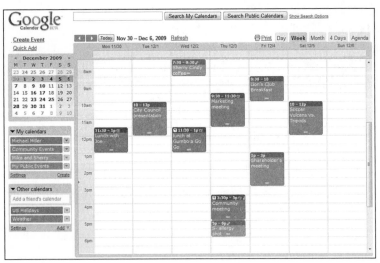

Google Calendar—a web-based calendar application.

What makes Google Calendar unique is that it's completely web based. This means that your calendar information is stored on Google's servers, not on your own computer. The advantage of this is that you can access your calendar from any computer anywhere in the world. Just log on to the Google Calendar page, and your calendar and all **events** are there.

Because Google Calendar is web based, you can use it to create not only a private calendar for yourself, but also public calendars for your company or organization. You can create one calendar for home, another for work, and yet another for your son's soccer team. Then you can view all your calendars from the same Google Calendar page.

Because Google Calendar is part of Google, it integrates smoothly with Gmail, Google's e-mail application. Google Calendar can scan your e-mail messages for dates and times. With a few clicks of the mouse, you can create events based on the content of your Gmail messages.

Creating Calendars

Google Calendar is designed to be easy to use. The first step is to create your calendar—or calendars.

Creating Your First Calendar

Setting up your first calendar is easy. In fact, there's nothing to set up. When you first sign in to the Google Calendar page, your calendar is already there waiting for your input. There's nothing to create and nothing to configure.

Creating Multiple Calendars

One of the most useful features of Google Calendar is the ease with which you can create and manage multiple calendars. For example, you might want to create one calendar with work events and another with social events.

To create a second (or third or fourth) calendar, go to the main Google Calendar page and click the Create link in the My Calendars pane. When the Create New Calendar page appears, give the calendar a name and description and then enter other appropriate information. Click the Create Calendar button when done.

9.1

All the calendars you create are listed in the My Calendars pane on the left side of the Google Calendars page. The main calendar on this page can display any single calendar individually or multiple calendars simultaneously. It all depends on which—and how many—calendars you enable.

By default, every calendar is displayed in the main calendar. To hide a calendar, click its name in the My Calendars pane; the name changes from the normal shaded box to just a link. Click the link again to redisplay the events from that calendar in the main calendar, color coded appropriately.

Viewing Your Calendar

Google Calendar lets you view your calendar in several different ways. You select each view by clicking the appropriate tab above the main calendar. You can view your calendar by day, week, month, next four days, or agenda.

For each view, you move backward and forward in time by clicking the left and right arrow buttons at the top of the calendar. To center the calendar on the current day, click the Today button.

You can also create customized calendar views that include any number of days. For this, you use the mini-calendar on the left side of the Google Calendar page. Just click and drag the mouse cursor across the mini-calendar from the first to the last day you want to view; the main calendar changes to reflect the number of days you select.

Working With Events

All the items scheduled on your calendar are called events. An event can include all sorts of information, some of which is augmented by information provided by the Google website.

Adding an Event

Google provides several different ways to add events to your calendar. Let's look at each in turn.

First, you can simply click the hour or the day on your calendar on which you'd like to create a new event. If you add an event to a daily calendar, click and drag the cursor over the entire time frame of the event. This opens a new event balloon. Enter the name of the event into the balloon and select which calendar you want to add the event to.

If you use this approach on a monthly calendar, unfortunately you can't easily determine the length of the event. To fine-tune these and other details of the event, click the Edit Event Details link in the event balloon. This opens a page where you can enter a variety of information, including the What (name), When (start and end times or days), and Where (location) for the event.

You can also add an event by clicking the Create Event link in the upper-left corner of the Google Calendar page. This opens a page where you enter the necessary information to create the event.

Quick Add

Perhaps the easiest way to add an event is with Google Calendar's Quick Add feature. When you click the Quick Add link (or type the letter Q), the Quick Add entry box appears. Enter the name and time of the event and then press Enter. This method is quite intelligent; if you enter **Lunch with George at noon Monday at Applebee's,** Quick Add translates the text and enters the appropriate event at the specified date and time.

Events from Gmail

If you use Gmail for your e-mail, you can add events from invitations you receive in e-mail messages. When you're reading a Gmail message that contains information pertaining to a possible event, just pull down the More Actions menu and select Create Event. This opens a New Event window; enter the appropriate information and click Save Changes. The event is added to your Google Calendar.

◁ *SEE ALSO 12.5, "Understanding Web E-mail"* ▷

Syncing with Microsoft Outlook

If you use Microsoft Outlook to manage your home or work schedules, you can import your Outlook events into Google Calendar—and export your Google Calendar events into Outlook. All you need is the Google Calendar Sync utility, which you can download for free at www.google.com/support/calendar/bin/answer.py?answer=89955.

When you first install Google Calendar Sync, you see a configuration window. Enter your Google Account info as well as how you want to sync:

▶ **2-way** automatically syncs events from each application to one another.

▶ **1-way: Google Calendar to Microsoft Outlook calendar** syncs your Google Calendar events to Outlook (Google Calendar is the master application).

▶ **1-way: Microsoft Outlook calendar to Google Calendar** syncs your Outlook events to Google Calendar (Outlook is the master application).

You also have to determine how often you want to synchronize your events, in minutes. Make your choices and then click the Save button. Now whenever your computer is online, your events are synchronized between your two calendars; events you add in the one application are automatically added to the other.

9.1

Receiving Phone Notifications

If you want to take your Google Calendar with you wherever you go, all you have to do is enable automatic phone notifications. Go to the Google Calendar home page and click the Settings link. When the Settings page appears, select the Mobile Setup tab.

The first time you access this page, you have to verify your mobile phone number, which you do by having Google send a verification number to your phone via text message. After this is done, enter the verification code into the appropriate box on the Settings page and then click the Finish Setup button.

The Notifications tab now changes to its final form. You can choose to be notified via SMS (text message), e-mail, or pop-up (if you have a web-enabled phone like the Apple iPhone). Select how long before each event you want to be notified, as well as how you want to be notified for each type of item (new invitations, changed invitations, and the like). Click the Save button and you're ready to go.

Inviting Others to an Event

When you first create an event, you have the option of adding guests to this event's information. If you do so, you are prompted to send e-mail invitations to those guests.

After you've created an event on your calendar, you can invite more guests at any time. Start by editing the selected event to display the event page. Click the Add Guests link and then enter the e-mail addresses of your guests into the text box. (Make sure you separate multiple addresses with commas.) Click the Save button. Google Calendar now displays the message, "Would you like to send invitations to new guests?" Click the Send button to do so.

Google now sends invitations to all the guests you added. Each invitation includes links for the guest's response—Yes, No, or Maybe. When the guest clicks one of these links, he or she is taken to a Submit Response web page. The response is then automatically entered into the event in your Google Calendar, as shown in the Guests section of the event page.

Sharing Your Calendar

One of the unique and useful features of a web-based calendar is that multiple users can share the same calendar. For example, you might create a family calendar that lets you, your spouse, and your children keep each other updated on what everyone is up to. Or you could create a public calendar for your child's sports team so that everyone is aware of upcoming games and practices.

To share a calendar, select that calendar in the My Calendars pane and then click the Settings link. This displays the Calendar Settings page with the Calendars tab selected. All of your calendars are listed in the My Calendars section of this page. Click the Share This Calendar link next to the calendar you want to share.

This displays the calendar Details page with the Share This Calendar tab selected. To make the calendar completely public so that anyone on the web can view it, check the Make This Calendar Public option. To selectively share the calendar with only certain people, enter their e-mail addresses into the Share With Specific People section. Pull down the Permission Settings list to select what each person can do—See All Event Details, See Free/Busy (Hide Details), Make Changes to Events, or Make Changes and Manage Sharing. Click the Add Person button to add this person to your calendar list; click the Save button when done sharing.

If you want your friends and family to only view your calendar—that is, to see what's happening but not add their own events or edit existing events—select the See All Event Details setting. If you want your friends and family to be able to add their own events and reschedule existing events, select the Make Changes to Events setting.

The people you add to your calendar list will receive an e-mail message notifying them of the new calendar. This e-mail will include a link to the calendar so that they can view it in their own web browsers.

9.1

WORDS TO GO . . .WORDS TO GO . . .WORDS TO GO

An **event** is an item scheduled on a calendar.

A **web-based application** is housed on and runs from computers connected to the Internet; you access web-based applications using your computer's web browser via any Internet connection.

9.2 UNDERSTANDING THE GOOGLE DOCS SUITE

Benefits

Privacy and Security Concerns

Should You Use Google Docs?

Navigating Google Docs

Creating New Documents

Saving a Document

Importing Microsoft Office Documents

Sharing and Collaborating

Publishing Your Document

Working Offline

You're probably familiar with Microsoft Office, Microsoft's suite of productivity applications. Office includes a word processor (Microsoft Word), spreadsheet program (Microsoft Excel), presentation program (Microsoft PowerPoint), and other applications that most people use every day.

Microsoft Office is traditional software; its applications are installed on and run from your computer's hard drive. But that's not the only way to do it; web-based applications perform the same functions but run from the Internet instead of from any single PC.

◄ *SEE ALSO 9.6, "Other Web-Based Applications"* ▶

One such web-based application is Google Docs, Google's answer to Microsoft Office. Google Docs is an **office suite** of word processor, spreadsheet, and presentation applications that mimics most of the key features of Office and other similar freestanding programs.

What's different about Google Docs, however, is that it's all web based. The application and all your documents reside on Google's servers, not on your computer. This results in some unique benefits.

Benefits

The most obvious benefit of using a web-based application is that you can access your documents wherever you are and from any computer (and from many handheld devices, such as your Blackberry Storm or iPhone). With Google Docs, you'll never experience the disappointment of realizing that the document you need is located on your office PC when you're using another PC, either at home or on the road.

Google Docs' web-based nature also lets you share your documents with others over the Internet. That makes real-time workgroup collaboration possible from anywhere around the globe, which is something you don't have with Microsoft Office and similar programs.

Another benefit of being web based is that you can't lose your work—theoretically, anyway. After you've named the document you're working on, Google Docs saves your file on its servers. From that point on, every change you make to the document gets saved to the Google servers automatically. Nothing gets lost if you close your web browser, navigate to another website, or even turn off your computer. Google saves everything you do.

The final unique feature of Google Docs is that it's free. It costs nothing to use, unlike the increasingly expensive Microsoft Office. Being free makes it easy to take for a test drive and even easier to add to your bag of applications. Many early users who've tried Google Docs have said that they're likely to switch from Office. It can do almost everything Word and Excel can do from a basic editing standpoint, which makes it perfect for corporate and small-business environments.

Privacy and Security Concerns

When you use Google Docs, you rely on Google to store your work on its servers. This raises some legitimate concerns about privacy and security; all your data is in Google's hands.

These sound like reasonable concerns, but Google says you shouldn't worry. Although Google stores your documents on its servers, it does not collect other personal information about you. In addition, Google uses a secure authentication method to control access to any document you create. Although you can grant access to others to share your documents, those documents are private by default. Unless you share a document URL, no one else can view it.

That said, you probably shouldn't use Google Docs to store or share highly sensitive documents. If you absolutely, positively don't want anyone seeing your work, don't put it on the web.

Should You Use Google Docs?

Before you jump into the Google Docs waters, you need to consider whether Google Docs is right for your particular needs. Here are the types of users for whom Google Docs holds promise:

▶ **Beginning users.** If you're just starting out with word processing, spreadsheets, or presentations, there's no better place to start than with Google Docs. The slightly limited functionality of Google's applications actually works to the benefit of beginning users; you aren't overwhelmed by all the advanced options that clutter the Word, Excel, and PowerPoint workspaces. Plus, Google Docs is extremely easy to use. Everything you need is out in the open, not hidden beneath layers of menus and dialog boxes.

▶ **Casual users.** Google Docs is also a good choice if you have modest word processing, spreadsheet, and presentation needs. If all you're doing is writing memos and letters, totaling a few numbers, or giving a short presentation, Google Docs gets the job done with ease.

▶ **Anyone who wants access to their documents from multiple locations.** If you work on the same data at work and at home (or on the road), you know what a hassle it is to carry your data around with you from computer to computer—and keep it synchronized. Google Docs solves this problem. Wherever you are (home, office, on the road), you always access the same version of your document, stored on Google's servers. There are no synchronization issues; you work on the same file wherever you go.

▶ **Anyone who needs to share their documents with others.** Sometimes you need others to view what you're working on. Maybe you have a family budget that you and your spouse both need to see. Maybe you have a soccer team schedule that other parents need to view. Whatever the need, Google Docs lets you share your documents with anyone you want over the web.

▶ **Anyone who needs to edit their documents in a collaborative environment.** Sharing is one thing; collaborative editing is another. If you need multiple users to both access and edit data in a document, Google Docs lets you do things that are impossible in Microsoft Office.

With all that said, Google Docs isn't for everyone. So who *shouldn't* use Google Docs?

▶ **Power users.** If you've created your own custom documents or spreadsheet applications in Microsoft Word, Excel, or PowerPoint, especially those with macros and pivot tables and the like, Google Docs is not for you. Google Docs lacks many of Office's most advanced features and simply won't get the job done.

▶ **Anyone who wants to create sophisticated printouts.** Google Docs lacks some of the more sophisticated formatting options that some Office users take for granted. With Google Docs, what you see onscreen is exactly what prints—for better or for worse. If you need fancy printouts, Google Docs will probably disappoint.

▶ **Anyone working on sensitive documents.** Web-based applications (and documents stored on the web) are not good tools if your company has trade secrets it wants to protect. In fact, some organizations may bar their employees from working on documents that don't reside on their own secured servers, which rules out Google's applications.

So if you're a beginning or casual user who doesn't need fancy charts or print-outs, or if you need to share your documents or collaborate online with other users, Google Docs is worth checking out.

Navigating Google Docs

You access Google Docs at docs.google.com. After you log on with your Google account, you see the Google Docs home page. This page is the gateway for all three Google Docs applications—word processing, spreadsheets, and presenta-tions. All your previously created documents are listed on this page.

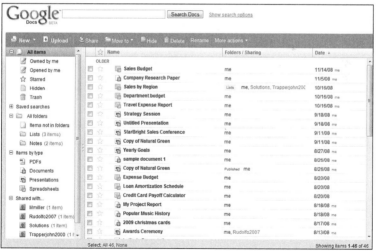

The Google Docs home page.

The left pane helps you organize your documents. You can store files in folders, view documents by type (word processing documents, spreadsheets, presenta-tions, or PDFs), see the results of saved searches, and display documents shared with specific people.

To create a new folder, click the New button, select Folder, and then give the new folder a name. To move a document to a folder, check the document, click the Add to Folder button, and then select the folder you want to add it to. To delete an item, select it and then click the Delete button.

The documents for the selected folder are displayed in the main part of the window. Word processing documents are noted with a document icon, spreadsheets have a spreadsheet icon, presentations have a slide icon, and PDF documents have the requisite Adobe PDF icon. To open any type of document, click the item's title; the document opens in a new window.

Creating New Documents

To create a new document of any type, click the New button and select the type of document you want to create: Document (for word processing), Spreadsheet, or Presentation. This opens a new, blank document of the chosen type in a new browser window.

Alternatively, you can create a new document based on a predesigned **template**— a combination of text styles, document formatting, and graphics to which you can add your own text, graphics, and numbers. When you click the New button and select From Template, Google opens a new Templates Gallery window. You can search or browse for templates; Google has templates for documents, spreadsheets, and presentations. Click the Preview link to see a quick view of the template. Then click the Use This Template button to create a new document based on the template.

Saving a Document

When you first save a new Google Docs file, you must do so manually—and give the file a name. After this first save, Google automatically resaves the file every time you make a change to it. In essence, this means that you have to save the file only once; Google saves all further changes automatically.

To save a new file of any type, click the Save button within the document. When the Save dialog box appears, enter a name for the file and then click the OK button. That's all there is to it. The file is now saved on Google's servers, and you don't have to bother resaving it at any future point.

Importing Microsoft Office Documents

To ensure compatibility with people still using Microsoft Office, you can use Google Docs to work on files you've previously created in your regular word processing or spreadsheet programs. You import these documents into Google Docs and can then work on them online using the Google Docs applications.

To import a file, follow these steps: Go to the Google Docs home page and click the Upload button. When the Upload a File page appears, click the Browse button and select the file to upload. Alternatively, if you want to import a file found on a website, enter the file's full URL into the Or Enter the URL of a File on the web box.

When you click the Upload File button, Google displays the uploaded document in your browser window. You can edit the document as you like; Google automatically saves a copy of the file on its servers for your future use.

Sharing and Collaborating

One unique feature of Google Docs is the ability to share a document with others—either for viewing or for collaborative editing. You can share your Google Docs documents with anyone who has a Google account.

To share a document for viewing or collaboration, click the Share button at the top right of that document and then select Share with Others. This displays the Share This Document panel.

In the Invite People box, enter the e-mail addresses of the people with whom you want to share the document (separate multiple addresses with commas). If you want others to simply view the document without being able to edit it, check the As Viewers option. If you want others to be able to edit the document, check the As Collaborators option. Click the Invite Viewers or Invite Collaborators button to send the invitations.

Your recipients will receive an invitation via e-mail. The invitation contains a link to the document; clicking this link opens the document in a new browser window.

Anyone invited as a viewer can navigate the entire file and also save that file to his or her personal Google Docs online storage area or as a file to his or her PC. Anyone invited as a collaborator can edit the file in real time. (In fact, multiple users can edit the document at the same time.)

WARNING . . .WARNING . . .WARNING . . .

Google permits more than one user at a time to make changes to an open document; the document isn't "locked" when the first user starts editing. This can create havoc if both users try to make changes to the same data or are unaware of the other changes being made. For this reason, you should always use caution while collaboratively editing a document.

Publishing Your Document

Another way to share a document is to publish it as a public web page or blog posting. When it is published, anyone can access the document for viewing; all the person needs is the URL for the page or blog post.

To publish your document, click the Share button for that document and then select Publish as Web Page. This displays the Publish This Document panel. To publish the document as a web page, click the Publish Document button. If you want to update the web page as the document is edited, also check the Automatically Re-Publish When Changes Are Made option. You're prompted to let anyone on the Internet see this document; click OK. The web page is now published, and Google Docs displays a link to the document's web page.

To post the document to your blog, click the Post to Blog button. The first time you do this, you're prompted to set your blog site settings; you need to provide your blog host, username, password, and the like. The document is then posted to your blog as a new post.

Working Offline

Originally, Google Docs was a web-only application, meaning that you had to be online to edit a document. If you weren't connected to the Internet, you couldn't access your Google Docs files. That changed with the introduction of Google Gears, a utility that lets you access all your Google Docs documents when you're offline.

To edit your documents offline, you have to install the Google Docs Offline application. Do this by clicking the Offline link at the top of the Google Docs home page and then clicking the Get Google Gears Now button. It's a short and simple installation; just follow the onscreen instructions to do the download.

After Google Gears has been installed, you can open the offline version of Google Docs by entering docs.google.com into your web browser or by clicking the Google Docs shortcut on your desktop. If you're not connected to the Internet, you open the offline version of Google Docs; if you are connected to the Internet, you open the normal online version. Whenever you're online, Google Docs automatically synchronizes the files stored on your computer with those stored online. It's a seamless and relatively invisible process.

If you use Google Chrome as your web browser, you have Google Gears already preinstalled. If you use Google Chrome to access Google Docs, it doesn't matter whether you're online or offline; the application launches in the Chrome browser either way.

An **office suite** contains applications for word processing, spreadsheets, and presentations.

A **template** is a predesigned combination of text styles, document formatting, and graphics used to create new documents.

9.2

9.3 USING GOOGLE DOCS FOR WORD PROCESSING

Navigating the Workspace

Entering and Formatting Text

Inserting Web Links

Inserting Images

Working With Tables

Checking Your Spelling

Printing a Document

Exporting to Microsoft Word

Google Docs consists of three different applications: the Google Docs word processor, Google Spreadsheets, and Google Presentations. In this section we'll examine the Google Docs word processor—Google's answer to Microsoft Word.

◀ *SEE ALSO 9.2, "Understanding the Google Docs Suite"* ▶

◀ *SEE ALSO 9.6, "Other Web-Based Applications"* ▶

Navigating the Workspace

You open a new word processing document by clicking the New button on the Google Docs home page and selecting Document. The new document looks like a big blank space in a new browser window, one with a menu bar and toolbar at the top.

You enter your text into the main window. Each pull-down menu is dedicated to a specific function; for example, you use the Edit menu to perform basic editing functions. You click the buttons on the toolbar to perform some of the most common file, editing, and formatting functions.

Entering and Formatting Text

Now to the main event—entering text into your document. It's as easy as positioning the cursor in the blank area of the document window and typing the text. Use the cursor keys on the keyboard to move back and forth through the text and use the Delete and Backspace keys to delete text you've entered.

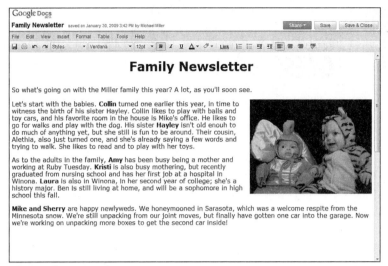

The Google Docs workspace.

Google Docs lets you format your text in a number of ways—bold, italic, underline, and the like. You can also change a selection's font, font size, and font color. Just select the text to format and then click the formatting option on the toolbar.

You can also create a numbered list by clicking the Numbered List button or a bulleted list by clicking the Bulleted List button. Additional formatting options are available from the Format menu, including three levels of headings, strikeout, superscript, subscript, and block quote formats.

Inserting Web Links

Because Google Docs is a web-based word processor, it's not surprising that you can include links to web pages in your documents. All you have to do is highlight the text you want to use for the link and then click the Link button; Google Docs now displays the Insert Link dialog box. Enter the URL you want to link to as well as any "flyover" text you want displayed when the link is hovered over. If you want the link to open in a new window, click the Open Link in New Window option. Click the OK button to create the link.

Inserting Images

To insert pictures and other images into a document, position the cursor where you want the image to appear and then select Insert, Picture. This displays the Insert Image dialog box; you can insert images from your computer (click the Browse button) or from the web (enter the URL of the image).

9.3

To see more configuration options, click the More Image Options link; this lets you resize and position the image, as well as wrap the text around the image. Click the Insert button to insert the image.

Working With Tables

Google Docs also lets you insert tables into your documents. Position the cursor where you want the table to appear and then select Insert, Table or Table, Insert Table. This displays the Insert Table dialog box; from here, you select the size of the table (in terms of rows and columns, as well as overall width and height) as well as other formatting options.

After the table is created, you can position the cursor within the cells to enter text. To further edit the look of the table, as well as to insert or delete rows and columns, right-click the table and make a selection from the pop-up menu.

Checking Your Spelling

A word processor wouldn't be complete without a way to check your spelling, which is why Google Docs includes its own spell checker. To check the spelling in a document, just click the Check Spelling button on the toolbar. Google Docs checks your document and highlights words that are either misspelled or not in its built-in dictionary. Click a highlighted word to see a list of suggested spellings or to add this word to the dictionary.

Printing a Document

Printing a Google Docs document is as simple as clicking the Print button on the toolbar. When the Print dialog box appears, make sure the correct printer is selected and click the Print button.

Exporting to Microsoft Word

By default, all the documents you work with in Google Docs are stored on Google's servers. You can, however, download files from Google to your computer's hard drive to work with in Microsoft Word. In essence, you're exporting your Google document to a .doc format Word file.

To export the current document, select File, Download File As, Word. When the File Download dialog box appears, click the Save button. When the Save As dialog box appears, select a location for the downloaded file, rename it if you like, and then click the Save button.

The Google Docs file is saved in .doc format on your hard disk. You can now open that file with Microsoft Word and work on it as you would any Word document. Know, however, that whatever changes you make to the file from within Word affect only the downloaded file, not the copy of the document that still resides on the Google Docs site. If you later want to reimport the Word file to Google Docs, you'll need to return to the main Google Docs page and use the Upload function.

WARNING . . .WARNING . . .WARNING

Not all document formatting translates when converting from one file format to another. You may need to manually tweak your document after saving it in another format.

9.3

9.4 USING GOOGLE SPREADSHEETS

Navigating the Workspace

Working With Multiple Sheets

Entering and Editing Data

Inserting and Deleting Rows and Columns

Working With Ranges

Sorting Data

Formatting Data

Entering Formulas

Using Functions

Charting Your Data

Printing a Spreadsheet

Expanding Functionality with Gadgets

Exporting to Excel Format

Google Spreadsheets is the spreadsheet application in the Google Docs suite. It's probably the most sophisticated of the three applications; unless your needs are overly advanced, you're apt to find Google Spreadsheets a worthy competitor to and replacement for the venerable Microsoft Excel.

◄ *SEE ALSO 9.2, "Understanding the Google Docs Suite"* ▶

◄ *SEE ALSO 9.6, "Other Web-Based Applications"* ▶

Navigating the Workspace

Google Spreadsheets looks and works a lot like every other PC-based spreadsheet application you've ever used. At the top of the workspace is a traditional menu bar. Below that is a toolbar with common formatting functions. Below that is the open spreadsheet itself.

A Google spreadsheet is arranged into rows and columns. **Rows** are horizontal and are numbered. **Columns** are vertical and are lettered alphabetically. A **cell** is the intersection of a row and a column and is where you enter data. The cell **address,** used to reference the cell in calculations, is the column letter followed by the row number. The first cell in the spreadsheet is A1.

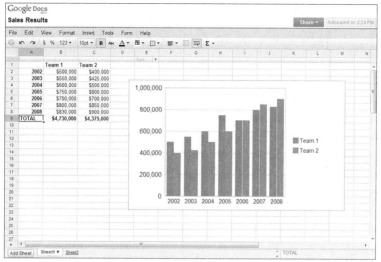

A typical Google Spreadsheets spreadsheet.

Working With Multiple Sheets

Like Excel, Google Spreadsheets lets you work with multiple sheets within a single spreadsheet file. Unlike Excel, which always starts with three sheets per spreadsheet, Google defaults to a single sheet. You can then add sheets to this first sheet.

To add a new sheet to your spreadsheet, all you have to do is click the Add Sheet button at the bottom of the main spreadsheet window. To switch to a different sheet, just click its link.

By default, Google names its sheets Sheet1, Sheet2, Sheet3, and so forth. If you'd like a somewhat more descriptive name for a sheet, select the sheet and then click its tab. When the pop-up menu appears, click Rename, enter a new name, and then click OK.

Entering and Editing Data

Google Spreadsheets lets you enter four different types of data. **Numbers** can be in a variety of formats, including currency and percent, and can be manipulated mathematically. **Text** can contain both alphabetic and numeric characters, and cannot be manipulated mathematically. **Dates** are specially formatted numbers. And **formulas** tell Google Spreadsheets how to make calculations using data in other cells.

9.4

Entering New Data

Entering data is as simple as selecting a particular cell and typing input. Just move the cursor to the desired cell, using either the mouse or the keyboard arrow keys, and begin typing.

This approach works for all types of data, with the exception of formulas. Entering a formula is almost as simple, except that you must enter an equals sign (=) first. Just go to the cell, press the = key on the keyboard, and then enter the formula.

As to how the individual data is formatted—that is, how Google Spreadsheets interprets numbers and letters—it depends on what type of data you enter:

▶ If you typed only numbers, the data is formatted as a number (with no commas or dollar signs).

▶ If you typed a number with a dollar sign in front of it, the data is formatted as currency.

▶ If you typed any alphabetic characters, the data is formatted as text.

▶ If you typed numbers separated by the – or / character (such as 12–31 or 1/2/09), the data is formatted as a date.

▶ If you typed numbers separated by the : character (such as 2:13), the data is formatted as a time.

Editing Previously Entered Data

Editing existing data in a cell is a fairly simple exercise; you actually edit within the cell. Just move the cursor to the desired cell and press the F2 key; this opens the cell for editing. Move the cursor to the data point within the cell you want to edit. Then use the Delete and Backspace keys to delete characters or use any other key to insert characters. Press Enter when you are finished editing, and your changes are accepted into the selected cell.

Inserting and Deleting Rows and Columns

To insert a new row or column into a spreadsheet, start by positioning the cursor in the row or column where you want to insert a new row or column. Click the Insert button and select whether you want to insert a row (above or below) or a column (to the right or left). Google Spreadsheets does the rest.

You can also delete entire rows and columns or clear the contents of individual cells. To delete a row or column, position the cursor in that row or column, click the Delete button, and select whether you want to delete the row or column.

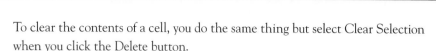

To clear the contents of a cell, you do the same thing but select Clear Selection when you click the Delete button.

Working With Ranges

When you reference data within a spreadsheet, you can reference individual cells or you can reference a few cells. When you reference more than one contiguous cell, that's called a **range.** You typically use ranges with specific functions, such as **SUM** (which totals a range of cells) or **AVERAGE** (which calculates the average value of a range of cells).

A range reference is expressed by listing the first and last cells in the range, separated by a colon (:). For example, the range that starts with cell A1 and ends with cell A9 is written like this:

A1:A9

You can select a range with either the mouse or keyboard. Using the mouse, you can simply click and drag the cursor to select all the cells in the range. Using the keyboard, position the cursor in the first cell in the range, hold down the Shift key, and then use the cursor keys to expand the range in the appropriate direction.

Finally, you can use a combination of mouse and keyboard to select a range. Use either the mouse or keyboard to select the first cell in the range. Then hold down the Shift key and click the mouse in the last cell in the range. All the cells between the two cells are automatically selected.

Sorting Data

9.4

Often you want your data to appear in a sorted order. You might want to sort your data by date, for example, or by quantity or dollar value. Fortunately, Google Spreadsheets lets you sort your data either alphabetically or numerically in either ascending or descending order.

Start by moving the cursor to any cell within the column you want to sort by. To sort in ascending order, select Tools, Sort by Column A>Z. To sort in descending order, select Tools, Sort by Column Z>A.

The A>Z and Z>A sorts don't just sort by letter; they also sort by number. An A>Z sort arranges numeric data from smallest to largest; a Z>A sort arranges numeric data from largest to smallest.

Formatting Data

A basic Google spreadsheet looks fairly plain; fortunately, you can spruce it up by changing font size, font family, and color and by changing the background color of individual cells. All you have to do is select the cell(s) you want to format and then use the formatting options on the toolbar. You can also use the formatting options on the Formatting menu.

WARNING . . .WARNING . . .WARNING

Although you can change text attributes for an entire cell or range of cells, Google Spreadsheets doesn't let you change attributes for selected characters *within* a cell.

You can also change how numbers are formatted within your spreadsheet. A number can be expressed as a whole number, a percentage, a fraction, currency, a date, and even exponentially. To apply a different number format, just select the cell or range, click the Format button on the toolbar, and then select a format.

Entering Formulas

After you've entered data into your spreadsheet, you need to work with those numbers to create other numbers. You do this as you would in the real world, by using common formulas to calculate your data by addition, subtraction, multiplication, and division. You can also use advanced formulas preprogrammed into Google Spreadsheets; these advanced formulas are called **functions.**

A formula can consist of numbers, mathematical operators, and the contents of other cells (referred to by the cell reference). You construct a formula from the following elements:

▶ An equals sign (=). This is necessary at the start of each formula.

▶ One or more specific numbers.

     and/or

▶ One or more cell references.

▶ A mathematical operator (such as + or –). This is needed if your formula contains more than one cell reference or number.

For example, to add the contents of cells A1 and A2, you enter this formula:

=A1+A2

To multiply the contents of cell A1 by 10, you enter this formula:

=A1*10

And so on. Table 9.1 shows the algebraic operators you can use within Google Spreadsheets formulas.

TABLE 9.1 ACCEPTED OPERATORS FOR GOOGLE SPREADSHEETS FORMULAS

Operator	Description
+	Addition
−	Subtraction
*	Multiplication
/	Division
^	Exponentiation (to the power of)
=	Equal to
>	Greater than
>=	Greater than or equal to
<	Less than
<=	Less than or equal to
<>	Not equal to
%	Percentage

To enter a formula in a cell, move the cursor to the desired cell, type = to start the formula, and then enter the rest of the formula. Remember to refer to specific cells by the A1, B1, and so on cell reference. Press Enter to accept the formula or press Esc to reject the formula.

When you're finished entering a formula, you no longer see the formula within the cell; instead, you see the results of the formula. For example, if you entered the formula =1+2, you see the number 3 in the cell. To view the formula itself, just select the cell and then look in the reference area in the lower-right corner of the spreadsheet window.

Using Functions

A function is a type of formula built into Google Spreadsheets. You can use Google's built-in functions instead of writing complex formulas in your spreadsheets; you can also include functions as part of your formulas.

Functions simplify the creation of complex formulas. For example, if you want to total the value of cells B4 through B7, you could enter the following formula:

=B4+B5+B6+B7

Or you could use the **SUM** function, which lets you total (sum) a column or row of numbers without having to type every cell into the formula. In this instance, the formula to total the cells B4 through B7 could be written using the **SUM** function, like this:

=sum(B4:B7)

This is much easier, don't you think?

Google Spreadsheets uses most of the same functions as those used in Microsoft Excel. All Google functions use the following format:

=function(argument)

Replace *function* with the name of the function and replace *argument* with a range reference. The argument always appears in parentheses.

You can enter a function into a formula either by typing the name of the function or by pasting the function into the formula from a list of functions. To access the full list of available functions, click the Formulas button on the toolbar and select More Formulas. When the Insert a Function dialog box appears, click the function you want to use. When you click the Close link, the function is pasted into the selected cell.

Charting Your Data

Google Spreadsheets also lets you present your data graphically. To create a chart, start by selecting the cells that include the data you want to graph and then select Insert, Chart.

This displays the Create Chart dialog box. You can create six types of charts—columns, bars, pie, lines, area, and scatter—and different subtypes within each major type. Select the type of chart you want along with the subtype, enter a chart title, and select any other desired options (such as a chart legend). When the preview looks like you want it to, click the Save Chart button. The chart is created and added to the current spreadsheet.

Printing a Spreadsheet

When you're finished creating your spreadsheet, you might want to print a hard copy. Just click the Print button on the selected spreadsheet page. When the Print dialog box appears, make sure that the correct printer is selected and then click the Print button.

Expanding Functionality with Gadgets

Unfortunately, Google Spreadsheets doesn't have all the functionality you find in Microsoft Excel. You can increase its functionality, however, by adding various **gadgets** to your spreadsheets.

In the Google Spreadsheets world, a gadget is a plug-in that adds functionality to the basic application. Gadgets are created both by Google and by other users; you can also create your own gadgets if you're so inclined. You can find gadgets that create more sophisticated chart types, add pivot table functionality, and the like. This is a great way for Google to make Google Spreadsheets better without having to alter the core application code.

To add a gadget to a spreadsheet, select Insert, Gadget. When the Add a Gadget dialog box appears, select the type of gadget you want and then click the Add to Spreadsheet button to add the gadget.

Exporting to Excel Format

By default, all the spreadsheets you work with in Google Spreadsheets are stored on Google's servers. You can, however, download files from Google to your computer's hard drive to work with in Excel. In essence, you're exporting your Google spreadsheet to an .xls format Excel file.

To export the current spreadsheet, click the File button and select Export, .xls. When the File Download dialog box appears, click the Save button. When the Save As dialog box appears, select a location for the downloaded file, rename it if you like, and then click the Save button.

The Google Spreadsheets file is saved in .xls format on your hard disk. You can now open that file with Excel and work on it as you would with any Excel spreadsheet. Know, however, that whatever changes you make to the file from within Excel affect only the downloaded file, not the copy of the spreadsheet that still resides on the Google Spreadsheets site. If you later want to reimport the Excel file to Google Spreadsheets, you'll need to return to the main Google Docs page and use the Upload function.

A **function** is an advanced formula preprogrammed into a spreadsheet application.

A **gadget** is a plug-in that adds functionality to the Google Spreadsheets application.

A **range** is a group of more than one contiguous cells in a spreadsheet.

9.5 USING GOOGLE PRESENTATIONS

Navigating the Workspace

Managing Slides

Changing Themes

Working With Text and Graphics

Animating Elements on a Slide

Printing Handouts and Speaker Notes

Giving Live Presentations

Exporting to PowerPoint Format

The final component of the Google Docs application suite is Google Presenta-tions. As the name implies, Google Presentations is an application, similar to Microsoft PowerPoint, that enables you to create and give slideshow-like pre-sentations. Due to its web-based nature, you can also use Google Presentations to give PowerPoint presentations when you're away from the office; you don't have to take any files with you—all you need is a computer with an Internet connection.

◀ *SEE ALSO 9.2, "Understanding the Google Docs Suite"* ▢

▢ *SEE ALSO 9.6, "Other Web-Based Applications"* ▶

9.5

Navigating the Workspace

A presentation is composed of a number of different slides. Each slide can hold text, images, videos, or any combination of these.

In the Google Presentations workspace, the slides in a presentation are displayed in the slide sorter pane to the left of the main part of the workspace. The larger part of the workspace, called the editing window, displays the current slide for editing. To edit a different slide, just select that slide in the slide sorter.

All the application's editing and formatting tools are at the top of the workspace. Editing functions are found on the editing toolbar; formatting commands are on the formatting toolbar.

The Google Presentations workspace.

Managing Slides

In Google Presentations, a slide can be based on one of five predesigned layouts: Title, Text, Two Columns, Caption, and Blank. Every new presentation starts with a single Title slide. To add a new slide, select Slide, New Slide. When the Choose Slide Layout dialog box appears, select the layout for the new slide. The new slide is now added to the slide sorter pane and displayed in the main window.

If you've created a slide with content or formatting that you'd like to repeat elsewhere in your presentation, you can duplicate that slide and then edit the duplicate. Select the slide you want to duplicate in the slide sorter and then select Slide, Duplicate Slide. A duplicate of the selected slide is created after the selected slide in the slide sorter.

Of course, you don't always want to keep every slide you create. To delete a slide, simply select it in the slide sorter and then click the Delete Slide link.

As your presentation develops, you may need to rethink the order of the slides in the presentation. You can rearrange your slides in the slide sorter using your mouse. Just select the slide you want to move and then drag it up or down to a new position.

Changing Themes

Few people want to give a presentation of black text on a plain white background. You gain more attention by using attractive background colors and graphics.

Google Presentations lets you choose from several predesigned **themes** for your presentations. A theme is a predesigned collection of background images, color schemes, and fonts that are applied to every slide in your presentation. You can also design your own themes by using custom background images on all of your slides.

To change the theme of your presentation, select Edit, Change Theme. When the Choose Theme dialog box appears, click the theme you want to use. This theme is now applied to all the slides in your presentation.

Working With Text and Graphics

Once you've chosen a slide layout, it's time to start adding content to that slide. Slide content can be in the form of text or images of various types.

Adding and Formatting Text

Each block of text on a slide is added via a separate text object. Just select an object to add, edit, or format the text within.

For example, most slides in a presentation have a title that appears at the top of the slide; this title area is an object labeled "Click to add title." Click this object and then type your title.

You add body text to a slide in a similar fashion. Just click the text object labeled "Click to add content" and then type your text. You can enter a block of text like a paragraph or (using the appropriate buttons on the formatting toolbar) bulleted or numbered lists.

Google Presentations also lets you format text on a slide pretty much the way you'd format text in a word-processing document. Just select the text object on the slide that contains the text you want to edit and then, within the text object, use your cursor to select the text you want to format. Now click the appropriate button on the toolbar to apply the formatting you want. For example, to change the font of the selected text, select a new font from the Font list; to boldface the selected text, click the Bold button.

9.5

Adding Images

Text isn't the only type of object you can add to a slide. Often you'll want to show a picture of some item on a slide or just add a graphic for visual interest.

To add a picture to a slide, position your cursor where you want the image to appear and select Insert, Image. When the Insert Image dialog box appears, click the Browse button and select the image file you want to include. Click OK, and the image is inserted into your slide as a new object.

After the image is inserted, you can now use your mouse to drag the image object to a new location on the slide. You can also resize the image by clicking and dragging the image's corner handles.

WARNING . . .WARNING . . .WARNING

Google Presentations does not currently include its own chart editor, so you can't create charts from within the application. You can, however, copy charts created in other applications into a Google Presentations slide. If you do this, you will not be able to edit the chart image.

◄ SEE ALSO 9.4, *"Using Google Spreadsheets"* ▷

Animating Elements on a Slide

While Google Presentations does not currently offer slide-to-slide transitions, you can animate the individual elements on a slide. That is, you can configure one element to appear after another element via what Google calls **incremental reveal.**

When you choose to incrementally reveal an object, it doesn't appear when you first display the slide during a presentation. To reveal an object, you press the Next button as if you were going to a new slide; this displays the first object you've chosen to reveal. If more than one object on a slide is formatted for incremental reveal, each successive object is displayed each time you press the next key.

It's even better when you select a bulleted or numbered list for incremental reveal. In this instance, only the first list item is displayed when you press the next button during the presentation. Continue pressing the next button to display successive items in the list.

To use incremental reveal, right-click the object you want to appear first and then select Incremental Reveal from the pop-up menu. A timer icon now appears next to that object on your slide.

Select the object you want to appear next and again select Incremental Reveal from that object's pop-up menu. A timer button with the number 2 now appears next to that object on your slide. Repeat this step for any other object you want to be revealed on the slide.

When you give the presentation, all you have to do is click the Next button to display each selected item in order.

Printing Handouts and Speaker Notes

Google Presentations lets you print your entire presentation, one slide per page, or create speaker notes for you to use when giving the presentation.

To create printed handouts, select File, Print. When the Print Preview dialog box appears, pull down the Layout list and select how many slides you want to print per page—1, 2, 4, 8, 9, or 12. Click the Print button, and your handouts will be printed as specified.

Beyond simple handouts, presenters often like to prepare speaker notes that they can reference while they're giving a presentation. To do this, go to the first slide of your presentation and click the View Speaker Notes button in the lower-right corner of the workspace. This changes the workspace to reveal a Speaker Notes pane. Enter your notes for this slide into the Speaker Notes pane. Then move to subsequent slides in your presentation and enter notes for those slides.

To print your speaker notes, select File, Print. When the Print Preview dialog box appears, check the Speaker Notes option and click the Print button. This prints your presentation one slide per page with speaker notes displayed beneath each slide.

Giving Live Presentations

After you've created and edited your presentation, you can connect your computer to a projector or large monitor and show it to any size group of people. In fact, you can take your presentation anywhere you travel just by connecting your computer to the Internet—where your presentation is stored.

To give a live presentation in person, start by opening the presentation and selecting the first slide; then click the Start Presentation button. This opens your live presentation in a new browser window. Press the F11 key on your keyboard to display the presentation full screen.

To advance to the next slide in the presentation, click the next slide (right) arrow or press the right-arrow key on your keyboard. If a slide includes objects formatted with incremental reveal, only the slide background and immediate reveal objects will appear when the slide first displays. To reveal the next object on the slide, click the next slide arrow or press the right-arrow key on your keyboard.

When the presentation is finished, you see an End of Presentation dialog box. Click the Restart button to start the presentation over or click the Exit button to close the presentation window.

9.5

Exporting to PowerPoint Format

Another way to share a presentation is to export it into PowerPoint format so that anyone using PowerPoint can view it. From within the current presentation window, select File, Download Presentation As, PPT. When the File Download dialog box appears, click the Save button. When the Save As dialog box appears, select a location for the downloaded file, rename it if you like, and then click the Save button.

The Google Presentations file is now saved in .ppt format on your hard disk. You can open this saved file with Microsoft PowerPoint and work on it as you would with any PowerPoint presentation.

WORDS TO GO . . . WORDS TO GO . . . WORDS TO GO

Incremental reveal is used in Google Presentations to animate individual elements on a slide.

A **theme** is a predesigned collection of background images, color schemes, and fonts that are applied to every slide in a Google Presentations presentation.

9.6 OTHER WEB-BASED APPLICATIONS

Calendars

Scheduling

To-Do Lists and Task Management

Office Suites

Word Processors

Spreadsheets

Presentations

With traditional desktop computing, you run copies of software programs on each computer you own. The documents you create are stored on the computer on which they were created. Although documents can be accessed from other computers on a network, they can't be accessed by computers outside the network.

Everything is different with web-based applications—or, as some call it, **cloud computing**—because everything is stored on a "cloud" of Internet-based computers. With web-based computing, the software programs you use aren't run from your personal computer, but rather are stored on servers accessed via the Internet. If your computer crashes, the software is still available for others to use. The same goes for the documents you create; they're stored on a collection of servers accessed via the Internet. Anyone with permission can not only access the documents, they can also edit and collaborate on those documents in real time. Which computer you use to access a document simply isn't important.

We've already examined some of the most popular web-based applications—Google Calendar and Google Docs. But there are many more applications out there in the cloud just waiting to be accessed via the Internet.

Calendars

A web-based calendar service stores your calendars on the Internet, where they can be accessed from any computer that has an Internet connection. This lets you check your schedule when you're on the road, even if your assistant in the office or your spouse at home has added new appointments since you left. Web-based calendars are also extremely easy to share with other users in any location, which make them great for collaborative projects.

9.6

Most web-based calendars are free and offer similar online sharing and collaboration features. The following are the most popular of these calendars:

- ▶ 30 Boxes (www.30boxes.com)
- ▶ AOL Calendar (calendar.aol.com)
- ▶ Apple MobileMe (www.apple.com/mobileme/)
- ▶ CalendarHub (www.calendarhub.com)
- ▶ Famundo (www.famundo.com)
- ▶ Google Calendar (calendar.google.com)
- ▶ Hunt Calendars (www.huntcal.com)
- ▶ Windows Live Calendar (mail.live.com/mail/calendar.aspx)
- ▶ Yahoo! Calendar (calendar.yahoo.com)

◀ *SEE ALSO 9.1, "Using Google Calendar"* ▶

Scheduling

An online scheduling application takes much of the pain out of scheduling meetings for both large and small groups. The typical application requires all users to enter their individual calendars beforehand. When you schedule a meeting, the application checks attendees' schedules for the first available free time for all. The application then generates automated e-mail messages to inform attendees of the meeting request (and the designated time), followed by automatic confirmation e-mails when attendees accept the invitation.

The following are the most popular web-based scheduling applications:

- ▶ Diarised (www.diarised.com)
- ▶ hitAppoint (www.hitappoint.com)
- ▶ Jiffle (www.jifflenow.com)
- ▶ Presdo (www.presdo.com)
- ▶ Schedulebook (www.schedulebook.com)
- ▶ Windows Live Events (home.services.spaces.live.com/events/)

To-Do Lists and Task Management

Now let's pivot from schedules to tasks. Planning and task management applications let you manage everything from simple to-do lists to complex group tasks, all over the Internet and collaboratively with other users. Here are the most popular:

- Bla-bla List (www.blablalist.com)
- HiTask (www.hitask.com)
- Hiveminder (www.hiveminder.com)
- iPrioritize (www.iprioritize.com)
- Remember the Milk (www.rememberthemilk.com)
- Ta-da List (www.tadalist.com)
- TaskTHIS (taskthis.darthapo.com)
- TracksLife (www.trackslife.com)
- Tudu List (www.tudulist.com)
- Vitalist (www.vitalist.com)
- Voo2do (www.voo2do.com)
- Zoho Planner (planner.zoho.com)

Office Suites

Microsoft Office is the most-used suite of applications on the market. To that end, several companies are offering web-based office suites to compete with Microsoft Office. Most of these suites offer word processing, spreadsheet, and presentation components.

The most popular of the web-based office suites are as follows:

- Glide Business (www.glidedigital.com)
- Google Docs (docs.google.com)
- Peepel Online Office (www.peepel.com)
- ThinkFree Office (www.thinkfree.com)
- WebEx WebOffice (www.weboffice.com)
- Zoho Office (office.zoho.com)

9.6

Word Processors

There are a number of web-based replacements for Microsoft's venerable Word software program. All of these programs let you write your letters and memos and reports from any computer, with no installed software necessary, as long as that computer has a connection to the Internet. Every document you create is housed on the web, so you don't have to worry about taking your work with you. It's cloud computing at its most useful, and it's here today.

The following are the most popular web-based word processors:

- ▶ Adobe Buzzword (buzzword.acrobat.com)
- ▶ Glide Write (www.glidedigital.com)
- ▶ Google Docs (docs.google.com)
- ▶ iNetWord (www.inetword.com)
- ▶ KBdocs (www.kbdocs.com)
- ▶ Peepel WebWriter (www.peepel.com)
- ▶ ThinkFree Write (www.thinkfree.com)
- ▶ Zoho Writer (writer.zoho.com)

◀ SEE ALSO 9.3, *"Using Google Docs for Word Processing"* ▶

Spreadsheets

Several web-based spreadsheet applications are worthy competitors to Microsoft Excel. If you're at all interested in moving your number crunching and financial analysis into the cloud, these web-based applications are worth checking out:

- ▶ EditGrid (www.editgrid.com)
- ▶ eXpresso (www.expressocorp.com)
- ▶ Glide Crunch (www.glidedigital.com)
- ▶ Google Spreadsheets (docs.google.com)
- ▶ Num Sum (www.numsum.com)
- ▶ Peepel WebSheet (www.peepel.com)
- ▶ ThinkFree Calc (www.thinkfree.com)
- ▶ Zoho Sheet (sheet.zoho.com)

◀ SEE ALSO 9.4, *"Using Google Spreadsheets"* ▶

Presentations

Web-based presentation programs enable you to create, collaborate, and give presentations over the Internet. While none of these programs has the full functionality of Microsoft PowerPoint, some do offer compelling experiences for groups who need to collaborate on presentations.

The best of these web-based presentation applications include the following:

- ▶ Brinkpad (www.brinkpad.com)
- ▶ Empressr (www.empressr.com)
- ▶ Google Presentations (docs.google.com)
- ▶ Preezo (www.preezo.com)
- ▶ Presentation Engine (www.presentationengine.com)
- ▶ PreZentit (www.prezentit.com)
- ▶ SlideRocket (www.sliderocket.com)
- ▶ ThinkFree Show (www.thinkfree.com)
- ▶ Zoho Show (show.zoho.com)

◀ *SEE ALSO 9.5, "Using Google Presentations"* ▶

WORDS TO GO . . . *WORDS TO GO . . . WORDS TO GO*

Cloud computing is another phrase for web-based applications, where the programs and related data are housed not on individual computers but on a "cloud" of computers connected to the Internet.

9.6

10

BLOGS AND PODCASTS

10.1 UNDERSTANDING BLOGS

Introducing the Blogosphere

Navigating a Blog

Much of the useful information found on the Internet doesn't come from big organizations, but rather from individuals posting their thoughts and comments on personal blogs. A **blog** (short for "web log") is a kind of online journal that its author updates frequently with new musings and information.

Introducing the Blogosphere

There are hundreds of thousands of blogs on the Internet from both private individuals and public companies. The people who contribute to blogs are called **bloggers,** the act of posting to a blog is called **blogging,** and the entire universe of blogs is called the **blogosphere.**

You can find blogs devoted to just about any topic, from industry news to political news to personal news. Most blogs, however, don't exist in and unto themselves; the blogosphere is an interlinking universe of individual blogs. That's because a big part of blogging is about linking to other blogs and to news and information on the web. Look at any blog, and you're likely to see a list of related blogs called a **blog roll.** Bloggers like to link to other blogs that they enjoy—as well as to news stories, photos, audio files, you name it.

◁ SEE ALSO 10.2, *"Searching for Blogs"* ▷

Navigating a Blog

A typical blog is a collection of individual **posts,** or articles. On most blogs these posts are short, typically no more than a paragraph or two. But some blogs feature longer posts in order for the blogger to go into more depth in his or her commentary.

Posts are arranged in reverse chronological order with the newest posts at the top; this way, visitors will always see the most recent comments. Older posts are typically relegated to the blog **archives,** which are generally accessible via a link in the sidebar column.

A blog's sidebar column is also where you'll find links to other items of interest, as determined by the blog's host. You might find links to the blogger's favorite books or videos or to related websites, for example.

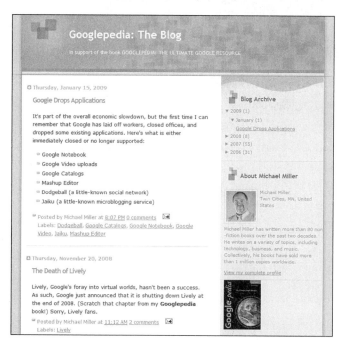

A typical blog.

Depending on the blog, readers may be able to post their own comments about any given post. Look for a "comments" link either above or below each post; click this link to read all the comments to date or to post your own comment.

Most blogs are all text, but blogs can also display photos, audio files, and even videos. It's all up to the blogger and how sophisticated he wants his blog to be. And while most blogs are maintained by a single individual, some professional blogs have posts from multiple authors in order to provide the most complete coverage of the topic.

◀ SEE ALSO 10.4, "Creating Your Own Blog" ▶

10.1

WORDS TO GO . . . WORDS TO GO . . . WORDS TO GO

A blog's **archives** contain older blog posts.

A **blog** (short for "web blog") is a frequently updated online journal containing news, information, and opinions.

A **blog roll** is a list of related blogs.

Bloggers are people who post to blogs.

The act of posting to a blog is called **blogging**.

The **blogosphere** is the entire universe of web-based blogs.

A **post** is a single blog entry.

10.2 SEARCHING FOR BLOGS

Blog Directories

Google Blog Search

The web has literally hundreds of thousands of blogs covering just about any topic you can think of. How do you find blogs of interest to you?

◀ SEE ALSO 10.1, *"Understanding Blogs"* ▶

Blog Directories

One way to find a particular blog is to search the various blog directories on the web. These include the following:

▶ BlogCatalog (www.blogcatalog.com)

▶ Blog Hints (www.bloghints.com)

▶ Blog Search Engine (www.blogsearchengine.com)

▶ Blogging Fusion (www.bloggingfusion.com)

▶ Bloghub.com (www.bloghub.com)

▶ Globe of Blogs (www.globeofblogs.com)

▶ Weblogs.com (www.weblogs.com)

Google Blog Search

Unfortunately, the blogosphere is quite chaotic and constantly changing, which means that no single blog directory can list all the blogs on the web. For that reason, many users turn to Google Blog Search to search not only for blogs but for individual blog postings.

How Google Blog Search Works

Google Blog Search works not by crawling the web, as Google's traditional search does, but by monitoring all of the **site feeds** in the blogosphere. A site feed is an automatically updated stream of a blog's contents, enabled by a special file format called **Really Simple Syndication** (RSS). When a blog has an RSS feed enabled, any updated content is automatically published as a special XML file that contains the RSS feed. The syndicated feed is then normally picked up by RSS feed reader programs and RSS aggregators for websites.

SEE ALSO 10.4, "Creating Your Own Blog" ▶

Google uses these RSS feeds to seed its blog search index. By aggregating RSS feeds into its index, Google Blog Search is constantly (and almost immediately) updated with new blog content. The structured format of the RSS files also makes it relatively easy to accurately search for specific information and date ranges within the blog index.

Searching for Blogs and Posts

To search for a given blog or a particular blog post, go to the Google Blog Search page (blogsearch.google.com). Enter your query into the search box and then click the Search Blogs button.

Google now searches its index of RSS feeds and returns a page of blogs and blog postings that best match your query. This page has two main parts.

At the top of the page is a short list of blogs that have some relevance to your query. Click the blog name to view the entire blog.

Below that is a list of individual blog posts. The title of the post is at the top of each listing; click the title to view the full posting. Below the title is a line that tells you when the posting was made and who posted it. Then there are the first few sentences of the post, serving as a summary. Finally, there's a link to the blog itself, listing both the blog's title and URL; click the link to view the entire blog.

WORDS TO GO . . .WORDS TO GO . . .WORDS TO GO

Really Simple Syndication (RSS) is a file format used to create site feeds. A **site feed** is an automatically updated stream of a blog's contents.

10.2

10.3 SUBSCRIBING TO BLOG CONTENT

Subscribing to a Feed
Feed Reader Programs
Feed Aggregator Websites

Many blogs let you subscribe to a feed of their posts. This is an updated list of all new posts. A feed subscription uses Really Simple Syndication (RSS) technology to notify you of all new posts made to that blog.

◀ *SEE ALSO 10.2, "Searching for Blogs"* ▷

Subscribing to a Feed

You typically subscribe to a blog's RSS feed directly from the blog itself. Look for a "subscribe" or "feed" or "RSS" button. (An alternative form of syndication, **Atom** feeds, is sometimes offered; it works the same way as RSS.) Click the button to display the feed page and then copy this page's URL into your feed reader program.

Feed Reader Programs

A feed reader (sometimes called a news reader) is a software program that monitors and displays all the RSS feeds you've subscribed to. Some of the more popular feed reader programs are as follows:

- ▶ FeedDemon (www.feeddemon.com)

- ▶ Feedreader (www.feedreader.com)

- ▶ RssReader (www.rssreader.com)

Some e-mail programs and web browsers also incorporate feed reader functionality. For example, Internet Explorer 8 includes a View Feeds button on its command bar. Click this button to view the feed subscription page for any blog with an RSS or Atom feed; you can then subscribe to the feed from that page. All your subscriptions are listed in the browser's Favorites center, which you display by clicking the Favorites button.

Feed Aggregator Websites

You can also monitor your RSS subscriptions with a web-based feed aggregator site. These sites work just like feed reader programs but from within your web browser. The most popular of these feed aggregator sites include the following:

- ▶ Bloglines (www.bloglines.com)
- ▶ Fastladder (www.fastladder.com)
- ▶ Google Reader (reader.google.com)

In addition, many personalized home pages, such as My Yahoo! (my.yahoo.com) and iGoogle (www.google.com/ig/), let you add RSS feeds to your customized page content. Follow the site's instructions to add a feed module to your page.

WORDS TO GO . . .WORDS TO GO . . .WORDS TO GO

Atom is a file format used to create site feeds.

10.3

231

10.4 CREATING YOUR OWN BLOG

Blog-Hosting Communities

Creating a Blogger Blog

Customizing Your Blog

Posting New Blog Entries

Adding a Site Feed

Bloggers typically update their blogs on a regular basis—weekly, daily, or even hourly, depending on the blogger. The process of updating a blog is facilitated by blogging software.

Fortunately, hosting a blog requires little or no technical expertise on the part of the blogger. All the heavy lifting is handled by the site that hosts the blog.

◄ *SEE ALSO 10.1, "Understanding Blogs"* ▷

Blog-Hosting Communities

A **blog-hosting community** is a site that offers easy-to-use tools to build and maintain your blog and then does all the hosting for you—typically for free. Creating your own blog on one of these sites is as simple as clicking a few buttons and filling out a few forms. After your blog is created, you can update it as frequently as you like, again by clicking a link or two.

The following are some of the most popular blog-hosting communities:

- ► BlogEasy (www.blogeasy.com)
- ► Blogger (www.blogger.com)
- ► Blogsome (www.blogsome.com)
- ► eBloggy (www.ebloggy.com)
- ► tBlog (www.tblog.com)
- ► TypePad (www.typepad.com)
- ► WordPress.com (www.wordpress.com)

In addition, most social networking communities, such as Facebook and MySpace, let you create blogs as part of your personal pages. If you use one of these sites, you can use it to host your blog.

Creating a Blogger Blog

Perhaps the most popular blog-hosting community on the web today is Blogger, which is owned by Google. Anyone with a Google account (or who registers for a free Blogger account) can have their blog hosted on Blogger.

After you've registered with Blogger, the home page (www.blogger.com) becomes the Blogger Dashboard. From here, you can manage all your blogs, create new blog posts, manage your Blogger account and profile, and access Blogger's help system.

To create a new blog, go to the Blogger Dashboard and then click the Create a Blog link. When the Name Your Blog page appears, enter a title for your blog and a corresponding blog address (the part of the URL that goes before Blogger's blogspot.com domain) and then click Continue. You are then asked to do a word verification for security purposes. Type in the word shown on the screen and click Continue.

Next you get to choose a template for your blog. This is a predesigned combination of page layout, colors, and fonts that gives your blog a unique visual style. After you make your choice, click the Continue button.

Blogger now creates your blog and displays a confirmation page. If now is a good time to write your first blog post, click the Start Blogging link. Otherwise, you can create posts later.

Customizing Your Blog

The blog templates that Blogger displays when you first create your blog are nice, but there aren't a lot of them. Fortunately, Blogger offers additional templates for your blog—and lets you fully customize the look and feel of your blog page.

Choosing a Different Template

If you no longer like the template you originally chose for your blog, you can change it. Blogger offers several dozen blog templates, and it's easy to switch from one to another. Your blog posts aren't lost when you switch.

To change templates, go to the Blogger Dashboard and click the Layout link next to your blog name. When the next page appears, select the Layout tab and click Pick New Template. This displays all of Blogger's available templates. This is a larger selection of templates than was visible when you first created your blog. To preview how your blog will look with a given template, click the Preview Template link beneath that template. To choose a new template, select that template's radio button and then click the Save Template button.

10.4

Personalizing Fonts and Colors

You don't have to settle for the stock templates that Blogger provides. Blogger lets you customize the fonts and colors used in any template with a few clicks of the mouse.

To customize the look of individual elements in your blog template, go to the Blogger Dashboard and click the Layout link next to your blog title. When the next page appears, select the Layout tab and click Fonts and Colors. This displays the Fonts and Colors page. From here you can change the color of all the elements on your page, from the background and main text to the sidebar and links. You can also change the font of the text and the page header.

For colors, making a change is as simple as selecting the element in the list and then clicking the new color in the color picker. To change the text font, select Text Font from the list and choose a font family, font style (normal, bold, or italic), and font size (smaller or larger). The preview of your blog, at the bottom of the page, reflects your changes. When you're satisfied with your changes, click the Save Changes button.

Adding New Gadgets

One of the more useful features of Blogger is the ability to add subsidiary page elements, called **gadgets,** in either the sidebar or the main column of the blog page. You can use these gadgets to add descriptive text, pictures, links, lists, and the like to your blog.

To work with gadgets, go to the Blogger Dashboard and click the Layout link next to your blog name. When the next page appears, select the Layout tab and click Page Elements. The resulting page displays all the current gadgets used in your blog. To rearrange existing gadgets, simply drag the selected element to a new position on the page.

To add a new gadget to your page, click the Add a Gadget link. This displays the Add a Gadget window; select a category on the left side to view all gadgets of that type. Click the "+" icon next to the element you want to add. You'll now see a window specific to the type of gadget you selected. Fill in the information required in this window and then click Save.

Your blog now contains the gadget you selected. You can then decide where on the page that gadget will appear by dragging it into place on the Add and Arrange Page Elements page.

Posting New Blog Entries

After you've created and customized your blog, it's time to write your first blog post.

Creating a Post

When you're ready to post, go to the Blogger Dashboard and click the New Post icon for this particular blog. When the Posting page appears, enter a title for this post. Next enter the text for your post into the large text box.

If you like you can format the text (bold, italic, colors, and so on) using the formatting toolbar above this text box. If you want to apply more sophisticated formatting (and you know how to code in HTML), click the Edit HTML tab and enter your own HTML codes.

To check the spelling in your post, click the Check Spelling button. Misspelled words are highlighted in yellow; click a word to see a list of suggested corrections.

To view a preview of your post, click the Preview link. Then when you're done writing and formatting, click the Publish Post button. Blogger publishes your post and displays a confirmation screen. Click the View Blog button to view your blog with the new post at the top of the page.

Adding Links

One of the neat things about a blog is the ability to link to other pages on the web via the use of inline hyperlinks. You add these links while you're creating the blog post. Just highlight the text from which you want to link and then click the Link button. This displays the Hyperlink dialog box; enter the URL for the link and then click OK.

Adding Pictures

10.4

Another way to make a visually interesting blog is to incorporate pictures into your blog entries. As with hyperlinks, you add pictures while you're creating your blog post. Just position the cursor where you want the picture to appear and click the Add Image button. This displays the Upload Images window.

To upload an image file from your computer, click the Browse button in the Add an Image from Your Computer section and then navigate to and select the image file. You can upload additional pictures by clicking the Add Another Image link.

To point to an image hosted elsewhere on the web, enter the full web address for that image into the URL box in the Or Add an Image from the Web section. Click the Add Another Image link to link to additional images.

After you select each image to include, you can choose how to display that image in the blog post. In the Choose a Layout section, select how you want the image aligned relative to the blog text: left, center, or right. In the Image Size section, select how big you want the image to appear: small, medium, or large.

Clicking the Upload Image button adds the photo to the selected blog post. Blog visitors can click the image to view it full size.

Adding Videos

Similarly, Blogger lets you add videos to your blog posts. You can upload videos in most popular file formats: AVI, MPEG, QuickTime, Real, and Windows Media Video (WMV). Videos can be uploaded from your own PC or linked to on the YouTube site. Your videos must be 100 MB in size or smaller.

◀ SEE ALSO 7.6, *"Watching Videos on YouTube"* ▶

To add a video to the current post, click the Add Video button; this displays the Add a Video to Your Blog Post window. Click the Browse button to select the video to upload and then enter the title of the video into the Video Title box. Check the box to agree to Blogger's terms and conditions and then click the Upload Video button.

The video is now uploaded to the Blogger site and inserted into the current blog post. Each video appears in its own video player in the post; visitors click the player's Play button to watch the video.

Adding Labels

When you get a lot of posts in your blog, it becomes increasingly difficult to find a particular post. You can make this easier for your blog visitors by using labels to categorize your posts. Visitors can then click a label in the label list to view all posts related to that particular topic.

To add a label to your post, enter the label into the Labels for This Post box at the bottom of the Create page. You can enter multiple labels for any post; just separate the labels with commas.

Adding a Site Feed

As noted previously, a site feed is an automatically updated stream of a blog's contents. When you activate a site feed for your blog, interested users can subscribe to that feed to be notified of all new posts that you make.

◀ SEE ALSO 10.3, *"Subscribing to Blog Content"* ▶

Blogger uses both RSS and Atom for its site feeds. When you add a site feed for your blog, Blogger automatically generates a machine-readable version of your blog that can be read by most feed readers and aggregators.

To add a site feed to your blog, go to the Blogger Dashboard and click the Settings link next to your blog name. When the Settings page appears, click the Site Feed link.

To create a feed for the full content of each post, pull down the Allow Blog Feeds list and select Full. To create a feed for just the first paragraph (or 255 characters) of each post, select Short. If you don't want to activate a feed, select None.

Click the Save Settings button to activate the feed.

WORDS TO GO . . .WORDS TO GO . . .WORDS TO GO

A **gadget** is a page element on a Blogger blog.

10.4

10.5 MICRO-BLOGGING WITH TWITTER

Using Twitter

Following Other Users

Following via Mobile Phone

Blocking Followers

Updating Your Profile

A blog is a great way to let people know your continuing thoughts and opinions. To that end, most people update their blogs at least weekly and some daily.

◄ *SEE ALSO 10.1, "Understanding Blogs"* ▶

If, however, you want your friends and family to know what you're doing or thinking at any given moment, a blog is too slow. Instead, you want to use a **micro-blogging** service, such as Twitter, that lets you create short (up to 140 characters in length) text posts with ease. Anyone subscribing to your posts receives updates via the Twitter site, RSS feed, or SMS text messages on their mobile phones.

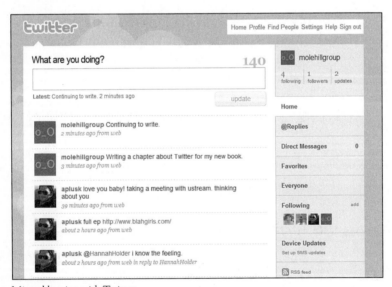

Micro-blogging with Twitter.

Using Twitter

To use Twitter, you first have to register as a user. This is free and is accomplished from the Twitter home page (www.twitter.com).

Once registered and signed in, the Twitter home page changes to a What Are You Doing? box. To **"tweet"** your current activity, just enter a short description of what you're doing into this box and then click the Update button.

Your most recent "tweets" are now displayed on your home page beneath this box—and are broadcast to anyone subscribing to your feed. In addition, tweets from people you're following are also displayed on the home page so that you know what they're up to.

Following Other Users

If friends or family members are on Twitter, you can follow their activities by subscribing to their "tweets." This is called **following** those users. (Although some might call it stalking ….)

To find people to follow, go to the Twitter home page and click the Find People link at the top of the page. When the next page appears, click the Find on Twitter tab to search for that person on the Twitter network. You can also find people on other networks or invite your friends to join Twitter; just click the appropriate tab.

To follow a Twitter user, go to his or her profile page and click the Follow link under the profile picture. All "tweets" from this user will now appear on your Twitter home page.

To stop following a user, revisit that user's profile page and click the Remove link.

WARNING . . .WARNING . . .WARNING

Some users protect their profiles so that strangers can't follow them without their permission. When you click the Follow link for these users, they have to register their approval before you can follow them.

Following via Mobile Phone

You can also follow fellow Twitterers from your mobile phone. You'll need to know their usernames in advance, but then it's a simple matter of sending a text message to twitter with the message **follow *username.*** To send a text message to Twitter in the United States, dial 40404 from your mobile phone. In Canada, dial 21212. In most other countries, dial +44 7624 801423.

After you've sent the text message, you'll receive a text message whenever that user makes a "tweet."

If you receive "tweets" via text messaging on your phone, normal text messaging charges will accrue.

Blocking Followers

If you don't want to be publically followed on Twitter, you can to protect your profile. Click the Settings link at the top of the Twitter home page and then select the Account tab. Scroll to the bottom of this page, check the Protect My Updates option, and then click Save. This requires you to approve a follower before he or she can receive your updates.

You can also block individual users from following you, which is a great way to evade cyberstalkers. Go to that person's profile page and click the Block link in the Actions section of the right-hand sidebar. This will block that user from receiving any "tweets" you make.

Updating Your Profile

As an active Twitterer, you probably want to customize the profile that other users see. You do this by clicking the Settings link at the top of the Twitter home page. Select the Account tab to edit your name, location, and bio; click the Picture tab to upload a personal picture; and click the Design tab to select a theme for your profile page. You can view your edited profile by clicking the Profile link at the top of the page.

WORDS TO GO . . .WORDS TO GO . . .WORDS TO GO

You **follow** a user on Twitter by subscribing to his or her "tweets."
Micro-blogging is a feed of short text posts that update others on one's current activities; Twitter is the web's most popular micro-blogging service.
A **tweet** is a text update on the Twitter service.

10.6 UNDERSTANDING PODCASTS

A text-based blog isn't the only way to find information and opinions online. You can also listen to audio blogs called **podcasts.** A podcast is essentially a home-grown radio program, distributed over the Internet, that you can download and play on your computer—or any portable audio player.

◄ *SEE ALSO 10.1, "Understanding Blogs"* ▶

Anyone with a microphone and a computer can create his or her own podcasts. That's because a podcast is nothing more than an MP3 file posted to the Internet. Most podcasters deliver their content via an RSS feed, which enables users to easily find future podcasts by subscribing to the podcaster's feed, just as a person would subscribe to blog feeds. The podcasts are then downloaded to the listener's computer or portable audio player and listened to at the user's convenience.

◄ *SEE ALSO 7.1, "Finding Music Online"* ▶

◄ *SEE ALSO 10.2, "Searching for Blogs"* ▶

WORDS TO GO . . .WORDS TO GO . . .WORDS TO GO

A **podcast** is an audio blog.

10.6

10.7 LISTENING TO PODCASTS

Finding Podcasts

Playing Podcasts on Your PC

Podcasts on the iPod

Listening to podcasts is easy—once you find the ones you want.

Finding Podcasts

Where can you find podcasts on the web? Your best bet is to browse through a podcast directory and see what's there for the listening. Some of the most popular podcast directories include the following:

- ▶ Digital Podcast (www.digitalpodcast.com)
- ▶ Podcast Alley (www.podcastalley.com)
- ▶ Podcast Bunker (www.podcastbunker.com)
- ▶ Podcast Directory (www.podcastdirectory.com)
- ▶ Podcast.com (www.podcast.com)
- ▶ Podcasting Station (www.podcasting-station.com)
- ▶ Podcast Pickle (www.podcastpickle.com)
- ▶ PodCastZoom (www.podcastzoom.com)
- ▶ Podfeed.net (www.podfeed.net)

Playing Podcasts on Your PC

When you find a podcast that interests you, you can typically listen to it on your computer via your web browser. Some podcasts are streamed in real time over the web, while others are contained in MP3 audio files that you first have to download to your PC.

◀ *SEE ALSO 7.1, "Finding Music Online"* ▶

On most sites, listening to a podcast is as simple as clicking the "listen" or "download" button. If the podcast is delivered via streaming audio, a separate window will typically open for podcast playback. You may have a selection of podcast episodes to choose from; select the episode you want and then click the Play button.

If the podcast is available as an MP3 file, you can download it to your PC for listening at your convenience. Just click the download button and specify where you want to save the file. You can then use any music player program, such as Windows Media Player or Apple's iTunes, to open and listen to the downloaded file.

Podcasts on the iPod

If you can download a podcast in MP3 format to your computer, you can also copy that file to your portable audio player for playback on the go. This is especially easy if you have an Apple iPod or iPhone.

You download podcasts to your iPod via the iTunes Podcast Directory. Open the iTunes software and click the iTunes Store link in the Source pane. When the iTunes Store opens, click the Podcasts link.

◀ *SEE ALSO 7.2, "Downloading Music from the iTunes Store"* ▶

You can now browse or search through the available podcasts, download the ones you like, and subscribe to the ones you want to hear again. Most of the podcasts available from the iTunes Store are free.

When you subscribe to a podcast, iTunes automatically checks for updates and downloads new episodes to your computer. Your downloaded podcasts are accessible by clicking the Podcasts link in the iTunes Source pane.

Naturally, the new podcasts are transferred to your iPod or iPhone when it's next connected and synced. Just access your iPod's Podcasts menu to display and listen to all downloaded podcasts.

10.7

10.8 CREATING YOUR OWN PODCAST

Equipment Needed

Making the Recording

Uploading the Podcast

Syndicating the Podcast

As noted previously, anyone can create a podcast; it's surprisingly easy to do.

Equipment Needed

To record a podcast, you'll need the following equipment and services:

▶ A microphone (any type will do, although one that connects to your computer via USB is easiest to use).

▶ A personal computer (Windows or Mac, no special technical requirements).

▶ Audio recording software such as Audacity (audacity.sourceforge.net), ePodcast Creator (www.industrialaudiosoftware.com), or Propaganda (www.makepropaganda.com). Alternately, many podcast-hosting communities supply their own podcast recording software.

▶ Headphones (optional but nice).

▶ A podcast hosting service or RSS syndicator.

◀ SEE ALSO 10.7, *"Listening to Podcasts"* ▶

Making the Recording

Making a podcast recording is a simple process. In general, you need to do the following:

1. Connect the microphone.

2. Launch the recording software.

3. Set the volume levels in the recording program.

4. Click the Record button.

5. Start talking (into the microphone).

Naturally, you can stop and restart the recording as necessary; you can even go back and rerecord any section that you don't like. Most podcast recording programs also let you edit your recordings by snipping out unwanted sections and moving sections around as necessary.

Your original recording should be saved in high-quality WAV format, and you should stay in the WAV format throughout the editing process. After your podcast is in its final form, you then export the file into MP3 format. If the podcast is voice only, a relatively low bitrate (32 or 64 kbps) is fine. If the podcast has a lot of music, consider a higher bitrate up to 128 kbps. Make sure you add the appropriate metatags for all the podcast info, and it's ready for distribution.

◀ *SEE ALSO 7.1, "Finding Music Online"* ▢

Uploading the Podcast

After you save your podcast in MP3 format, you have to upload the MP3 file to a server. If you have your own personal website, you can use that server to store your podcasts. You'll need a fair amount of storage space; audio files can get large, depending on the recording quality and length. For example, a 30-minute podcast saved at 64 kbps in mono will be about 8 MB in size. If you use a higher bitrate, the file size goes up accordingly.

If you don't have your own server, consider using a podcast hosting service such as Hipcast (www.hipcast.com), Podbean.com (www.podbean.com), Podbus.com (www.podbus.com), Switchpod (www.switchpod.com), or any of the podcast directories discussed previously. Some of these hosting services are free; others charge $5 to $10 per month for file storage. Most of these sites will also help you with the RSS syndication of your podcasts.

Syndicating the Podcast

The final stage of the podcast-creation process is creating an RSS feed for all of your podcasts. This is best accomplished via a podcast hosting service or via blogging software. Most blogging software and services can generate an RSS feed, or you can use FeedBurner (www.feedburner.com) to do the work for you (for free). If you use FeedBurner, you'll have to create a link on your website to the FeedBurner file so that people can find the feed.

◀ *SEE ALSO 10.1, "Understanding Blogs"* ▢

And that's that. All you have to do now is wait for users to find your podcasts, subscribe to your feed, and start listening.

11
SOCIAL NETWORKING

11.1 UNDERSTANDING SOCIAL NETWORKING

How Social Networks Work

Using Social Networks

Friending

The Biggest Social Networks

One of the biggest things on the Internet today is **social networking.** Put simply, social networking enables people to share experiences and opinions with each other via community-based websites. While that technically includes blogs, micro-blogs, and podcasts, most social networking communities are much more social and interactive than blogs and their ilk.

◄ *SEE ALSO 10.1, "Understanding Blogs"* ▷

◄ *SEE ALSO 10.5, "Micro-Blogging with Twitter"* ▷

◄ *SEE ALSO 10.6, "Understanding Podcasts"* ▷

How Social Networks Work

In practice, a social network is a large website that aims to create a community of users. Each user posts his or her own personal profile on the site in the form of a **profile page.** There's enough personal information in each profile to enable other users with similar interests to connect as "friends." One's growing collection of friends helps to build a succession of personal communities.

Most profile pages include some form of blog, discussion forum, or chat space so that friends can communicate with the person profiled. In many instances, individual users also post a running list of their current activities so that their friends always know what they're up to.

Using Social Networks

Social networks are all about hanging out—virtually. Typical users spend a fair amount of time cruising through the profiles, looking for people they know or who share similar interests. They play music and watch videos posted on other profile pages. They see who's online, and they send instant messages, bulletins (short messages), and e-mails to each other.

In addition, users spend time updating their own profile pages—their face to the online world. They redecorate their pages by changing templates, changing color schemes, adding new backgrounds and images, even adding pictures of themselves and their friends. They also post updates about their own activities, which is how their friends know what they've been doing.

Friending

Social networks are all about connecting to new and existing friends. The process of finding new friends is called **friending**, and some specific rules are involved.

First, it's important to be connected to all your real-world friends and acquaintances. Second, you want to be connected to people whom you might not personally know but whom you've heard of and respect. Third, although it's important to have a lot of friends, the coolness of your friends matters more. In other words, it's better to have 10 high-profile friends than 100 low-profile friends.

Know, however, that when you add someone as friend, that doesn't imply they're a friend in the traditional use of the word. It doesn't even mean that you know that person or want to know that person—only that you've added him or her to your friends list.

After a time, linking from one friend to a friend of that friend to a friend of a friend of a friend leads to a kind of "six degrees of separation" thing. It's fun to see how many friends it takes to connect you to various people, and you get to find new friends by seeing who your friends are friends with.

The Biggest Social Networks

Chances are, you've at least heard of the two leading social networks, MySpace and Facebook—especially if you have a teenager in the household. Many younger users access their favorite social networking sites several times a day. Not only do they post new information to their own social networking profiles, they're constantly checking the status of their friends' profiles. It's addictive.

11.1

SEE ALSO 11.3, "Using MySpace" ▶

SEE ALSO 11.4, "Using Facebook" ▶

Of these two social networking communities, Facebook is more of a site for older youngsters, typically high school and college aged and older; it also boasts an increasing number of adult users. MySpace is more of a site for younger teenagers and preteens, although it also has a large presence among amateur and professional musicians.

Friending is the process of finding new friends on a social network.

A **profile page** on a social network displays a user's personal information—and is the home page for comments and messages.

Social networking enables people to share experiences and opinions with each other via community-based websites; the most popular social networks today are Facebook and MySpace.

11.2 SOCIAL NETWORKING—SAFELY AND SANELY

Self-Policing Policies

Parental Supervision

Protect Yourself

Given that MySpace and Facebook are so popular among teenagers and preteens, many parents worry about their children being cyberstalked on these sites. That worry is not ill-founded, especially given the amount of personal information that most users post on their social networking profiles.

◀ SEE ALSO 11.1, *"Understanding Social Networking"* ▶

Self-Policing Policies

It's important to note that both MySpace and Facebook try to police themselves. For example, on MySpace, users with ages set to 14 or 15 years automatically have private profiles—that is, they're not browsable by the mass MySpace public. Users age 16 or older have the option to restrict profile access to people on their friends list, although most teens don't exercise this option. (Of course, MySpace doesn't actually verify ages, so a younger child can claim to be older to get more access.)

In addition, both MySpace and Facebook work to keep known sex offenders off their sites. In February 2009, MySpace announced that it had purged the profiles of almost 90,000 known sex offenders, thus helping to protect their younger users. Facebook has similar programs in place.

Parental Supervision

11.2

As a parent, it's important that you become "friends" with your children on MySpace and Facebook and visit their profile pages on a regular basis. You might be surprised at what you find there.

It's an unfortunate fact that not all teens and preteens are wise about what they put online. It's not unusual to find provocative pictures posted on their social networking profiles; you probably don't want your children exposing themselves in this fashion.

You also need to warn your kids that not everyone on MySpace or Facebook is truly a "friend." They should be circumspect about the information they make public and about whom they personally communicate with. It's also worth noting that kids shouldn't arrange to meet in person strangers who they're "friends" with online; it's not unheard of for unsavory adults to use social networks as a stalking ground.

In other words, teach your kids to be careful. Hanging out at MySpace or Facebook is normally no more dangerous than hanging out at the mall, but even malls aren't completely safe. Caution and common sense are always called for.

Protect Yourself

The advice you give to your children regarding social networks also applies to yourself online. Think twice before posting personal information or incriminating photographs, don't broadcast your every move on your profile page, and don't automatically accept friend requests from people you don't know.

Most important, don't view MySpace or Facebook as online dating services. Yes, you may meet new friends on these social networks, but use caution about transferring online friendships into the physical world. If you decide to meet an online friend offline, do so in a public place and perhaps with another friend along. Don't put yourself at risk when meeting strangers—until you get to know them in person, anyone you correspond with online remains a stranger.

11.3 USING MYSPACE

MySpace Users

Friending

Viewing a Profile

Commenting

Creating Your Own Profile

Adding Photos

The number-two social network today is MySpace, which tends to target younger teenagers and preteens. MySpace (www.myspace.com) is a collection of millions of individual web pages, posted and updated by users, that combine to create an interactive social network. Users' profile pages contain blog postings, photos, music, videos, and links to lots and lots of online friends.

◀ *SEE ALSO 11.1, "Understanding Social Networking"* ▶

MySpace is totally free to use, although you do need to sign up for an account to access many of the site's features. (You don't need an account to browse other users' profiles, however.)

MySpace Users

Interestingly, MySpace started (in 2003) as a site for twenty-somethings in the Los Angeles indie music scene. Other musicians soon discovered the site, and that attracted a larger (and younger) audience. Today, users as young as 14 frequent the MySpace site, updating their profile pages and browsing the site for new friends.

You can still find plenty of musicians on MySpace—along with artists, movie stars, comedians, and many wannabe celebrities. Many bands and performers use MySpace as their home base to launch new CDs and support their latest tours.

11.3

Today, the average MySpace user is in the 14–24 age range. The site sports more than 100 million accounts and gets close to a quarter-million visitors every day— which makes it one of the top five sites on the web, up there with Google and eBay.

Friending

You can find new friends by either browsing or searching. You browse for friends by selecting Friends, Browse from the MySpace menu bar. This displays the Browse Users page, where you set your browse criteria. The Basic tab on this page lets you filter your browsing by gender, age range, location, and other criteria.

For more sophisticated browsing, click the Advanced tab on this page. This adds more browsing options, including ethnicity, body type, height, and lifestyle (smoker, drinker, sexual orientation, education, religion, income, children). You can choose to sort results by recently updated, last login, new to MySpace, or physical distance from your location.

If you know who you're looking for, you can search the MySpace profiles for a specific user. All you have to do is click the Web link inside the search box at the top of the page and select People. Enter the user's actual name or profile name into the search box and then click the Search button. MySpace returns a list of matching profiles; make sure you click the Next button if the profile you want doesn't show up in the first page of results.

Once you find the person you want to make your friend, click the Add to Friends icon next to that person's name. You're now prompted to confirm your friend request; when you do so, that person is sent a message asking if he or she wants to be your friend. If the person says yes, you're friends. If he or she doesn't know you or doesn't want to be your friend, that's that.

Once someone is your friend, you can follow that person's activities and comments from the MySpace home page. Your friends' activities are displayed at the top middle of your home page, so you'll always know what they're up to.

Viewing a Profile

Because users can personalize their profile pages, few MySpace profiles look the same. Most profiles, however, include some common page elements, including Blurbs (about the user), Interests, Contact Info, Comments (from other users), and the like.

All MySpace profile pages are fully customizable. In fact, if the user is conversant with HTML, CSS, and JavaScript, some fancy customization is possible. Otherwise, users can choose their own themes, backgrounds, colors, and content modules.

A typical MySpace profile.

Commenting

If a friend has a Comments module on his or her page, you can leave your comments for that friend (and all of his or her other friends) to read. Simply scroll down to the Comments module and click the Add Comment link. When the next page appears, enter your message in the box provided and then click the Post a Comment button. (You can also add a photo to your comment, if you wish.) Your comment now appears at the top of your friend's public comments.

Creating Your Own Profile

To create your own MySpace profile, you first have to sign up with MySpace. You do this from the MySpace home page by clicking the Sign Up! button.

Signing up is simple (and free). All you have to provide is your name, e-mail address, country and postal code, birthday, and desired password.

After you've signed up, you're prompted to upload a photo of yourself. The photo can be in JPG or GIF format, must be smaller than 600 KB, and shouldn't contain any nudity.

Next you're encouraged to invite your friends to view your MySpace page. Enter their e-mail addresses, if you want, and then click the Invite button.

MySpace now displays your personal account page. This is your home page on the MySpace site; it lists any e-mail or bulletins you've received as well as all your friends. It also includes the URLs for your profile and blog pages.

To personalize your profile, start by clicking the Pick Your MySpace Name/URL link. This lets you choose your MySpace display name—the name that others will know you by.

WARNING . . .WARNING . . .WARNING

Once you've chosen your MySpace name, you can't change it—so choose it carefully.

Next, return to your home page and select Profile, Edit Profile. This takes you to the Profile Edit page, which is where you start constructing your profile page. Fill in the blanks as appropriate and then click the Save All Changes button. Click through the links at the top of the pages to tab to additional content pages—Interests & Personality, Name, Basic Info, Background & Lifestyle, Schools, Companies, Networking, and Song & Video on Profile.

To change the look of your profile, return to your home page and select Profile, Customize Profile. From here you can select which page elements to display (and where) and choose a predesigned theme for your page. To more fully customize your page, select either the Advanced Edit or (to use HTML code) CSS options. Click the Publish button when you're done making changes.

Adding Photos

To add photos to your MySpace profile page, select Profile, My Photos from the toolbar. When the My Photos page appears, click the Upload Photos link.

The first time you upload photos, MySpace installs the necessary MySpace Image Loader software in your browser. You can then navigate to and select the photos on your hard drive that you want to upload. Click the Upload button to upload the photos.

A Photos link now appears at the top of your profile page. Your friends can view your photos by clicking this link.

11.4 USING FACEBOOK

Friending

Viewing Profiles

Creating Your Own Profile

Uploading Photos

Writing on the Wall

E-mailing Other Users

The leading social network today is Facebook (www.facebook.com). This site attracts an older audience than MySpace, including many adult users.

◀ *SEE ALSO 11.1, "Understanding Social Networking"* ▶

Friending

Finding people on Facebook is a matter of using the search function. Just enter the user's real name or username into the search box at the top of any Facebook page and then press Enter. The search results page will display all matching users; click the Add as Friend link to send that person a friend invite. If he or she accepts your invitation, you'll be added to each other's friends list.

Once someone is on your friends list, all of that person's activities are displayed on your Facebook home page. Just go to the home page and select the News Feed tab; all friend activity is displayed there. Alternatively, you can select the Status Updates tab to view updates to your friends' status; the Photos tab to see your friends' latest pictures; the Posted Items tab to view links, videos, and the like posted by your friends; or the Live Feed tab to view friend activity in real time.

Viewing Profiles

11.4

A Facebook profile is much like a MySpace profile but without as much customization. There are actually multiple tabs on each profile page, including tabs for the Wall (your recent activity and notes from friends), Info (your personal information), and Photos. Key information about yourself and your friends list are displayed in a left-hand sidebar; additional features can be accessed by clicking the icons in the toolbar at the bottom of the screen.

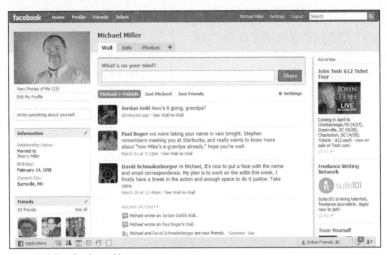

A *typical Facebook profile.*

Creating Your Own Profile

You create your profile when you first sign up for the Facebook service. You can also edit your profile at any time by going to your profile page and clicking the Edit My Profile link.

The Profile Info page displays all the information you need to supply for your Facebook profile, including personal contact, and education and work information. You can also add a personal photo to your profile by clicking the profile picture area (or your current picture, if you've already added one but want to change it). When the next page appears, click Change Profile Picture. When prompted, select which photo you want to upload and then upload it.

Uploading Photos

Facebook lets you upload personal photos to the site and create themed photo albums. Your photos appear on the Photos tab on your Profile page.

To upload a photo, go to your Profile page, select the Photos tab, and then click the Create a Photo Album button. When the next page appears, give the album a name, enter your location (or the location where you shot the photos), and provide a description of what's included. If you want your photos to be public for all to see, make sure Everyone is selected from the Privacy list; you can also opt for your photos to be seen by Only Friends or Friends of Friends. Click Create Album to proceed.

If this is the first time you're adding photos, Facebook now installs its photo up-loading software within your web browser. When the next page appears, select the Add Photos tab and navigate to where the photos are stored on your computer's hard drive. Select the photos you want to upload and then click the Upload button.

You can change the order of the photos in your album by opening the album and selecting Organize Photos. To "tag" individuals within a photo (that is, to identify your Facebook friends in your photos), select Edit Photos. To add more photos to the album, click Add More Photos.

Writing on the Wall

Want to tell your friends what you're doing at this moment? It's easy to do. Just go to your home page or profile page and enter a few words into the What Are You Doing Right Now? box. Click the Post button and your updated activity is dis-played on your Wall and on the Walls of all your friends.

If you want to write a comment directly on a friend's Wall, go to that person's profile page and select the Wall tab. Enter your message into the Write Some-thing box at the top of the page, and your comments will immediately appear on that person's Wall.

E-mailing Other Users

Writing on someone's Wall is one way to "talk" with him or her online, but it's a public conversation—all of that person's friends can read what you wrote. If you prefer a more private conversation, Facebook offers e-mail functionality that lets you send messages directly to other users.

To send an e-mail via Facebook, select Inbox, Compose New Message from the toolbar. When the new message page appears, enter the recipient's username into the To: box, the subject of the message into the Subject: box, and the text of your message into the Message: box. Click the Send button to send the message to your friend's Facebook inbox.

11.4

To view messages in your own inbox, select Inbox, View Message Inbox. This displays all recent messages; click a message header to view the text of a specific message. You can then reply to that message by entering your text into the Mes-sage: box at the bottom of the message page. Click the Send button to send your reply on its way.

Managing your Facebook inbox is easy. To delete older or unwanted messages, just check those messages and then click Delete. You can also mark unread mes-sages as read and vice versa.

11.5 USING USENET NEWSGROUPS

How Usenet Works

Choosing a Newsreader

Searching Newsgroups with Google Groups

Before MySpace and Facebook were developed, social networking took place on a part of the Internet called **Usenet,** which is a collection of more than 130,000 online discussion groups. These discussion groups, called **newsgroups,** are organized by topic and let interested users interact with others with the same interests.

How Usenet Works

Usenet is a network that piggybacks on the larger Internet. In fact, it was one of the first components of the Internet, predating the web and the public Internet.

In essence, a Usenet newsgroup is an electronic gathering place for people with similar interests. Within a newsgroup, users post messages (called **articles**) about a variety of topics; other users read these articles and, when so disposed, respond. The result is a kind of ongoing, freeform discussion in which dozens—or hundreds—of interested users can participate.

WARNING . . . WARNING . . . WARNING

Unlike blogs or other web-based discussion forums, most Usenet newsgroups are unmoderated—which means that no one is watching the message content to ensure that subject discussions stay on track. The result is a kind of only slightly organized chaos, typically with a lot of off-topic messages and thinly concealed advertisements mixed in with the on-topic and useful messages.

A newsgroup name looks a little like a website address, with single words or phrases separated by periods. Newsgroup names are more logical, however, in that each break in the name signifies a level of greater granularity. The leftmost part of the name places the newsgroup in one of several major domains, with each subsequent component denoting a subset of the major domain—which is kind of like moving through the folders and subfolders on your hard disk.

As you read a newsgroup name, your focus moves from left to right until you zero in on a very specific topic. For example, the **rec.arts.cinema** group tells you that the newsgroup is in the *recreational* section of Usenet and that it discusses the *art* of the *cinema*.

Choosing a Newsreader

To read newsgroup articles, you need a software program called a **newsreader.** These programs download newsgroup articles from Usenet for your reading and posting pleasure.

Some of the most popular newsreader programs include the following:

▶ Agent Newsreader (www.forteinc.com)

▶ News Rover (www.newsrover.com)

▶ SBNews/Newsbot (www.newsrobot.com)

In addition, Outlook Express (included with Windows XP) and Windows Mail (included with Windows Vista and optional with Windows 7) have built-in Usenet newsreader capability. You can also use a web-based newsreader, such as that provided with Google Groups (groups.google.com), to read Usenet articles.

Searching Newsgroups with Google Groups

Usenet is a kind of living beast, with new articles being posted daily and old articles fading into the ether—except that old articles don't really fade away. They still exist in the Usenet archive.

To find older articles that no longer exist on your normal newsgroup server, use Google Groups (groups.google.com). Google Groups is a website that functions as a newsreader for both current and archived newsgroup postings. (It's also host to non-Usenet groups that users create.)

▣ *SEE ALSO 11.6, "Using Web Groups"* ▶

Searching for Newsgroups

11.5

To find a specific newsgroup, go to the Explore Groups section of the Google Groups page. Enter your query into the search box and then click the Search for a Group button.

The search results page lists several different items. At the top of the page is a series of filters you can click to list only those matching groups within a specific topic, language, activity level, or size (number of members). Below that is a list of the groups themselves, listed in order of activity (high to low).

For each group, Google lists the group name, the language of the group, the group's activity level and number of users, and whether or not it's a Usenet newsgroup. (If the word "Usenet" doesn't appear, it's a user-created Google Group.)

Browsing for Newsgroups

You can also browse for newsgroups by category. Just scroll down to the bottom of the Google Groups page and click the Browse All Group Categories link. This displays the Group Directory; click through a major category and its various subcategories until you find the specific group you want.

Alternatively, you can browse through Usenet newsgroups by hierarchy. Just click the Browse All of Usenet link on the Group Directory page.

Searching Across All Groups

If, instead of reading the messages in a specific group, you want to search for messages about a given topic across all newsgroups (and user-created Google groups), you can do that. Searching the Google Groups archive is as simple as entering a query into the search box at the top of the Google Groups page and then clicking the Search button.

This displays a list of individual messages that match your search criteria. Click a message header to read that message or click the group name below that message to go to the hosting group.

WORDS TO GO . . .WORDS TO GO . . .WORDS TO GO

An **article** is an individual post or message in a Usenet newsgroup.

A **newsgroup** is a Usenet online discussion forum; newsgroups are organized in hierarchies by topic.

A **newsreader** is a software program used to read and post Usenet newsgroup articles.

Usenet is a part of the Internet that hosts online discussion groups called newsgroups.

11.6 USING WEB GROUPS

Using Google Groups
Using Yahoo! Groups

Usenet is just one type of online community on the web—and one that's diminishing in importance. In reality, Usenet newsgroups are being supplanted by easier-to-use **web groups.** These groups don't require any special software; they can be accessed over the web using any web browser.

◀ *SEE ALSO 11.5, "Using Usenet Newsgroups"* ▷

A web group is similar to a Usenet newsgroup in that it's a community for users devoted to a particular topic or hobby. The community aspect comes from the site's forum or message board, where users gather to exchange messages about the topic at hand.

The message forum in a web group is like an old-fashioned bulletin board. A user begins by posting a message regarding a specific topic. Other members of the group respond to that message and post replies. Before long you have an intricate **thread** of messages, all branching out from that initial posting.

The two biggest web group communities today are Google Groups and Yahoo! Groups. Both operate in similar fashion.

Using Google Groups

You're already familiar with Google Groups (groups.google.com) from its functionality as a Usenet archive and newsreader. In addition to these Usenet features, Google Groups also hosts tens of thousands of web groups that any user can use or create. Each group includes a message forum (for text-based messages), the ability to upload and share files, and group notices and e-mails.

Visiting Groups and Reading Messages

To view any Google group, all you have to do is search for or browse to the group and then click the group name. This displays the main page for the group.

A list of the most recent topics (in Google parlance, "discussions") is on the left side of the page; a full list of topics can be accessed by selecting the Discussions tab on the right side of the page. Groups can also contain specialized pages (on the Pages tab) and files for downloading (on the Files tab).

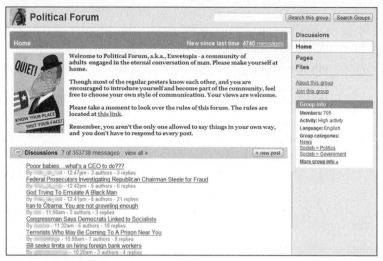

Viewing a Google group.

To read all the messages on a given topic (in a given thread or discussion, that is), just click the title of the thread. This displays the message page, with messages listed in chronological order (the first message at the top and the last at the bottom).

Joining a Group

If you want to keep up-to-date on all the new messages in a group, you may want to join that group. When you join a group, you're automatically notified of new messages posted to the group via e-mail; you don't have to visit the group page to manually read messages.

To join a group, just go to the main group page and click the Join This Group link at the top of the page. When the Join page appears, select how you want to be notified of new messages. You can select to receive no notification, an abridged e-mail (a once-a-day summary), a digest e-mail (25 e-mails per message), or an e-mail for every new message.

Once you've made your selection, enter the nickname you want to use and then click the Join This Group button. If you later want to unsubscribe from that group, return to that group's page, click the Edit My Membership link, and then click the Unsubscribe button on the following page.

Posting to a Group

Once you're on a group page, you have the option of simply reading messages, replying to messages, or posting a message on a new topic.

To reply to a message, start by opening the message thread. At the bottom of each message in the thread is a Reply link; click this link and the page expands to show a Reply box. Enter your reply into the box and then click the Post button. Your reply will be added to the end of the current thread.

Creating a New Message Thread

You're not limited to replying to existing message topics. You can also start a new message thread (or "discussion") with a new message.

To do this, go to the main group page and click the New Post button at the top of the page. This displays the Start a New Discussion page. Enter a name for the new discussion into the Subject box and then enter the text of your message into the Message box. When you click the Post Message button, your new message appears as the first in a new topic/thread on the main group page.

Using Yahoo! Groups

Similar to Google Groups is Yahoo! Groups (groups.yahoo.com), which also offers message forums and file uploading, as well as photo libraries, group calendars, and polls.

Finding and Joining Groups

You search for Yahoo! groups by going to the main Yahoo! Groups page, entering your query into the search box, and then clicking the Search button. You can also browse groups by category.

Most Yahoo! groups are private groups, meaning that they require membership before you can read and post messages. To join a group, click the Join this Group! button on the group's home page. You'll then need to supply your Yahoo! username and password and select how you wish to be notified of group messages. You can opt to receive individual e-mails for each message posted, a daily digest of posts made in the past 24 hours, or no notification—that is, to read messages on the web only.

11.6

Some groups will automatically approve your membership; others require approval by the group's moderator, which can take anywhere from a few hours to a few days. You should receive e-mail notification when your membership is approved.

Reading and Replying to Posts

Once you've joined a group, the group's home page displays the most recent messages posted. To read a message, simply click the message header. To add your comments to an ongoing message thread, scroll to the bottom of the message and click the Reply button.

Other sections of the group can be accessed by the navigation sidebar on the left. You can view the Home page, recent Messages, Files for downloading, Photos posted by group members, Links to related websites, and other pertinent information.

Creating a New Message Thread

To create a new message thread in a group, click the Start Topic link on either the Home or Message page. When the next page appears, enter a subject for your post and then write what you want. Click the Send button when you're done, and a new topic thread will be created with your message at the top.

WORDS TO GO . . .WORDS TO GO . . .WORDS TO GO

A **thread** is a collection of messages and replies about a given topic.

A **web group** is a web-based community for users devoted to a particular topic or hobby; the two biggest web group communities are Google Groups and Yahoo! Groups.

12

E-MAIL

12.1 HOW E-MAIL WORKS

E-mail Addresses
Routing E-mail Messages
POP vs. Web E-mail

E-mail—short for "electronic mail"—is the modern way to communicate with friends, family, and colleagues. An e-mail message is like a regular letter except that it's composed electronically and delivered almost immediately via the Internet.

When you send an e-mail message to another Internet user, that message travels from your PC to your recipient's PC through a series of Internet connections and servers almost instantaneously. E-mail messages can be of any length and can include file attachments of various types.

E-mail Addresses

To make sure your message goes to the right recipient, you have to use your recipient's **e-mail address.** Every Internet user has a unique e-mail address composed of three parts:

▶ The user's login name

▶ The @ sign

▶ The user's domain name, usually the name of his or her Internet service provider (ISP)

As an example, if you use Comcast as your Internet provider (with the domain name **comcast.net**) and your log-in name is **bigbob,** your e-mail address is **bigbob@comcast.net.**

◀ SEE ALSO 12.3, "Setting Up a POP E-mail Account" ▶

Routing E-mail Messages

When you send an e-mail message, it doesn't go directly to the recipient. Instead, it is sent (via the Internet) to your ISP's or mail service's e-mail servers. The message is then sent from those servers to the e-mail servers of your recipient's ISP. The next time the recipient accesses his or her ISP account, your e-mail message is downloaded to the recipient's personal computer—and stored in that person's e-mail program's inbox.

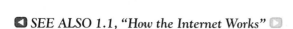

◀ *SEE ALSO 1.1, "How the Internet Works"* ▷

The same process works in reverse for messages sent to your e-mail address. The message starts out on the sender's computer, is uploaded to his or her ISP's e-mail servers, is sent to your ISP's servers, and then is downloaded to your computer (and your e-mail program's inbox) the next time you connect and check your e-mail.

POP vs. Web E-mail

There are actually two different ways to send and receive e-mail via the Internet.

The traditional way to send and receive e-mail uses a protocol called the **Post Office Protocol** (POP). POP e-mail requires the use of a dedicated e-mail client program and—at the ISP level—separate e-mail servers to send and receive messages.

The other way to send and receive e-mail is via web-based e-mail services, also known as **HTTP e-mail.** Unlike POP e-mail, **web e-mail** can be accessed from any computer using any web browser; no special software is required.

POP E-mail

POP e-mail is the standard type of e-mail account you receive when you sign up with an ISP. You're assigned an e-mail account, allowed to select an e-mail address, and provided with the necessary information to configure your e-mail program to access this account.

To use POP e-mail, you have to use a POP e-mail program such as Outlook Express, Windows Mail, Windows Live Mail, or the Mail program included with Apple's OS X. That e-mail program has to be configured to send e-mail to your ISP's outgoing mail server (called an **SMTP server**) and to receive e-mail from your ISP's incoming mail server (called a POP3 or **IMAP server**). If you want to access your e-mail account from another computer, you'll have to use a similar e-mail program and go through the entire configuration process all over again on the second computer.

◀ *SEE ALSO 12.3, "Setting Up a POP E-mail Account"* ▷

12.1

Web E-mail

You're not limited to using the "hard-wired" POP e-mail offered by your ISP; you can also send and receive e-mail from special web-based e-mail services. These services—such as Yahoo! Mail, Google's Gmail, and Microsoft's Windows Live Hotmail—enable you to access your e-mail from any computer and using any web browser.

If you use a PC at work or on the road, web e-mail is a convenient way to check your e-mail at any time of day, no matter where you are. You don't have to go through the same sort of complicated configuration routine that you have with POP e-mail; all you have to do is go to the e-mail service's website, enter your user ID and password, and you're ready to send and receive messages.

◁ *SEE ALSO 12.5, "Understanding Web E-mail"* ▷

WORDS TO GO . . . WORDS TO GO . . . WORDS TO GO

E-mail, short for "electronic mail," is a means of sending and receiving letter-like messages via the Internet.

An **e-mail address** is necessary to send an e-mail to a recipient; all e-mail addresses are composed of the user's log-in name, the @ sign, and the user's domain name.

HTTP e-mail is web-based e-mail.

IMAP servers are used by ISPs to receive POP e-mail messages.

The **Post Office Protocol** (POP) is one technology used to send e-mail over the Internet via dedicated e-mail servers; POP e-mail requires the use of special e-mail client software.

SMTP servers are used by ISPs to send POP e-mail messages.

Web e-mail sends and receives e-mail over the web using any web browser.

12.2 CHOOSING AN E-MAIL PROGRAM

Microsoft Outlook

Outlook Express

Windows Mail and Windows Live Mail

Apple Mail

Mozilla Thunderbird

There are several programs you can use to send and receive POP e-mail. Many (but not all) e-mail programs are free, and most offer similar features and functionality.

◀ *SEE ALSO 12.1, "How E-mail Works"* ▶

Microsoft Outlook

If you're in a corporate environment or running Microsoft Office, Microsoft Outlook is often the e-mail program of choice. Outlook is part of the Microsoft Office suite (Standard, Small Business, and Professional versions only) or is available for purchase as a freestanding program.

WARNING . . .WARNING . . .WARNING

Microsoft Outlook is *not* included as part of the popularly priced Home and Student version of Microsoft Office.

One advantage to using Outlook as your e-mail program is that it also functions as a fully featured contact management and scheduling program. As such, Outlook's contacts integrate fully with Outlook's e-mail functionality.

Microsoft Outlook sells for $109.95. Learn more at office.microsoft.com/outlook.

Outlook Express

12.2

Microsoft's Outlook Express offers the e-mail functionality of Microsoft Outlook in a freestanding program. It was included for free with the Windows 98, Windows Me, and Windows XP operating systems. If you have a PC that's running one of these older versions of Windows, chances are you already have Outlook Express installed.

Outlook Express functions as both an e-mail client and a Usenet newsreader. It includes its own address book for storing recipient names and addresses.

Unfortunately, Outlook Express is no longer available for purchase or download, having been replaced by the Windows Mail and Windows Live Mail programs.

Windows Mail and Windows Live Mail

The replacement for Outlook Express in Windows Vista was Windows Mail. With Windows 7, Windows Mail is succeeded by Windows Live Mail. Windows Mail and Windows Live Mail are essentially the same program—for all intents and purposes, Outlook Express with a new name and slightly different interface.

◀ *SEE ALSO 12.4, "Using Windows Live Mail"* ▶

Like Outlook Express, Windows Mail/Live Mail functions both as an e-mail client and Usenet newsreader. While it's optimized for POP e-mail, it can also be used to access Hotmail, Gmail, and other web e-mail services. The latest version, Windows Live Mail, also includes a built-in calendar and RSS newsreader.

Windows Mail is included for free with Windows Vista; it's preinstalled on your system, so no downloading is necessary. Windows Live Mail is an optional download for Windows 7; it can be downloaded for free from download.live.com/wlmail.

Apple Mail

Apple's Mail program is the program of choice for most Mac users, as it's built into the OS X operating system. It functions as both an e-mail client and an RSS newsreader and can interface with Gmail, Yahoo! Mail, and other web e-mail services.

Learn more about Apple Mail at www.apple.com/macosx/features/mail.html.

Mozilla Thunderbird

Just as Mozilla Firefox is a popular alternative to the Internet Explorer web browser, Mozilla Thunderbird is an alternative to Microsoft's Outlook Express and Windows Mail e-mail programs. It works with both POP and web e-mail services and offers robust anti-spam and anti-phishing protection.

Thunderbird is available for free download at www.mozilla.com/thunderbird.

12.3 SETTING UP A POP E-MAIL ACCOUNT

If you're using POP e-mail, you need to configure your e-mail program to work with your e-mail account. To do so, you need to know specific information about your account, as provided by your ISP. This information includes the following:

▶ The e-mail address assigned by your ISP, in the format *name@domain.com*.

▶ The type of e-mail server you'll be using; it's probably a POP3 server. (It could also be an HTTP, IMAP, or SMTP server, but POP3 is more common.)

▶ The address of the incoming e-mail server and the outgoing mail server.

▶ The account name and password you will use to connect to the e-mail servers. (The account name is probably your e-mail address or the first part of the address—before the @ sign.)

◀ *SEE ALSO 12.1, "How E-mail Works"* ▷

Once you have this information (which should be supplied by your ISP), you enter it into the appropriate configuration or settings section of your e-mail program. Many e-mail programs automate this process by using some type of new e-mail account wizard.

For example, if you're using Windows Live Mail, you start by clicking the Add E-mail Account link in the folders pane. You'll now be guided through a series of screens that ask for specific pieces of information such as your e-mail address, password, e-mail server names, and the like. Enter what's asked for, and a new e-mail account will be created within the program.

◀ *SEE ALSO 12.4, "Using Windows Live Mail"* ▷

12.3

12.4 USING WINDOWS LIVE MAIL

Navigating Windows Live Mail

Reading Messages

Replying to a Message

Composing a New Message

Since Windows Live Mail can be downloaded for free for use with any computer running the Windows operating system, we'll focus on this program as an example of how POP e-mail programs work. Know that Windows Live Mail is almost identical to the Windows Mail and Outlook Express programs, so if you use one of these older programs, most of what you see here is directly applicable. In fact, most of what's here also works with Microsoft Outlook, Apple Mail, and even Mozilla Thunderbird; all of these e-mail programs look and act quite similarly.

Navigating Windows Live Mail

The basic Windows Live Mail window is divided into three panes. The pane on the left is called the Folder list, and it's where you access your Inbox, message folders, and other program functions. The top pane on the right is the Message pane, and it lists all the messages stored in the selected folder. Below that is the Preview pane, and it displays the contents of the selected message.

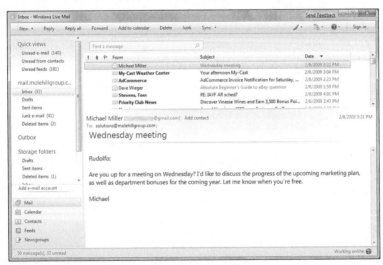

Using Windows Live Mail to send and receive e-mail.

Reading Messages

When you receive new e-mail messages, they're stored in the Inbox for that e-mail account. To display all new messages, select the Inbox item from the Folders list. All waiting messages now appear in the Message pane.

To read a specific message, select its header in the Message pane. The contents of that message are displayed in the Preview pane. You also can double-click a message header to display the message in a separate window.

Replying to a Message

To reply to an e-mail message in your Inbox, select the header for that message in the Message pane. Click the Reply button on the toolbar. This opens a Re: window, which is just like a New Message window except with the text from the original message "quoted" in the text area and the e-mail address of the recipient (the person who sent the original message) pre-entered in the To: field.

Enter your reply text in the message window and then click the Send button to send your reply back to the original sender.

Composing a New Message

It's easy to create a new e-mail message with Windows Live Mail. Start by selecting New, E-mail Message from the toolbar; this launches a New Message window.

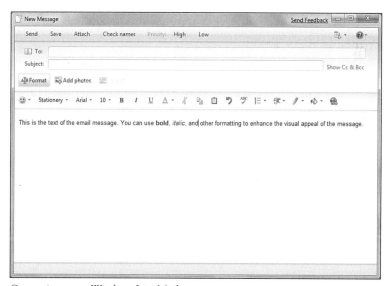

Composing a new Windows Live Mail message.

12.4

Enter the e-mail address of the recipient in the To: field. To enter multiple addresses, separate each address with a semicolon (;) like this:

solutions@molehillgroup.com;gjetson@sprockets.com

Instead of entering e-mail addresses manually, you can select addresses from the Windows Live Mail address book. When you click the To: button, you see a list of saved contacts. Double-click a contact to add it to your To: list and click OK when done.

You can also **carbon copy** (cc:) and **blind carbon copy** (bcc:) other recipients to your message. A carbon copy sends a copy of the message to selected recipients, with all recipients visible to each other; a blind carbon copy sends a copy to selected recipients, without other recipients knowing. To cc: and bcc: recipients, click the Show Cc and Bcc link and then enter recipient addresses into the Cc and Bcc boxes.

Once you've entered all the recipient addresses, move your cursor to the main message area and type your message. You can use the formatting options present on the window's toolbar to enhance your message's visual appeal.

When your message is complete, send it on its way by clicking the Send button.

WORDS TO GO . . .WORDS TO GO . . .WORDS TO GO

When you **blind carbon copy** (bcc:) an e-mail recipient, he or she receives a copy of the message but his or her name is hidden from other recipients.

When you **carbon copy** (cc:) an e-mail recipient, he or she receives a copy of the e-mail message, and others see his or her name in the recipient list.

12.5 UNDERSTANDING WEB E-MAIL

How Web E-mail Works

Choosing a Web E-mail Service

Web-based, or HTTP, e-mail is fast becoming the e-mail of choice for many users. That's because it can be accessed from any computer at any location. It's great if you want to check e-mail from both work and home or when you're on the road.

◄ *SEE ALSO 12.1, "How E-mail Works"* ▷

How Web E-mail Works

Web e-mail is much easier to set up than traditional POP e-mail. All you need to know is the URL of the e-mail service, your user ID, and your password. In most instances, there's no further configuration.

To access web e-mail, all you need is a web browser and an Internet connection. You may also be able to check your web e-mail from your iPhone or other Internet-enabled mobile phone.

When you access your web e-mail service, you see a page that lets you view the contents of your inbox, read and reply to messages, create new messages, and (in many cases) store messages in folders. You can even, on some services, use your web e-mail account to access your ISP's POP e-mail.

Choosing a Web E-mail Service

Dozens of web e-mail services are available. In fact, your ISP may offer web-based access to its traditional POP e-mail, which is convenient when you're away from home and need to check your e-mail.

Most web e-mail services are completely free to use. Some services offer both free versions and paid versions, with paid subscriptions offering additional message storage and functionality.

12.5

The largest web e-mail services include the following:

▶ AOL Mail (webmail.aol.com)

▶ Gmail (mail.google.com)

▶ Lycos Mail (mail.lycos.com)

- Mail.com (www.mail.com)
- Windows Live Hotmail (www.hotmail.com)
- Yahoo! Mail (mail.yahoo.com)

Most of these services let you store several gigabytes of data, which makes it convenient to archive old messages—including those with large file attachments. Many web e-mail services also can be configured to interface with your ISP's POP e-mail account. Check for these and other features before you sign up.

12.6 USING GMAIL

Navigating Gmail
Reading Messages
Viewing Conversations
Replying to a Message
Composing a New Message

One of the largest web e-mail services today is Google's Gmail. We'll use Gmail as an example of how these web e-mail services work; most services offer similar features.

Navigating Gmail

You access the Gmail home page at mail.google.com. If you don't yet have a Google account, you'll be prompted to sign up for one. Do so now; signing up is free.

After you activate your Gmail account, you're assigned an e-mail address (in the form of *name*@gmail.com), and you get access to the Gmail inbox page.

The Gmail inbox.

The default view of the Gmail page is the inbox, which contains all your received messages. You can switch to other views by clicking the appropriate links on the left side, top, or bottom of the page. For example, to view all your sent mail, simply click the Sent Mail link on the left; to view only unread messages, click the Unread link at the top or bottom.

12.6

Each message is listed with the message's sender, the message's subject, a snippet from the message itself, and the date or time the message was sent. (The snippet typically is the first line of the message text.) Unread messages are listed in bold; after a message has been read, it's displayed in normal, nonbold text with a shaded background. And if you've assigned a label to a message, the label appears before the message subject.

To perform an action on a message or group of messages, put a check mark by the message(s), and then click one of the buttons at the top or bottom of the list. Alternatively, you can pull down the More Actions list and select another action to perform.

Reading Messages

To read a message, all you have to do is click the message title in the inbox. This displays the full text of the message on a new page.

If you want to display this message in a new window, click the New Window link. To print the message, click the Print All link. To return to the inbox, click the Back to Inbox link.

Viewing Conversations

One of the unique things about Gmail is that all related e-mail messages are grouped in what Google calls **conversations**. A conversation might be an initial message and all its replies (and replies to replies). A conversation might also be all the daily e-mails from a single source with a common subject, such as messages you receive from subscribed-to mailing lists.

A conversation is noted in the inbox list by a number in parentheses after the sender name(s). If a conversation has replies from more than one person, more than one name is listed.

To view a conversation, simply click the message title; this displays the most recent message in full. To view the text of any individual message in a conversation, click that message's subject. To expand *all* the messages in a conversation, click the Expand All link. All the messages in the conversation are stacked on top of each other, with the text of the newest message fully displayed.

Replying to a Message

Whether you're reading a single message or a conversation, it's easy enough to send a reply. In the original message, click the Reply button; this expands the message to include a reply box. Or, if a conversation has multiple participants, you can reply to all of them by clicking the down arrow next to the Reply button and then selecting Reply to All.

The text of the original message is already quoted in the reply. Add your new text above the original text. Since the original sender's address is automatically added to the To: line, all you have to do to send the message is click the Send button.

Composing a New Message

To compose and send a new message, click the Compose Mail link at the top of any Gmail page. When the Compose Mail page appears, enter the recipient's e-mail address in the To: box; separate multiple recipients with commas.

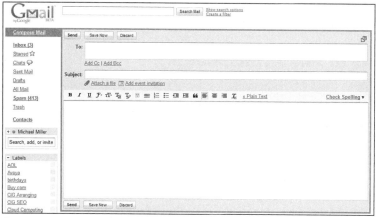

Composing a new Gmail message.

You can also carbon copy and blind carbon copy additional recipients by clicking the Add Cc and Add Bcc links. This expands the message to include Cc or Bcc boxes, into which you enter the recipients' addresses.

Once you've entered the recipient addresses, enter a subject for the message into the Subject box. Next, enter the text of your message in the large text box. Use the formatting controls (bold, italic, font, and so forth) to enhance your message as desired. When you're done composing your message, click the Send button.

WORDS TO GO . . . WORDS TO GO . . . WORDS TO GO

12.6

A **conversation** is an e-mail message thread in Gmail.

12.7 WORKING WITH FILE ATTACHMENTS

Dangers of File Attachments
File Attachments in Windows Live Mail
File Attachments in Gmail

When you need to send a digital photo or other file to a friend or colleague, you can do so via e-mail. To send a file via e-mail, you attach that file to a standard e-mail message. When the message is sent, the **file attachment** travels along with it; when the message is received, the file is right there waiting to be opened.

Dangers of File Attachments

It's an unfortunate fact that e-mail file attachments are the biggest sources of computer viruses and spyware infections. Malicious users attach viruses and spyware to e-mail messages, oftentimes disguised as legitimate files; when a user clicks to open the file, his or her computer is infected with the virus or spyware.

◄ *SEE ALSO 3.2, "Protecting Against Computer Viruses"* ▷

◄ *SEE ALSO 3.3, "Protecting Against Spyware"* ▷

This doesn't mean that all file attachments are dangerous, simply that opening file attachments—especially those you weren't expecting—is risky. You should avoid opening the following types of file attachments:

▶ Executable program files, with an EXE extension, sent from any user

▶ Any file sent from any user you don't know

▶ Any file sent from a friend or colleague that you weren't expecting

The only relatively safe file attachments are those coming from people you know who previously told you they were being sent. So if your Aunt Matilda previously e-mailed you to tell you she'd be sending you some vacation pictures, and you later get an e-mail from Aunt Matilda containing a handful of JPG files, those files are probably safe to open. On the other hand, if you receive an e-mail from a complete stranger with an unknown file attached, that's probably a malicious file that you shouldn't open.

What should you do when you receive an unexpected or unwanted file attachment? Fortunately, just receiving an e-mail attachment doesn't activate it; you have to open the file to launch the virus or spyware. What you should do, then, is delete the entire message. Don't open the file attachment, just delete the whole thing—message and attachment together. What's deleted can't harm you or your computer.

File Attachments in Windows Live Mail

It's easy to both send and receive e-mail file attachments. As an example, we'll examine how to do so in Windows Live Mail.

◀ *SEE ALSO 12.4, "Using Windows Live Mail"* ▶

Attaching a File

To attach a file to an outgoing e-mail message, click the Attach button in the message's toolbar. When the Open dialog box appears, browse for and select the file you want to attach.

The attached file is now listed below the Subject: field in the message window. When you click the Send button, the e-mail message and its attached file are sent to the recipient.

Opening an Attachment

When you receive a message that contains a file attachment, you'll see a paper clip icon in the message header and a paper clip button in the preview pane header. You can choose to view (open) the attached file or save it to your hard disk.

To view or open an attachment, double-click the paper clip button in the Preview pane header. When the Mail Attachment dialog box appears, click the Open button. This opens the attachment in its associated application. (If you're asked whether you want to save or view the attachment, select view.)

To save an attachment to your hard disk, right-click the paper clip button in the Preview pane header and then select Save As. When the Save Attachments As dialog box appears, select a location for the file and click the Save button.

File Attachments in Gmail

12.7

Sending and opening file attachments in a web e-mail application is similar to doing so in a POP e-mail program. As our example, we'll look at how to perform these tasks in Gmail.

◀ *SEE ALSO 12.6, "Using Gmail"* ▶

Attaching a File

To attach a file to a Gmail message, compose a new message and then click the Attach a File link. When the Choose File to Upload dialog box appears, navigate to and select the file you want to attach, and then click the Open button.

The file you selected appears under the Subject box on the new message page. To attach another file to this same message, click the Attach Another File link; otherwise, continue to compose and then send your message as normal.

WARNING . . .WARNING . . .WARNING . . .

Although you can send Word documents, Excel spreadsheets, MP3 music files, JPG picture files, and the like, Gmail won't let you send any executable program files. (These are files that have an EXE extension.) Gmail blocks the transmittal of all EXE files, including those in ZIP files, in an attempt to prevent potential computer viruses.

Opening an Attachment

When you receive a message with an attachment, you see a paper clip icon next to the message subject/snippet. To view or save an attachment, click the message to open it. Now scroll to the bottom of the message, and you'll see the attached file.

If you can view the attachment in Gmail, you'll see a View As link (this may be a View as HTML link); click this link to view the file. To save the file to your hard disk, click the Download link. When the File Download dialog box appears, click the Save button, select a location for the file, and then click the second Save button.

WORDS TO GO . . .WORDS TO GO . . .WORDS TO GO

A **file attachment** is a file that piggybacks on an e-mail message.

12.8 REDUCING SPAM

Understanding E-mail Spam
How to Stop Spam
Dealing With Blacklists

Viruses and spyware aside, the biggest e-mail-related annoyance is **spam,** otherwise known as unsolicited commercial e-mail (UCE). Spam is any unrequested marketing message sent via e-mail—the online equivalent of postal junk mail.

Understanding E-mail Spam

Spam messages are sent in bulk and indiscriminately, hawking adult websites, male enhancement pills, mortgage refinancing, penny stocks, and other schlocky products and services. The only good thing about spam is that it's easy enough to get rid of—by hitting the Delete key in your e-mail program.

Why is spam such a big problem? It's simple—spam is a low-cost, low-risk way to generate substantial profit. For a budding direct marketer, there is no lower-cost medium than e-mail. Unlike postal mail, where you have to put a stamp on every envelope or catalog, e-mail messages are essentially sent for free; it costs the same amount (zero) to send a hundred thousand messages as it does to send a single message.

How Spam Works

Spam works like any other e-mail message, except in bulk. The spammer creates his message, gathers a list of e-mail addresses, and then bulk e-mails his message to all the names on his list. The spam message then travels across the Internet to your ISP's e-mail server and eventually to your e-mail inbox.

Because spam is such a problem, most ISPs try to block it by monitoring or filtering large numbers of outgoing messages. To that end, the spammer has to perform some high-tech tricks to get around these outbound message limits.

One such trick is to use hundreds or thousands of hijacked computers to send the spam. The spammer infects these computers with a virus that opens a backdoor to control the computer via remote control. Then he instructs the e-mail program on each zombie computer to send his spam message to a designated list of addresses; to the recipients, it looks as if the spam came from the hijacked computer—which it did.

◄ *SEE ALSO 3.1, "Protecting Against Computer Attack"*

12.8

Finding Names to Spam

How do spammers find out your e-mail address? There are several ways:

▶ **Spam lists**—Spammers can purchase lists of tens of millions of e-mail addresses for just a few hundred dollars over the web and then use these names for their mailings.

▶ **E-mail harvesting**—More sophisticated spammers use automated software—called **spambots**—to scour the Internet for publicly available e-mail addresses. These e-mail addresses can come from a variety of sources—public web pages, blog postings, message forums, public directories, and so forth. Aggressive spammers can even scour Google, Yahoo!, and other search engines for publicly posted e-mail addresses. If your e-mail address is on a web page that is listed at the search site, it's visible to a spambot via a quick query of the search engine.

▶ **Phishing and social engineering**—Some spammers work by tricking you into providing your e-mail address. For example, some spammers send out "blind" spams to all the possible addresses in a given domain, asking you to reply to the message. When you reply, the spammer scrapes your address off the reply e-mail and adds it to his or her database of valid addresses. Phishing is also popular; when you're lured to a phony website by a phishing message, the e-mail address you enter is used for future spam mailings (and is sold to other spammers, of course).

▶ **Automatic name generation**—Perhaps the most common means of generating e-mail addresses today is via **dictionary spam.** This type of spam occurs when the spammer uses special software to guess every possible name in a given domain. For example, the spammer might start sending e-mail to **aaa@thisdomain.com** and end with a message to *zzz@thisdomain.com.* More sophisticated dictionary spammers make sure to include all known given names (and possible first- and last-name combinations), so if you have a common name at a major ISP—**mike@hotmail.com** or **jimbrown@gmail.com**—you're likely to get hit with an inordinate amount of spam.

Spoofing E-mail Addresses

Have you ever looked closely at a spam message and discovered that it appears to come from a friend's e-mail account—or even from your own address? Spammers use these fake addresses to trick you—or your spam filter—into not deleting them. This technique is called **e-mail spoofing.**

How does a spammer spoof a specific e-mail address? It's all in the software. There are spoofing programs available today that make it relatively easy to insert any e-mail address into the spam message's header. Some software even works interactively, inserting the recipient's address into the sender's address field so that it looks as if the e-mail you receive is actually coming from you.

The problems posed by these types of header spoofs are obvious. Because it spoofs a trusted address or domain, a spam message is less likely to be filtered by spam-blocking software and services. In addition, you're more likely to open a message if it looks as if it's coming from some person or organization you know.

How to Stop Spam

Want to decrease the amount of spam in your inbox? There are several things you can do to keep off spam lists and reduce the number of spam messages you receive.

Keep Your E-mail Address Private

The first step to cutting down on spam is to make sure as few people as possible know your e-mail address. If the spammers don't know where you are, they can't bother you.

What you want is the online equivalent of an unlisted phone number. Although it might be impossible to have a totally anonymous e-mail address, there are ways to minimize your exposure to spammers and thus decrease the amount of spam you receive.

Here are some tips for minimizing the public exposure of your e-mail address:

▶ **Don't give out your e-mail address.** It's obvious, really; the best way to hide your e-mail address from spammers is to not give it out. This means that you shouldn't do any of the following: fill out web-based registration forms, fill out online surveys, include your e-mail address when you post on public message boards or blogs, or add your name and address to any user directory. In addition, you should definitely not put your e-mail address on your website or blog; that's just inviting spammers who skim the web for e-mail addresses. Of course, this approach becomes problematic, especially when a website requires an e-mail address for registration— which might make alternative approaches more viable.

▶ **Create a less-common e-mail address.** Dictionary spam adds common names to popular Internet domains to "guess" at valid e-mail addresses. For this reason, the address **bob@myisp.com** will receive more spam than **b2qb475@myisp.com.** So learn from the dictionary spammers and create an e-mail address that looks as random as possible; it will be harder to guess, and you'll get less spam.

12.8

▶ **Use a spamblock.** If you need to publicize your e-mail address, you can do so in a way that foils automated spambots. The best method is to use a **spamblock,** an e-mail address that has been altered by the insertion of supplementary characters. For example, if your e-mail address is **johnjones@myisp.com,** you might change the address to read **johnSPAMBLOCKjones@myisp.com.** Other users will know to remove the SPAMBLOCK from the address before e-mailing you, but the spambots will be foiled.

▶ **Use two addresses.** This is kind of a workaround, but it's effective. Use a free web-based e-mail service, such as Gmail or Hotmail, to create a second e-mail address and then use that address for all public correspondence and such. Keep your other, ISP-based e-mail address private, known only to selected friends and family. All the spam will go to the more public address, which you can easily ignore. Your main address will remain relatively spam-free.

▶ **Use a disposable e-mail address.** Another alternative is to generate what is called a disposable e-mail address. This provides a working e-mail address to any site that requires it, without divulging your real e-mail address. You can obtain disposable e-mail addresses from spamgourmet (www.spamgourmet.com), Spamex (www.spamex.com), ZoE-mail (www.zoe-mail.com), and similar sites.

▶ **Don't reply to spammers.** Remember, many spammers get your address when you give it to them. For that reason, you don't want to reply to any spam messages—period. It's when you reply that they harvest your e-mail address; don't reply, and they're left empty-handed.

▶ **Don't unsubscribe to spam.** Along the same lines, don't click the "unsubscribe" link found in many spam messages. This link seldom leads to a legitimate unsubscribe function, and more often it just adds your e-mail address to the spammer's e-mail database—unlike the functioning unsubscribe link found in legitimate e-mail marketing messages.

Use Your ISP's Spam-Blocking Features

Many Internet service providers provide their own spam-blocking services. Some ISPs activate their spam blocking automatically, in the background; others provide a set of tools you can choose to use on the e-mail you receive. To cut down on the spam you receive, you should avail yourself of your ISP's spam blocking.

Most ISPs have such spam-blocking features, although they're not often well publicized. If in doubt, check with your ISP's technical support department to find out what spam-blocking services it offers.

Use Your E-mail Program's Spam Filter

Most e-mail programs and web mail services include some sort of spam filtering. You should activate these spam filters to cut down on the amount of spam that reaches your inbox.

Use Anti-Spam Software

If the amount of spam in your inbox becomes overwhelming, you might want to consider using an anti-spam software program. Most anti-spam software uses some combination of spam blocking and content filtering to keep spam messages from ever reaching your inbox; their effectiveness varies, but they do decrease the amount of spam you receive to some degree.

The most popular anti-spam software offerings include the following:

- ANT 4 MailChecking (www.ant4.com)
- MailWasher (www.mailwasher.net)
- SonicWALL Anti-Spam and E-mail Security (www.sonicwall.com)
- SpamCatcher (my.smithmicro.com)
- Vanquish vqME (www.vanquish.com)

In addition, many anti-virus and content-filtering programs, as well as so-called "Internet security suites," include anti-spam modules. If you're already using an anti-virus program or security suite, check whether it offers spam e-mail filtering.

Use a Spam-Filtering Service

If anti-spam software isn't powerful enough for you, you can subscribe to one of the several online services that interactively block spam using a variety of filtering and blocking techniques. Many of these services are also available for small business and large corporate networks; most are priced on a per-month subscription basis.

Here are some of the more popular spam-filtering services:

- Mailshell (www.mailshell.com)
- OnlyMyE-mail (www.onlymye-mail.com)
- SpamCop (www.spamcop.net)
- SpamMotel (www.spammotel.com)

12.8

Dealing With Blacklists

One feature of most of anti-spam services is that they use blacklists to filter out potential spam content. A blacklist is simply a list of known or suspected spammers, either by unique IP address or general domain.

Filtering by blacklist is somewhat effective, as spammers tend to use unprotected computers or domains to do their dirty deeds. If a computer or domain is known to be frequently used by spammers, it makes sense to block traffic from that computer or domain.

The problem with a blacklist is that it blocks *all* traffic from that computer or domain, not just spam traffic. It's inevitable that some messages from legitimate users will get blocked along with the spam messages. That isn't a good thing for either the intended recipients of those legitimate messages or the senders, who can't get their messages out to companies employing those blacklist filters.

If you find yourself the victim of an unintended blacklist, your first step is to contact the owner of that blacklist and plead your case. In most instances, that means finding out which anti-spam service a recipient uses, and then contacting that company. Some companies are easier to deal with than others; the bad news is, some companies don't honor any requests for blacklist removal as long as you're using an offending server.

If you can't get your address removed from the blacklist, your only recourse is to use a different e-mail address for the duration of the blacklist. Alternatively, you can change ISPs or web hosts to one that isn't frequently blacklisted.

WORDS TO GO . . . WORDS TO GO . . . WORDS TO GO

Dictionary spam is e-mail spam sent to every possible name in a given domain.

E-mail spoofing involves making a spam message look as if it came from another e-mail account instead of from the one it was actually sent from.

Spam is the online equivalent of junk mail—unwanted marketing messages sent via e-mail.

A **spamblock** is used to block spam by inserting supplementary characters into your e-mail address, thus foiling spambots from harvesting your legitimate address.

A **spambot** is an automated software program used by spammers to scour the Internet for publicly available e-mail addresses.

13

OTHER ONLINE COMMUNICATIONS

13.1 CHATTING AND MESSAGING ONLINE

Understanding Chat and Messaging

Chat Shorthand

Emoticons

Even though e-mail is relatively new to some users, it's old technology for many others. Many people—especially younger users—consider e-mail too slow and involved for their fast-paced lives and instead communicate via text-based chat and instant messages.

◀ SEE ALSO 12.1, *"How E-mail Works"* ▶

Understanding Chat and Messaging

There are two ways to send and receive text messages online. When you want a private one-on-one conversation with another user, you use an **instant messaging** (IM) program, such as AOL Instant Messenger or Yahoo! Messenger. IM consists of a series of short text messages sent from one user to another, with all messages displayed in a **message window** on your computer desktop.

◀ SEE ALSO 13.2, *"Instant Messaging"* ▶

Online chat is similar to instant messaging in that it's text-based. However, online chat takes place in a public **chat room** where others can see what you're saying; all your conversations are public.

◀ SEE ALSO 13.3, *"Chat Rooms"* ▶

Chat Shorthand

When you're chatting online or using instant messaging, quickness takes precedence over accuracy—which means that many users talk in their own unique shorthand, which is easier and faster to type than spelling out complete words and sentences.

Part of this shorthand is the use of acronyms in place of common phrases. For your online chatting convenience, Table 13.1 lists those acronyms you're most likely to encounter online.

TABLE 13.1 POPULAR ONLINE ACRONYMS

Acronym	Meaning
AKA	Also known as
ASAP	As soon as possible
BRB	Be right back
BTW	By the way
FWIW	For what it's worth
FYI	For your information
GDR	Grinning, ducking, and running
IMHO	In my humble opinion
IOW	In other words
LMAO	Laughing my a** off
LOL	Laughing out loud
NP	No problem
OTOH	On the other hand
PMJI	Pardon me for jumping in
ROFL	Rolling on the floor laughing
RT	Real time (as in, arrange a real-time meeting)
RTFM	Read the frickin' manual!
TLA	Three letter acronym
TTFN	Ta ta for now!

It's also okay to abbreviate longer words and to type in all lowercase (but *never* in all UPPERCASE!). It goes without saying that spelling, grammar, and punctuation really don't count for much in chat and IM sessions, but you should at least try to make your messages understandable. Keep it short and to the point, and you'll fit right in.

Emoticons

Another way to accentuate your chat and IM sessions is to use **emoticons** or **smileys.** These are groups of symbols that represent specific emotions. For example, the emoticon :) means that you're smiling (look at it sideways to see a smiley face); the emoticon ;) means that you're winking.

13.1

293

In some chat rooms and with some IM clients, typing one of these text-based emoticons will display a graphic emoticon. Some chat rooms and IM clients offer additional graphic emoticons that you can select from a list or pull-down menu.

WORDS TO GO . . .WORDS TO GO . . .WORDS TO GO

A **chat room** is a web-based forum for public text messaging.

An **emoticon** is a series of symbols used to represent a particular emotion during online chat or instant messaging.

Instant messaging (IM) enables two users to send text messages to each other in real time over the Internet.

The **message window** is where you enter and view your IM conversations.

Online chat is a public exchange of text messages with a group of other users.

A **smiley** is another word for an emoticon.

13.2 INSTANT MESSAGING

IM Networks

Using AOL Instant Messenger

When you want to talk one-on-one with another computer user in real time, but you don't have time for a phone call, instant messaging is the way to go. Instant messaging is the computer equivalent of phone-based text messaging, but it's done over the Internet. It's faster than e-mail and less chaotic than chat rooms.

◀ SEE ALSO 12.1, "How E-mail Works" ▶

◀ SEE ALSO 13.3, "Chat Rooms" ▶

IM Networks

The following are several big players in the instant messaging market today:

- ▶ AOL Instant Messenger (www.aim.com)
- ▶ Google Talk (www.google.com/talk)
- ▶ ICQ (www.icq.com)
- ▶ Windows Live Messenger (messenger.live.com)
- ▶ Yahoo! Messenger (messenger.yahoo.com)

Unfortunately, these are all separate IM networks, and the networks are not interconnected. If you're using Yahoo! Messenger, for example, you won't be able to communicate with someone running AOL Instant Messenger. That means you'll want to use the IM program that all your friends and colleagues are using—so find that out before you download any software.

That said, several of these IM networks are starting to interface with one another. For example, the Windows Live Messenger and Yahoo! Messenger networks do talk to each other, as do AOL Instant Messenger and some versions of Google Talk. But the general rule still holds—subscribe to the IM network that your contacts are using.

13.2

WARNING . . .WARNING . . .WARNING

Instant messaging only works if both parties are online at the same time; you can't send an instant message to someone who isn't available. However, some IM programs save your messages until the recipient returns online and then sends them.

Using AOL Instant Messenger

The most popular instant messaging program today is AOL Instant Messenger (AIM), with Yahoo! Messenger a close second. AIM is especially popular among the teen and preteen crowd, although people of all ages can and do use it. We'll use AIM for the examples in this chapter, but know that all instant messaging programs work in pretty much the same fashion.

Downloading the AIM Software

To use AIM, you first have to download the AIM client software. AIM is free to both download and use on a daily basis.

Go to the AIM website (www.aim.com) and click the Downloads menu. Several different versions of AIM are available; the most current version, as of March 2009, is AIM 6.8. (Be on the lookout for newer versions, however.) Select the version you want to download; when the next page appears, click the Install Now link. This downloads the AIM software and installs it on your PC.

Launching AIM and Signing In

When you first launch the AIM program, you'll need to choose a screen name before you can start using the program. You do this by clicking the Get a Screen Name link in the AIM window. Follow the onscreen instructions to choose a screen name and password for your account.

After you have your screen name and password, you have to sign in to the AIM service before you can start messaging. When you launch the AIM software, enter your screen name and password and then click the Sign In button. This connects you to the service and notifies any of your friends that you're online and ready to chat.

Navigating AIM

The AIM application consists of two separate windows, only one of which appears when you first launch the program. The main AIM window contains a list of your friends and colleagues who are also AIM users. These people are your buddies, in AIM parlance, and the list of buddies is your **buddy list.** This window is also where you configure the program and initiate various actions.

The main AIM window, complete with buddy list.

When you launch a conversation with one of your buddies, AIM opens a second window called the message window. This is where the conversation takes place; you can open individual message windows at the same time for conversations with multiple buddies.

Adding New Buddies

To send an instant message to another user, that person has to be on your buddy list. To add a new buddy to the list, click the Buddy List Setup button at the bottom of the AIM window (that's the +/- button) and select Add Buddy. When the New Buddy window appears, enter the person's AIM screen name and then click the Save button. This person is now added to your buddy list.

After you've added people to your buddy list, they show up in the main AIM window. Buddies who are online and ready to chat are displayed at the top of the list; buddies who aren't currently online appear at the bottom of the list in the Offline section.

13.2

Sending a Message

To send an instant message to one of your buddies, double-click that person's name in your buddies list. This opens a separate message window. Enter your message in the lower part of the window and then press Enter.

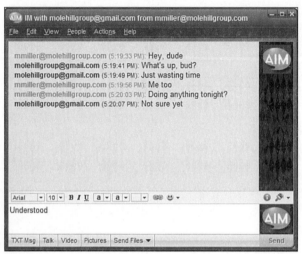

Send and receive instant messages via the AIM message window.

Your message appears in the top part of the window, as does any reply from your buddy. Continue talking like this, one message after another. Your entire conversation is displayed in the top part of the window, and you can scroll up to reread earlier messages.

Receiving a Message

When you're logged on to the AIM service and someone else sends you an instant message, AIM displays an alert in the lower-right corner of your screen, accompanied by an alert sound. To reply to the message, click the alert; this opens a new IM window for your chat.

Sending Pictures and Other Files

You also can use AIM to display pictures and send files to other users during the course of a message session.

To show a picture to your buddy, click the Pictures button at the bottom of the message window. When the Sharing Pictures window appears, click the Send Pictures button. When the Open Image Files window appears, navigate to and select the pictures you want to display. This will open a similar Sharing Pictures window for your messaging buddy; your pictures are shown in an automatic slideshow.

If you'd rather send a picture file (or any other type of file) directly to your buddy, click the Send Files button in the message window and then select Send File. When the Send File window appears, navigate to and select the file you want to send. Your buddy will be notified that he has a file waiting to download.

Voice and Video Chats

In addition to traditional text messaging, AIM can also be used for voice and video messaging if you and your buddy both have microphones and/or webcams connected to your computers. To initiate an audio chat, click the Talk button at the bottom of the open message window. To initiate a video chat, click the Video button.

WORDS TO GO . . .WORDS TO GO . . .WORDS TO GO

A **buddy** (or friend) is someone with whom you converse via instant messaging.
Your **buddy list** is your list of IM buddies.

13.2

13.3 CHAT ROOMS

Understanding Online Chat

Finding a Chat Site

Chat Tips

Chatting at TalkCity

An online chat is different from an instant message session. Whereas instant messaging describes a one-to-one conversation between two users, online chat involves real-time discussions among large groups of users. These chats take place in public chat rooms.

◄ *SEE ALSO 13.2, "Instant Messaging"* ▷

You can find chat rooms at any number of websites. These chat rooms are accessible via any web browser.

Understanding Online Chat

No matter which chat room you visit, be prepared for a very informal, very hectic experience. Some busy chat rooms are populated by several dozen users at a time and often feature as many different conversations taking place as there are users. As the lines of text go scrolling by, faster than you can read them, you'll have to work hard to figure out which comments go with which conversations and which users to pay attention to and which to ignore.

If this all seems intimidating to you, don't worry. It may take a little practice, but before long you'll be right in the middle of things, chatting along with the best of them.

Finding a Chat Site

Many individual websites offer chat rooms as part of their regular content. These sites typically have a single chat room devoted to the site's main focus that all site users can access.

Chat rooms can also be found on larger chat community websites. These sites offer numerous chat rooms, each devoted to a particular topic. The biggest of these chat communities include the following:

- ▶ #1 Chat Avenue (www.chat-avenue.com)

- ▶ 321 Teen Chat (www.321teenchat.com)

- ▶ AIM Chat (chat.aim.com)

- ▶ ChitChatting.Com (www.chitchatting.com)

- ▶ Cool Teen Chat (www.coolteenchat.com)

- ▶ Java Chat Rooms (www.javachatrooms.net)

- ▶ Talk City (www.talkcity.com)

- ▶ Teenage Chat Rooms (www.teenagechatrooms.com)

- ▶ TeenChat (www.teenchat.com)

In addition, some IM services offer public chat rooms that are accessible via the IM clients. For example, Yahoo! Chat is available from within Yahoo! Messenger; just click the Yahoo! Chat item on the Messenger menu.

Chat Tips

Chatting can be fun—if you're ready for it. With that in mind, here's a list of tips for a more enjoyable chat experience:

- ▶ Don't feel like you have to jump right in and participate in every single discussion. It's okay to sit back, take your time, and watch the conversations flow before you decide to add your two cents' worth.

- ▶ Don't assume you're really talking to the person you *think* you're talking to. It's easy to hide behind a nickname and create a totally different persona online.

- ▶ For that matter, it's okay to create an online persona for yourself that bears no relation to the real you. It's actually kind of fun to pretend to be someone else when you're chatting online—and see how others respond to the "new" you.

- ▶ If you want to get personal with someone you meet in a chat channel, send a private message (sometimes called a whisper). Don't subject everyone in a room to your private conversations.

- ▶ Don't give out your real name, address, or phone number in any chat session—period.

- ▶ Think twice before agreeing to meet someone from a chat session in person. There *are* cyber predators out there who use chat rooms to set up real-time meetings for all sorts of nefarious purposes. Don't be a victim. If you do meet someone offline, do so in a public place and with some sort of "escape plan" in case things go wrong.

13.3

▶ Along the same lines, beware of law enforcement personnel posing as potential chat room victims. If you're thinking of discussing anything remotely illegal, just remember that the person you're chatting with could be a member of your local police force!

▶ Watch out for your kids. The online world is part of the real world, and chat channels are good places for unsavory sorts to stalk unknowing youngsters. Make sure that your kids are well informed, that they use good judgment, and that they never, *ever* arrange to meet a chat mate without your supervision.

◀ SEE ALSO 3.6, *"Safe Surfing for Children"* ▶

▶ Be very careful about accepting files sent to you during a chat session. Since many chat rooms exist for the purpose of creating online hookups between users, it's not uncommon for users to send pictures of themselves to people they're chatting with. It's okay to accept picture files (typically in JPG or GIF format), as these files are nonexecutable and can't carry any viruses. If you're not vigilant, however, you'll find yourself mindlessly accepting any file sent your way—which is a surefire way to infect your system with a computer virus or spyware. Examine carefully any file sent to you in a chat session and reject anything that is the least bit suspicious.

◀ SEE ALSO 3.2, *"Protecting Against Computer Viruses"* ▶

◀ SEE ALSO 3.3, *"Protecting Against Spyware"* ▶

Chatting at TalkCity

One of the most popular chat community websites is TalkCity. This site offers several hundred chat rooms, each devoted to a particular topic or type of user; it works similarly to other chat communities.

Entering a Chat Room

TalkCity's chat rooms are categorized along the left side of the page. Click a major category to see the individual rooms within that category and then click a room title to enter that room.

When you first use TalkCity, you're prompted to create a user account, which includes your member name and password. After you've done this, you're prompted to enter this information each subsequent time you enter a chat room.

When you click to enter a chat room, you see the home page for that room. This page contains basic information about the room, including recent visitors and message threads. To begin chatting, click the Chat Now button; this opens a separate chat window for that room.

Chatting

Once you've entered a TalkCity chat room, all messages are displayed in the main pane in the middle of the window. Everyone chatting in the room is listed in the Chatter List to the right of the chat pane.

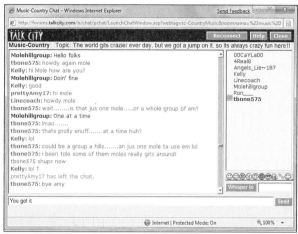

A *TalkCity chat room.*

To display information about a given user, click that user's name and select Launch Profile from the pop-up menu. This displays the member's profile in a new window.

To send a message to the room, enter that message in the message box under the chat pane and then click the Send button. After you send a message, it appears in the main chat pane, listed in line with all the other messages.

Sending Private Messages

To initiate a private conversation with another chatter, click that user's name in the Chatter list and then click Whisper from the pop-up menu. Enter your message into the message box and then click the Whisper To button.

13.4 WEBCAMS

Why Webcast?

How Webcams Work

Finding Webcams on the Internet

Viewing a Webcam

Hooking Up Your Own Webcam

A **webcam** is a small camera (typically with a built-in microphone) that you attach to your computer to record moving and still images. Many people use webcams to send photos and videos to other users, often via live video instant messaging and chat.

Webcams can also be connected to the Internet to provide continuous images or streaming video. When you point your browser to a webcam page, you get a live look at whatever the camera is pointing at; this is called a **webcast.** (If you're looking at a still image, that image will be updated periodically—typically once a minute or so.)

Why Webcast?

Webcams can be voyeuristic, webcasting personal details of an individual's life, but they can also be practical. For example, many cities have webcams aimed at busy intersections or stretches of highway; you can check out the traffic cam to see how busy the roads are before you head out and about. In addition, thousands of webcams are installed at various vacation spots around the globe. Watching the webcam for a day or two is a good way to prepare for an upcoming vacation.

That doesn't even address the webcams you can set up for your own personal use. For example, a parent can set up a webcam broadcasting live pictures from her baby's bedroom—so the parent can see how the baby's doing while she's away from home. For that matter, you can set up a webcam to keep an eye on your dog or cat in your absence, or you can set up a webcam in your children's play-room and give the URL to other members of your family so that your parents can watch their grandkids at play.

How Webcams Work

A webcam is nothing more than a simple digital video camera attached to a computer. The camera connects to the PC, typically via the USB port, and feeds images into a special webcam software program. This program can be configured to stream or capture moving video images or to periodically grab single frames from the camera, saving the pictures as individual JPG graphic files. In the latter configuration, the individual JPG files are then fed to a web server, which embeds the pictures into a constantly refreshing web page.

While some webcams broadcast continuous streaming video, most shoot out one frame at a time with new frames posting every few seconds or minutes. As a user, this latter approach is ideal and requires no special viewing software—all you're looking at is a series of JPG picture files, which are automatically updated by the host site.

WARNING . . . WARNING . . . WARNING

Many personal webcams are actually paid adult services, not suitable for viewing by youngsters.

Finding Webcams on the Internet

There are thousands of webcams on the Internet. Some are outdoor cams, some are indoor cams, some are pointed at really interesting people and things, and some are pointed at potted plants and coffee machines. With all these cams available, how do you find an interesting one to watch?

Several large webcam directories on the Internet list hundreds of different sites by type. Some of these directories also provide webcam hosting services and function as a one-stop shop for anyone looking to set up his or her own webcast.

If you want to see what's playing on your favorite webcam, check out these sites:

- ▶ Camvista (www.camvista.com)
- ▶ EarthCam (www.earthcam.com)
- ▶ Live Webcam Directory (www.live-webcam-directory.com)
- ▶ OnlineCamera (www.onlinecamera.com)
- ▶ WebCam Central (www.camcentral.com)
- ▶ Webcam World (www.webcamworld.com)
- ▶ WebcamSearch.com (www.webcamsearch.com)

13.4

Viewing a Webcam

Viewing a webcam is typically as simple as using your web browser to navigate to the webcam page. The pictures from the webcam should automatically appear in your browser. Some webcams update their pictures automatically every minute or so; others can be refreshed manually by clicking a button.

A live webcam from San Diego.

Hooking Up Your Own Webcam

Setting up your own webcam isn't hard. Here's what you need:

▶ A webcam

▶ Webcam software

▶ A web server to host your webcam

It's relatively easy to hook up a webcam to your PC, and the webcam software isn't hard to install or configure. The biggest challenge is finding a host server—although you can always run your own server if you're technically adept.

Webcam Hardware

The webcam itself is nothing more than a very small, very simple, full-motion video camera that attaches to any personal computer. Webcams are designed for both frame capture and continuous video and can feed images for e-mail attachments, video conferencing, and other uses. Most webcams connect via USB.

Webcams today typically sell for less than $100. Most models include a built-in microphone for use in live video chats.

Webcam Software

Webcam software typically performs a variety of functions, including grabbing frames from your webcam, uploading those frames to a server or saving them to individual files, and managing streaming broadcasts for either webcam or video chat purposes. You can find commercial webcam software at your local consumer electronics store; there are also a number of freeware and shareware programs that you can download from the web. In addition, many webcams come with their own webcam software with no additional purchase necessary.

Some of the more popular freestanding webcam programs include the following:

- CoffeeCup WebCam (www.coffeecup.com/webcam/)
- EyeSpyFX (www.eyespyfx.com)
- ImageSalsa (www.imagesalsa.com)
- TinCam (www.tincam.com)
- visionGS (www.visiongs.de)
- Yawcam (www.yawcam.com)

Finding a Webcam Host

The final piece in the webcam puzzle is the server that hosts your live webcasts. That server might be based at a standard website hosting service, or it might be at a site that specializes in webcam hosting.

Wherever your server is, you'll need a relatively persistent connection between your home computer and the host server—which means an always-on broadband connection. That's because the connection has to be up all the time in order for your webcam images to be constantly updated.

◄ SEE ALSO 1.2, "Broadband vs. Dial-Up" ▷

For most users, the best solution is one of the sites that specialize in hosting and listing webcams. Most of the sites listed in the "Finding Webcams on the Internet" section of this chapter also offer webcam hosting services and can serve as a one-stop shop when you're first getting set up.

WORDS TO GO . . .WORDS TO GO . . .WORDS TO GO

13.4

A **webcam** is a small camera that attaches to your computer and records video, audio, and still pictures. The word "webcam" also refers to hardware webcams connected to the Internet that stream continuous images or video to other computer users.

A **webcast** is streaming video sent from a webcam over the Internet.

13.5 ONLINE PHONE SERVICE

How VoIP Works

Different Ways to Call

VoIP Services

Making a Call

Here's another way to communicate over the Internet: by phone. **Internet telephony** enables users to place phone calls directly from their PCs over the Internet, either to other Internet users or to regular telephones. When you place a call over the Internet, you avoid paying some or all of the long-distance charges associated with normal phone calls.

How VoIP Works

Internet telephony is possible because of **Voice over Internet Protocol** (VoIP) technology. VoIP breaks normal analog voice conversations into the type of digital data packets that are typical of other Internet data and then routes those packets over the Internet from your PC to another PC, where the packets are reassembled into a voice stream.

In the early days of Internet telephony, voice quality was abysmal. As the technology has improved, however, so has the quality of the communication. Using a relatively new, relatively fast computer with the latest software and a fast broadband Internet connection, the quality of a PC-based conversation approaches that of today's mobile phones.

◁ *SEE ALSO 1.2, "Broadband vs. Dial-Up"* ▷

Most VoIP services have two operating modes:

▶ **PC-to-PC,** where you can talk directly to another user of the same program using the microphones and speakers in your personal computer systems or using Internet phone handsets. In PC-to-PC telephony, no long-distance charges accrue—no matter where in the world you're calling.

▶ **PC-to-phone,** where you dial from your computer to any telephone number in the world. You use the microphone and speaker in your PC or an Internet phone handset, and the person you're talking to uses a regular landline or mobile phone. In PC-to-phone telephony, you're subject to at least some of the standard long-distance charges—although typically at a much-reduced rate because most of the call takes place using the Internet backbone as opposed to the telco backbone.

WARNING . . .WARNING . . .WARNING

For PC-to-PC telephony to work, both users must be using the same software or service. For example, if both participants are using Skype, the PC-to-PC connection is easy to complete. If, on the other hand, one user is using Skype and the other is using Net2Phone, a connection cannot be made.

Different Ways to Call

There are many ways to use VoIP technology on your computer:

▶ **Instant messaging.** All of the major instant messaging programs include Internet telephony capability for PC-to-PC calls; some include technology for PC-to-phone service.

◀ *SEE ALSO 13.2, "Instant Messaging"* ▷

▶ **Videoconferencing.** Most videoconferencing programs let you make PC-to-PC calls; some programs also have PC-to-phone capability.

▶ **VoIP services.** Several companies offer dedicated Internet telephony services for both PC-to-PC and PC-to-phone calls. Most of these services charge a fee for use, but this fee is less than traditional landline or mobile telephone service.

VoIP Services

VoIP services enable you to make PC-to-PC and PC-to-phone calls from your computer over the Internet to any location around the globe. Many services offer free PC-to-PC calling to others using the same service and then charge by the minute for PC-to-phone calls—but with rates lower than that of traditional telephone service.

To use these services, all you need is a computer connected to the Internet (a broadband connection is preferred) and a web browser. In addition, you may have to download and install that service's proprietary calling software. You'll also need some hardware to complete your calls—either a PC microphone and speakers, a headset with microphone, or a telephone handset adapted for computer use (typically connected via USB).

The most popular of these services include the following:

▶ iConnectHere (www.iconnecthere.com)

▶ MediaRing Talk (www.mediaringtalk.com)

▶ Net2Phone (www.net2phone.com)

13.5

▶ Skype (www.skype.com)

▶ WebPhone (www.webphone.com)

▶ Yahoo! Voice (voice.yahoo.com)

Making a Call

Making a VoIP call with an Internet telephony service is relatively easy. Once you have the service's software installed (and are connected to the Internet), you can choose to place a call to anyone on your contact list or manually dial a number.

Once you're connected, you listen to the call through your PC's speakers and talk through the connected microphone. Alternatively, you can connect a telephone headset (headphones and microphone combined) or use a handset designed for PC use. These handsets typically connect to your computer's USB port.

Any PC-to-phone calls you make will likely be charged. You may need to provide billing information when you first sign up or purchase "credits" for use with future calls.

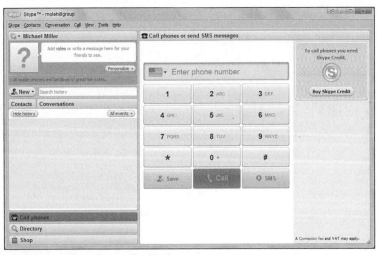

Making an Internet phone call with Skype.

Internet telephony enables users to place phone calls directly from their computers over the Internet.

PC-to-phone calls are made from a computer to a traditional landline or mobile phone over the Internet.

PC-to-PC calls are made from one computer to another computer over the Internet.

Voice over Internet Protocol (VoIP) is the technology that enables Internet telephony.

13.5

14

PLAYING ONLINE GAMES

14.1 Finding and Playing Games Online

14.2 Second Life and Other Virtual Worlds

14.3 Sites for Gamers

14.1 FINDING AND PLAYING GAMES ONLINE

Types of Online Games

Connection Considerations

Finding Online Game Sites

Game playing is serious business, especially on the Internet. Whether you're looking for a quick game of checkers or an evening-long session of a difficult **multiplayer game,** you can find dozens of sites on the web to satisfy your gaming needs.

Types of Online Games

There are two general types of games available online: simple games and multiplayer games.

Simple games require no previous purchase of game software, nor any complex multiple-player networking software. These games are either single-player or very basic multiple-player games such as card games or board games. Some of these games run within your normal web browser using HTML coding; others run in a separate gaming window using either Java, Flash, or Shockwave technology. Most of these simple games are free to play.

Multiplayer games are those that use the Internet to connect multiple users together in a single game. Most of these games are complex action and strategy games; many require that separate game software be installed on your PC before you connect to a dedicated gaming website to network with other players.

Casual gamers should probably stick to the simple games. Multiplayer gaming is more difficult to set up, often requires an investment in game software, and is typically played by much more serious gamers.

Connection Considerations

If you're playing games online in real time, you want as fast an Internet connection as you can afford—which means broadband cable or DSL. Slower dial-up connections may suffice for some simple single-player games, but more sophisticated and multiplayer games beam a lot of data back and forth, and a slow connection can seriously disrupt continuous game play.

◄ *SEE ALSO 1.2, "Broadband vs. Dial-Up"* ▷

When you're playing some of the more demanding multiplayer games, you need to consider the **latency** of your Internet connection. Latency is the "lag time" between when a command is sent and when it is received. High latency can be as disruptive as a slow Internet connection; you want as close to instant response as you can get so that your game playing takes place in real time. Ask your ISP about connection latency; some ISPs offer faster (and more expensive) packages that have lower latency for better game playing.

Finding Online Game Sites

If you're interested in playing online games, check out these websites:

- ▶ All Games Free (www.allgamesfree.com)
- ▶ Arcade Temple (www.arcadetemple.com)
- ▶ ArcadeTown.com (www.arcadetown.com)
- ▶ Boxerjam (www.boxerjam.com)
- ▶ Dailygames.com (www.dailygames.com)
- ▶ Games.com (www.games.com)
- ▶ Gamesville (www.gamesville.com)
- ▶ Internet Chess Club (www.chessclub.com)
- ▶ Internet Park (www.internet-park.com)
- ▶ iWin.com (www.iwin.com)
- ▶ Miniclip (www.miniclip.com)
- ▶ MSN Games (zone.msn.com)
- ▶ OnlineGames.net (www.onlinegames.net)
- ▶ PlayedOnline.com (www.playedonline.com)
- ▶ Pogo.com (www.pogo.com)
- ▶ Uproar (www.uproar.com)
- ▶ Yahoo! Games (games.yahoo.com)

Most of these sites offer both simple single-player games and more sophisticated multiplayer games.

14.1

Latency is the lag time between when a command is sent and when it is received; you want low latency when playing online games.

Multiplayer games let multiple users play against each other online.

14.2 SECOND LIFE AND OTHER VIRTUAL WORLDS

Understanding Virtual Worlds

Second Life

Virtual worlds are online games with a twist. They function more like social networks than they do traditional blast-'em-up games.

◀ *SEE ALSO 11.1, "Understanding Social Networking"* ▷

Understanding Virtual Worlds

A virtual world is a simulated onscreen environment that is part chat room, part multiplayer game; some people refer to them as **massively multiplayer online role-playing games** (MMORPGs). You access the virtual world over the Internet via your web browser. The world itself is a three-dimensional space that you and other users inhabit.

◀ *SEE ALSO 13.3, "Chat Rooms"* ▷

◀ *SEE ALSO 14.1, "Finding and Playing Games Online"* ▷

You are represented by an onscreen character called an **avatar.** Your avatar can be personalized to suit your personality, and you move it around onscreen in the three-dimensional virtual space. Your avatar can walk and talk (you put the words into its mouth, of course) and participate in various onscreen activities.

What can you do in a virtual world? Virtually everything you can do in the physical world. You can talk to other others, play games with them, shop for virtual merchandise, even participate in virtual political campaigns. It's a computerized version of the real world that you play on your computer over the Internet.

Some virtual worlds closely resemble the real world. Others present fantasy worlds in which your avatar might be a wizard or a knight or a superhero. These latter games are more obviously descendents of traditional role-playing games, although all virtual worlds incorporate role playing to some extent.

The most popular virtual worlds today include the following:

▶ Active Worlds (www.activeworlds.com)

▶ City of Heroes (www.cityofheroes.com)

14.2

- Habbo (www.habbo.com)

- Kaneva (www.kaneva.com)

- MapleStory (www.maplestory.com)

- Nicktropolis (www.nick.com/nicktropolis/game/)

- Poptropica (www.poptropica.com)

- Second Life (www.secondlife.com)

- There (www.there.com)

- World of Warcraft (www.worldofwarcraft.com)

Some of these virtual worlds, such as Nicktropolis and Poptropica, cater more to children and preteens. Others, such as City of Heroes and World of Warcraft, are more game oriented than chat oriented. In any case, you need to spend some time getting a feel for any particular virtual world before you decide to dive in on a more serious basis.

Second Life

One of the most popular virtual worlds today is Second Life (www.secondlife. com), with millions of participants. Like most virtual worlds, Second Life is free to play, although subscriptions are available for more sophisticated game play. You can also purchase virtual dollars (called **Linden Dollars,** named after the game developer) to participate in the world's virtual economy.

Getting Started

You have to create a (free) account to play Second Life. Click the Get Started link on the home page, and you're prompted to choose an initial look for your avatar and enter your name and e-mail address. Once your account is confirmed (via e-mail), you're prompted to download and install the Second Life viewer, which is necessary to access the virtual world.

Exploring the Virtual World

When you enter Second Life, your avatar appears at the bottom of the screen. You move around the world by using the arrow keys on your computer keypad; press and hold a key to walk in that particular direction.

Exploring Second Life.

The people you meet within Second Life are called **residents.** Residents can explore the Second Life world (called the **grid**), socialize with other residents, participate in individual and group activities, and create and trade virtual properties and services with each other.

The room that you're in is just a small part of the Second Life world. To view a map of the world, click the Map button; click a point on the map to travel to that area.

To chat in Second Life, enter your comments in the Local Chat box below the main screen. The ongoing conversation in a room appears in a chat box overlaid in the bottom left corner of the screen.

Customizing Your Avatar

After a while, you'll get bored with your initial avatar and want to change your appearance. You do this by selecting Edit, Appearance from the Second Life menu. This displays an editing window that lets you customize your avatar's body parts and clothing to a fine degree of detail. Make the changes you want and then click the Save button.

And More ...

This is only a small look at what you can do in Second Life. Most people spend untold hours exploring the grid and interacting with other residents. There's a

14.2

lot to do here; the Second Life world is every bit as rich as the real world outside your computer screen.

WORDS TO GO . . . WORDS TO GO . . . WORDS TO GO

An **avatar** is your physical onscreen representation in a virtual world.

The **grid** is the virtual world in Second Life.

Linden Dollars are the virtual currency in Second Life.

A **massively multiplayer online role-playing game** (MMORPG) is another phrase for a virtual world.

The other players in Second Life are called **residents.**

A **virtual world** is an online environment that is part multiplayer role-playing game, part online chat room.

14.3 SITES FOR GAMERS

In addition to sites that let you play games online, the Internet is also host to numerous sites that provide news, information, reviews, instructions, hints, and cheats for the most popular computer games and videogame systems. Among the best of these sites are the following:

- ▶ Cheat Code Central (www.cheatcc.com)
- ▶ GameRankings.com (www.gamerankings.com)
- ▶ GameDaily (www.gamedaily.com)
- ▶ GamePro (www.gamepro.com)
- ▶ GamesRadar (www.gamesradar.com)
- ▶ GameSpot (www.gamespot.com)
- ▶ GameZone (www.gamezone.com)
- ▶ IGN.com (www.ign.com)
- ▶ The Magic Box (www.the-magicbox.com)

15

CREATING YOUR OWN WEBSITE

15.1 CREATING A SIMPLE WEB PAGE

How Web Pages Work
Home Page Communities
Using Tripod

There are many ways to establish your own personal presence on the web. You can create a personal profile on a social networking site such as Facebook or MySpace. You can write your own blog. Or, best of all, you can create your own personal web page or website.

◄ SEE ALSO 11.1, *"Understanding Social Networking"* ▷

◄ SEE ALSO 10.1, *"Understanding Blogs"* ▷

Creating a full-blown website can be complicated, but creating a personal web page or two is actually quite easy—especially if you use one of the many **home page communities** on the Internet. These sites make it easy to generate good-looking pages without you having to learn any fancy **HTML** coding, and then they post your pages on the web where all your friends and family can visit them.

How Web Pages Work

No matter the content, a web page is nothing more than a computer file, a document composed in a certain language or **code.** Just like a word processing document, a web page document consists of lines of text with other elements (pictures, sounds, and links) included as necessary.

◄ SEE ALSO 1.1, *"How the Internet Works"* ▷

The code used to create a web page document is called HTML, which stands for Hypertext Markup Language. The codes in HTML work in the background to define what you see when you view a web page from your web browser.

◄ SEE ALSO 15.2, *"Basic HTML Editing"* ▷

HTML is a versatile language. It's simple enough that just about anyone can create a basic web page, but it contains enough advanced codes that professional web page developers can create more complex and lively pages. However you create your page, the final product is an assemblage of these HTML codes.

For a web page to be viewed by other users, that page must reside on a **web server,** which is nothing more than a computer with a large amount of hard disk storage that is continuously connected to the Internet. When a web page is **hosted** by a server, that page receives its own specific address or URL; any user can enter that address in a web browser and view the corresponding page.

When you have more than one page together on a server, then you have a website. Again, anybody can create a website; the pros just build bigger and fancier sites than do most individuals.

Home Page Communities

The easiest way to get your own personal web page is to use a service that specializes in the creation and hosting of individual web pages. These sites—some of which host millions of unique pages—are called home page communities, and they typically offer a variety of web page creation tools and hosting options. More often than not, these sites are free.

When you join a home page community, you're provided with a specified amount of space on its servers, anywhere from 15 MB to a full 1 GB—which should be more than enough to host your personal pages. You can then use the tools on the site to create your web pages or upload previously created pages to the site.

All of the major home page communities work in a similar fashion. Those that don't charge fees try to make their money by posting ads on your pages; they collect the advertising revenues, not you. Even those that purport to be free sometimes offer a variety of additional (not free) services and will be glad to charge you for additional storage space, domain name registration, e-commerce tools, and the like.

When you're looking to create your first home page on the web, here are the most popular communities to choose from:

> ▶ Angelfire (angelfire.lycos.com)

> ▶ Bravenet (www.bravenet.com)

> ▶ FortuneCity (www.fortunecity.com)

> ▶ Freeservers (www.freeservers.com)

> ▶ Google Sites (sites.google.com)

> ▶ Homestead (www.homestead.com)

- ▶ Office Live Small Business (www.officelive.com/free-website)
- ▶ Rediff (homepages.rediff.com)
- ▶ Tripod (tripod.lycos.com)
- ▶ Webs (www.webs.com)

Many Internet service providers also offer free personal home pages to their subscribers; check with your ISP to see what services are available.

Using Tripod

Tripod (tripod.lycos.com) is one of the largest and most established home page communities, and we'll use it as an example for how to create your own simple web pages. Most home page communities function in a similar fashion.

Like all home page communities, Tripod is essentially a collection of personal web pages. Tripod offers both free and paid hosting plans; the paid plans offer more storage, bandwidth, and features.

Free Hosting

What do you get for free with Tripod? The free plan provides the following to users:

- ▶ Hosting for an unlimited number of web pages (within the storage limit)
- ▶ 20 MB of storage for web pages, images, and related files
- ▶ 1 GB of monthly bandwidth for visitors to your site
- ▶ Easy-to-use page creation tools, including predesigned templates

WARNING . . .WARNING . . .WARNING

Tripod subsidizes its free plan by placing advertisements on all the web pages you create. If you want to avoid ads on your pages, you'll have to sign up for one of Tripod's paid plans.

Tripod also offers domain name registration and various other features for additional cost. The Plus plan ($4.95/month) adds blog hosting and photo albums and ups storage to 1 GB and bandwidth to 100 GB per month. The Pro plan ($8.95/month) adds a free domain name and e-mail accounts and ups storage to 3 GB and bandwidth to 300 GB per month. Other plans offer even more storage and bandwidth.

Creating a Web Page

To sign up for free hosting, go to Tripod's home page and click the Start Now button. When the next page appears, click the Sign Up button for the Tripod Free plan. You then have to create the customary username and password as well as provide other pertinent information.

Once you've created your free account, it's time to create your first web page. Tripod now displays your account management page; click the Site Builder button on the page's toolbar.

The next page provides two options. You can create a multipage site or a single-page express site. The multipage option offers more flexibility, so click the Start with a Multi-Page Template link.

The next page displays several categories of templates. Click a category to see the available templates and then click the Choose link next to the template you want to use.

Tripod now displays a form page for you to fill out. Enter the required information about the site you want to create and then click Continue.

Now you see a suggested visual design for your page. If you like this design, click the Use the Suggested Design button. To view more designs, click the Choose from All Designs button. Click any design to view a preview and then click the Use This Design button to select a design.

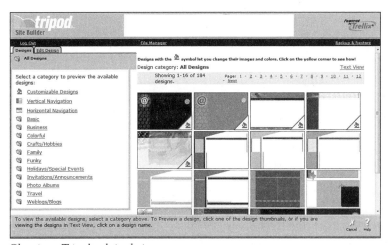

Choosing a Tripod website design.

Tripod now displays the first page of your site with placeholder text and graphics. To enter your own text, click the Edit Text button next to each text block. When the text editing page appears, enter your text. Use the formatting controls to change font, font size, font color, and formatting.

To insert your own picture, click the Edit Picture button next to a placeholder image. When the next page appears, browse your hard disk for the picture you want to upload and then click the Done button. When the Picture Gallery page appears, click the Choose link next to the photo you want to insert; when the Edit the Picture Settings page appears, click the Done button.

To add any other features to the page, scroll down and click the Edit Site Add-On button. This lets you add a variety of content modules, including search boxes, page counters, an interactive guestbook, and more.

When you're done editing this page, you have to publish it to put it on the web. To do this, click the Publish to Web icon at the bottom of the window. This saves your page, publishes it to the web, and displays a congratulations page. This page also includes the URL for your website in the form of *username*.tripod.com, with your username in the place of the italics. To view your web page, click the link on this page or enter the URL into your web browser.

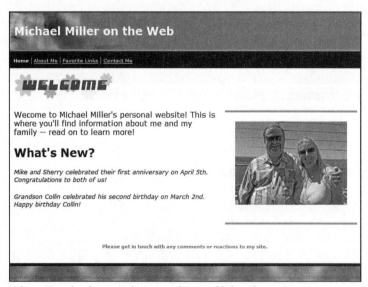

A basic Tripod web page; ads appear above and below this content.

Managing Your Web Pages

To edit the page you just created, return to the Tripod home page and click the Site Builder button again. Go to the All My Sites pane and click the link for your site. When the editing page appears, make whatever changes are necessary and then click the Publish to Web icon.

To edit other pages on your site, return to the editing page and click the Site Organizer icon. This displays the Site Organizer page, which lists all the pages you've created. Click the Edit Page link to edit a particular page.

To add new pages to your site, go to the Site Organizer page and click the Add Page icon. When the Add Page page appears, tell Tripod what kind of page you want to create and then enter all necessary information about that page. Click the Done button to display the new page for editing, with placeholder text and graphics in place.

To delete a page from your site, go to the Site Organizer page and click the Delete link next to the unwanted page.

Remember, whenever you add, delete, or change a page, you have to click the Publish to Web icon, or your changes won't be saved.

WORDS TO GO . . .*WORDS TO GO . . .WORDS TO GO*

A **home page community** is a service that hosts personal websites, often for free.

Hosting is the process of storing all the files for a website on a web server and then serving those files to other users via the Internet.

HTML (short for Hypertext Markup Language) is the coding language used to create all web pages.

A **web server** is a computer that hosts one or more websites.

15.2 BASIC HTML EDITING

How HTML Works

Codes to Get Started

Codes for Backgrounds

Codes for Text

Codes That Insert Things

Codes for Lists

Codes for Tables

HTML Editors

Beyond HTML

If you want to create more sophisticated web pages or a complete website, you need to learn HTML, which is the language behind all the pages on the web. By manipulating the various HTML codes, you can add all sorts of formatting and special effects to your web pages.

How HTML Works

Hypertext Markup Language (HTML) is the engine that drives the creation of web pages. In reality, HTML is nothing more than a series of codes that tell web browsers how to display different types of text and graphics. The codes are embedded in a document, so you can't see them; instead, you see the results of the codes.

To understand HTML, it's important to know that it's nothing more than text surrounded by instructions in the form of simple codes, called **tags.** Tags are distinguished from normal text by the fact that they're enclosed within angle brackets. Each particular tag turns on or off a particular effect such as boldface or italic text. Most tags are in sets of "on/off" pairs; you turn "on" the code before the text you want to affect and then turn "off" the code after the text.

For example, the tag **<h1>** is used to turn specified type into a level-one heading; the tag **</h1>** turns off the heading formatting. And the tag **<i>** is used to italicize text; **</i>** turns off the italics.

As you can see, an "off" code is merely the "on" code with a slash before it, **</like this>**. Any text *not* surrounded by tags uses HTML's default formatting—normal Times Roman text.

When you view the HTML code for a document, you're actually viewing a plain text document. Because of this, you can use any text editor—such as Windows Notepad or Apple's TextEdit—to edit HTML documents. While this makes for easy editing, entering raw code is not always the most intuitive way to build a web page.

A better and easier way to create and edit web pages is with an HTML editing program. These programs let you create a web page in a "what you see is what you get" (WYSIWYG) environment and then translate your designs into the appropriate HTML code.

Just because you use an **HTML editor,** however, doesn't mean that you don't need to know basic HTML coding. Some special effects can only be coded manually, and sometimes it's easier to make simple changes directly to the code itself rather than launching the cumbersome HTML editing program.

Codes to Get Started

When you first create a new web page, you have to insert some codes to identify the document as an HTML document. These tags are mandatory; you should get used to typing them in whenever you start to work on a new web page.

In fact, the best way to think of these tags is as a "shell" into which you then insert the rest of your text and other codes. For a typical document, here's the shell you use:

```
<html>
<head>
<title>insert the title of the document here</title>
</head>
<body>
insert your entire document—including other HTML codes—in-between
the body and /body tags
</body>
</html>
```

So you enter the **<html>** and **<body>** tags and insert everything else in between—including the **<head>** and **<title>** tags.

Codes for Backgrounds

The **<body>** tag can be expanded to define document-wide **attributes** for your web page. The most common use of **<body>** attributes is to assign a color or image to the background of your web page.

Background Color

You assign a background color by adding a special **bgcolor** code (called an **attribute**) within the brackets of the "on" **<body>** tag, like this:

```
<body bgcolor="xxxxxx">
```

Of course, you still have to use the **</body>** "off" tag at the end of your document; that doesn't change.

In the **bgcolor** code, you replace the *xxxxxx* with the six-digit hexadecimal code for a specific background color—surrounded by quotation marks. (Remember to precede each code with a number sign: #). Table 15.1 lists some basic color codes.

TABLE 15.1   COMMON COLOR CODES

Color	Code
Black	000000
Blue	0000FF
Cyan	00FFFF
Green	008000
Gray	808080
Silver	COCOCO
Lime	00FF00
Fuschia	FF00FF
Orange	FFA500
Purple	800080
Red	FF0000
White	FFFFFF
Yellow	FFFF00

As an example, suppose you wanted to set the background color for your document to silver. You would enter the following code:

```
<body bgcolor="COCOCO">
```

Background Graphics

You can also incorporate graphic images for the background of your web pages, much like how you can configure your Mac or Windows desktop with a certain wallpaper. When you specify a graphics file to use as a background, that file is loaded before the rest of the page loads—and, if it isn't big enough to fill the whole page, repeats down the page as often as necessary.

You add a background to your page with the **background** attribute used within the **<body>** tag. The code should look something like this:

```
<body background="URL">
```

In this code, the **URL** should be the name and location of your graphics file (it can be either a JPG or GIF file). It needs to be enclosed in quotation marks and include the complete URL or directory path.

As an example, if your background graphic is the file **background.jpg** located at www.webserver.com/mydirectory/, you insert this code:

```
<body background="http://www.webserver.com/mydirectory/background.
jpg">
```

Codes for Text

Now you enter the text of your web page between the "on" and "off" **<body>** tags. This creates a document that contains nothing but plain text—which looks pretty plain. Fortunately, you can use a variety of text-formatting tags to add variety and emphasis to specific text on your page.

Headings

HTML includes special tags for the headings of a document. You can use up to six levels of heading tags, from **<h1>** (the largest) to **<h6>** (the smallest). You enclose the text for each heading between the "on" and "off" tags, like this:

```
<h1>formats text as the largest heading</h1>
```

Formatting

You can use several HTML tags to format the way selected text looks in your listing. These are detailed in Table 15.2.

TABLE 15.2   HTML TEXT FORMATTING CODES

Codes (on/off)	Formatting
`<b></b>`	Boldface
`<strong></strong>`	Strong emphasis—similar to boldface, replaces the <b> tag
`<i></i>`	Italics

continues

TABLE 15.2   HTML TEXT FORMATTING CODES *(continued)*

Codes (on/off)	Formatting
`<em></em>`	Emphasis—similar to italics, replaces the `<i>` tag
`<u></u>`	Underline
`<tt></tt>`	Monospaced, typewriter-style text
`<center></center>`	Centers text
`<pre></pre>`	Displays text as "preformatted," for when you need to preserve line breaks and other formatting

Just insert the "on" tag right before the text you want formatted and insert the "off" tag right after the selected text. For example, if you have a sentence where you want to give strong emphasis (boldface) to a single word, it should look like this:

```
This is the sentence with the <strong>highlighted</strong> word.
```

Fonts

You don't have to settle for the standard font used by default on many web pages; you can make your page stand out with your own special font.

HTML uses the **<font>** tag (in "on" and "off" pairs) to change font attributes for specified text. You place specific attributes within the brackets for the **<font>** tag; you can change the font type (called a **face**), size, and color.

To specify a different font face for a piece of text, use the following code:

```
<font face="xxxx">text</font>
```

Replace *xxxx* with the name of the font you want. For example, if you wanted to change the font to Garamond, you would enter this code:

```
<font face="Garamond">text</font>
```

WARNING . . .WARNING . . .WARNING

Just because you specify a font doesn't necessarily mean that all the other users who'll be viewing your page have the same font available to them. If you change fonts on your page, change to a common font such as Arial, Helvetica, or Times Roman. Going more obscure could ensure an unpredictable display for your listing for many users.

Size

If you want to change the size of your text, use this code:

```
<font size="x">text</font>
```

Replace the *x* with the size you want, from 1 to 7, with 1 being the smallest and 7 the biggest.

You can also string these font codes together. Let's say you wanted to change your text to the largest possible Times Roman; you would enter this code:

```
<font face="Times Roman" size="7">text</font>
```

WARNING . . .WARNING . . .WARNING

Be careful about changing fonts within your description. Too many different fonts look garish.

Color

Adding color to your text works much the same as changing the font face or size. The code you use looks like this:

```
<font color="#xxxxxx">text</font>
```

As with the **bgcolor** code, replace the six *x*'s with the code for a specific color. Suppose you wanted to color some text red. You would use this code:

```
<font color="#FF0000">red text</font>
```

Codes That Insert Things

So far we've examined HTML codes that format selected text. Now let's take a look at codes that insert elements into your text.

Paragraphs

To create a paragraph within your text, you use the **<p>** and **</p>** on and off pairs. Insert the **<p>** tag before the start of the paragraph and the **</p>** tag after the end.

Lines and Line Breaks

Two HTML codes do not require "on/off" pairs. These are codes that insert simple elements into your document, like this:

```
<br> inserts a line break
<hr> inserts a horizontal rule (line)
```

So if you want to break a paragraph so that the next word starts on a new line, insert a **
** where you want the line to break. If you want to put a line between two paragraphs, you insert a **<hr>**.

Images

Inserting pictures and other graphics adds excitement to an otherwise boring web page. If you want to add a graphic to your page, you need to know the address of that graphic (in the form of a web page URL) and then use the following code:

```
<img src="URL">
```

There is no "off" code for inserted graphics. Note that the location is enclosed in quotation marks—and that you have to insert the **http://** part of the URL.

For example, if your graphic is the file **graphic01.jpg** located at www.webserver. com/mydirectory/, you insert this code:

```
<img src="http://www.webserver.com/mydirectory/graphic01.jpg">
```

You can size your graphic by using the **width** and **height** attributes and affixing the desired dimensions (in pixels). For example, to force your graphic to a 100×150 pixel size, use the following code:

```
<img src="http://www.webserver.com/mydirectory/graphic01.jpg"
width=100 height=150>
```

You can also place a border around the graphic with the **border** attribute; the size of the border (in pixels) must also be specified, as follows:

```
<img src="http://www.webserver.com/mydirectory/graphic01.jpg"
border=2>
```

You can also align the graphic on your page by using the **align** attribute. You can choose to align the graphic left, right, center, top, bottom, middle, or absolute; if you don't specify an alignment, your graphic will use the default left alignment.

For example, to center your picture on a line, the code should read as follows.

```
<img src="http://www.webserver.com/mydirectory/graphic01.jpg"
align=center>
```

Links

Web pages are all about hyperlinks to other web pages. If you want to include a hyperlink to another web page, you use the "on/off" versions of the **<a>** tag. The linked page is specified by using the **href** attribute within the brackets of the **<a>** tag.

The **<a>** and **</a>** tags surround the text that you wish to hyperlink, as follows:

```
<a href="URL">this is the link</a>
```

The text between the on and off codes appears onscreen as a typical underlined hyperlink; when users click that text, they are linked to the URL you specified in the code. Note that the URL is enclosed in quotation marks and that you have to include the **http://** part of the address.

Here's what a representative hyperlink code looks like:

```
<a href="http://www.webserver.com/mydirectory/mypage.htm">This is a
link to my Web page</a>
```

You can also hyperlink a graphic by surrounding the **<img>** tag with the **<a>** and **</a>** tags, like this:

```
<a href="http://www.webserver.com/mydirectory/mypage.htm"><img
src="http://www.webserver.com/mydirectory/graphic01.jpg"></a>
```

When users click the hyperlinked graphic, they jump to the linked page.

You can also add a link that users can click to send e-mail to you. Here's the code:

```
<a href="mailto:yourname@domain.com">click here to e-mail me</a>
```

Codes for Lists

If you have a list of items somewhere on your page, you might want to format them in a bulleted list. Using HTML codes, it's easy to create a neatly organized list.

Bulleted Lists

First enclose your bulleted list with the **<ul>** and **</ul>** tags. Then precede each bulleted item with the **<li>** tag. (There's no "off" code for bulleted items, by the way.)

The code for a typical bulleted list looks like this:

```
<ul>
    <li>item one
    <li>item two
    <li>item three
</ul>
```

When you're dealing with complex coding like this, it's sometimes easier to visually understand what's going on if you indent different levels of the code; the indentation isn't necessary for the code to work.

Numbered Lists

A numbered list works pretty much like a bulleted list but with ordered numbers instead of bullets. The difference is that you use the **<ol>** tag instead of the **<ul>** tag, like this:

```
<ol>
    <li>item one
    <li>item two
    <li>item three
</ol>
```

Codes for Tables

In addition to making pretty text and inserting links and graphics, one of the other interesting things you can do with HTML is add a table. The code to create a table, although it looks complex, is quite simple—at least in theory.

You start off by enclosing your table with <table> and </table> tags. Then you enclose each individual row in the table with **<tr>** and **</tr>** tags and each cell in each row with **<td>** and **</td>** tags. You can then insert any type of item within any individual cell—plain text, formatted text, bulleted lists, background shading, even graphics.

A basic table with two rows and two columns (four cells total) would be coded like this:

```
<table>
   <tr>
      <td>row 1 cell 1</td>
      <td>row 1 cell 2</td>
   </tr>
   <tr>
      <td>row 2 cell 1</td>
      <td>row 2 cell 2</td>
   </tr>
</table>
```

You can format both the table as a whole and the cells within a table to some degree:

▶ To dictate the width of the table border, use the **border** attribute within the **<table>** tag, like this: **<table border=*xx*>** (*xx* is in pixels).

▶ To shade the background of a cell, use the **bgcolor** attribute within the **<td>** tag, like this: **<td bgcolor="#*xxxxxx*">**.

▶ To dictate the width of a cell, use the **width** attribute within the <td> tag, like this: **<td width="*xx*%">** (*xx* is a percentage of the total table width).

HTML Editors

All of the coding presented in this chapter can be done by using any text editor and saving the resulting document with an **.html** or **.htm** extension. For more complex web pages, however, it may be easier to "draw" your page in a WYSIWYG environment and have the code generated automatically for you; to do this, you'll need to invest in special HTML editor software.

All HTML editors work in pretty much the same fashion, even if their particular menus and toolbars differ somewhat. You enter your text as you would in a word processor and then use menu or toolbar commands to format selected text. You also use menu or toolbar commands to insert graphics, create hyperlinks, and add other special effects. The resulting document is automatically saved in HTML format.

The two most popular HTML editors today are Microsoft Expression Web (www. microsoft.com/expression) and Adobe Dreamweaver (www.adobe.com/products/ dreamweaver). Both of these programs let you create individual web pages and complete multipage websites.

Beyond HTML

HTML is the solid backbone of all web page design. However, several other standards are now available that extend beyond basic HTML and make it easier to apply more complex designs and effects.

The most basic addition to HTML is another scripting language called **JavaScript.** JavaScript is written just like HTML code, and its code is inserted directly into your HTML code. With JavaScript you can perform a number of special effects, from scrolling tickers to those annoying pop-up windows that appear when you visit some commercial websites.

JavaScript is an offshoot of a more robust programming language called **Java.** Java is meant to be a platform-independent programming language so that an application written in Java can be used on any machine—Windows, Macintosh, Unix, or whatever. Many of the more sophisticated applets found on some state-of-the-art web pages are written in Java.

In addition, the HTML language itself is being supplanted in many instances by a new language called **eXtensible HTML** (XHTML). XHMTL moves beyond basic HTML to provide developers more control over the look of the final page. This enhanced control is accomplished via the use of **Cascading Style Sheets** (CSS), which more precisely define page elements.

While you don't need to know Java, JavaScript, or XHTML to create basic web pages, knowledge of these beyond-HTML languages is necessary to create sophisticated effects and truly state-of-the-art websites. If you're serious about website development, you need to master these and any other new programming languages as they become available.

An **attribute** is a subset of some HTML tags that define specific page or text formatting.

Cascading Style Sheets (CSS) are used in XHTML to precisely define page elements.

In HTML, a font **face** defines a font type or family.

An **HTML editor** is a software program that creates sophisticated web pages in a WYSIWYG environment.

Java is a programming language used to develop full-blown applications and sophisticated web page applets.

JavaScript is a scripting language used to insert special effects into web pages.

A **tag** is an HTML code used to insert instructions that define the look and content of a web page.

eXtensible HTML (XHTML) is the next generation of HTML, which provides more control over the look of web pages.

15.3 REGISTERING A DOMAIN NAME

Top-Level Domains

Where to Register

How to Register

If you want your website to be unique, it needs its own unique URL. The key component of the URL—the part *after* the **www.**—is called the domain. It consists of a unique domain name (before the dot) and a top-level domain (after the dot) such as .com or .net, like this: **domainname.domain.** You put a **www.** in front of this to denote your website; you put a unique address and an @ sign in front of it to create an e-mail address.

◀ *SEE ALSO 1.1, "How the Internet Works"* ▶

Choosing a domain name is just part of the process. Once you have a name in mind, that name needs to be listed with the Internet's **domain name system** (DNS) so that users entering your URL into their browsers are connected to the appropriate IP address where your site is actually hosted. Most website hosting services will provide DNS services if you provide a unique domain name; some will even handle the registration process for you.

◀ *SEE ALSO 15.4, "Website and Domain Hosting"* ▶

If you want to receive e-mail at your new domain, you'll also need to have your hosting service (or your ISP) link your domain name to your existing e-mail account. You can typically set up any number of specific addresses within a single domain and have them all forwarded to the same e-mail account.

Top-Level Domains

When you choose a domain name, you have a choice of a number of different top-level domains. While .com is the most common top-level domain, it's also the one with the fewest unique domain names left. In fact, if you want a short and relatively common domain name, it's probably already taken in the .com domain.

For that reason, you should be aware of the other top-level domains available. Table 15.3 lists the most common of these domains.

TABLE 15.3   TOP-LEVEL DOMAINS

Domain	Usage
.aero	Aviation industry
.asia	For any site based in Asia, Australia, and the general Pacific region
.biz	Business
.cat	For sites in the Catalan language
.com	Originally designated for commercial purposes but now for general use
.coop	Business cooperatives
.edu	Schools and educational institutions
.gov	U.S. government agencies
.info	General use (similar to .com)
.int	International organizations
.mil	U.S. military
.mobi	Sites compatible with cellular phones and other mobile devices
.museum	Museums
.name	General use (similar to .com)
.net	Originally designated for network providers but now for general use (similar to .com)
.org	Originally for nonprofit organizations but now for general use (similar to .com)
.pro	Professionals such as accountants, lawyers, physicians, and engineers
.tel	Internet telecommunications services
.travel	Travel and tourism-related sites

In addition, all non–U.S. countries have their own unique top-level domains. For example, England's domain name is .uk, and Canada's is .ca. Sites registered in those countries typically have their country domain tacked on at the end of an otherwise normal URL, such as www.widgets.co.uk.

Where to Register

Numerous firms perform domain name registration. All of these firms operate on behalf of the Internet Corporation for Assigned Names and Numbers (ICANN), a nonprofit corporation created to oversee a number of Internet-related management tasks, including domain name registration.

So where can you register for your domain name of choice? Most website hosting firms and home page communities offer domain name registration as part of their services; if you're using one of these sites, this is probably the easiest way to proceed.

◀ *SEE ALSO 15.1, "Creating a Simple Web Page"* ▷

You can also register directly with a variety of domain name registrars. Some of the largest domain name registrars include the following:

- ▶ Answerable.com (www.answerable.com)
- ▶ Domain-It (www.domainit.com)
- ▶ Go Daddy (www.godaddy.com)
- ▶ Lunarpages (www.lunarpages.com)
- ▶ MyDomain (www.mydomain.com)
- ▶ Namescout.com (www.namescout.com)
- ▶ Network Solutions (www.networksolutions.com)
- ▶ Register.com (www.register.com)

The cost for registering a domain varies from registrar to registrar, as well as by the length of registration desired. Expect to pay anywhere from a few dollars to $35 per year—although some hosting firms offer free domain registration as part of their hosting plans.

How to Register

Registering your domain is as easy as following these general steps:

1. Go to a domain registration site and search to see if the name you want is available.

2. If your name is available, reserve it by entering the appropriate contact information.

3. Arrange payment with the domain registration service, typically via credit card.

4. Contact your website hosting service and arrange for your domain name to be linked to a specific IP address and added to the Internet DNS system.

5. Arrange for your website hosting service to link your domain name to your e-mail account.

WORDS TO GO . . . WORDS TO GO . . . WORDS TO GO

The Internet's **domain name system** (DNS) is where all domain names are registered.

15.4 WEBSITE AND DOMAIN HOSTING

Building a Professional Website

Important Services

Finding a Host

Home page communities are fine if all you want to do is post a few basic pages about your family or hobby. However, if you want a more robust web presence or to create an online retail site, you have to enter the realm of professional websites.

◀ SEE ALSO 15.1, *"Creating a Simple Web Page"* ▶

Building a Professional Website

A professional website is more than just a collection of web pages. It's a complete, thoughtfully envisioned, well-laid-out experience where the home page leads naturally to subsidiary pages and where all the pages share a similar design and navigation system. No matter which page users ultimately gravitate to, they should know that that page is part of a greater site and be able to navigate back to a home page that truly serves as a portal to all that lies within.

To create a professional website, you need to use professional site-creation tools. You don't build a complex website using Microsoft Notepad or FrontPage Express. You need to use a full-featured program, such as Microsoft Expression Web or Adobe Dreamweaver, that lets you view your entire site as a single project and that automatically applies uniform formatting and navigation to any new pages you add. (It also helps to know your way around HTML, XHTML, and JavaScript coding, of course.)

◀ SEE ALSO 15.2, *"Basic HTML Editing"* ▶

You also can't upload a complex website to Yahoo! GeoCities or most other home page communities. These communities are designed to host individual web pages, not complete sites. You certainly don't want your professional site to be burdened with a URL that looks something like www.geocities.com/thisismysite/. Instead, you need to find a professional **website hosting service,** a master site that will provide hundreds of megabytes of disk space, robust site management tools, and the ability to use your own unique domain name. (With your own domain name, your site's URL will read www.*yourname*.com—just like the big sites do.)

◄ *SEE ALSO 15.3, "Registering a Domain Name"* ▷

All of these services will cost you, of course; that's part and parcel of going pro. Most website hosting services start at around $5 a month and go up from there, depending on the storage space and services you avail yourself of.

Important Services

A professional web hosting service, at the most basic level, provides large amounts of reliable storage space for your website—normally for a monthly or yearly fee. Most hosting services also provide other types of services, as discussed next.

So when you're shopping for a hosting service for your website, what should you look for? Here's a short list:

- ▶ **Adequate storage space.** The main reason you want a website hosting service is to host your website. That means you need a certain amount of disk space. Most sites offer different levels of service depending on the amount of disk space you need. If you start to run out of space, you can normally upgrade to the next highest plan.

- ▶ **Unlimited bandwidth.** If you start to get a lot of traffic to your site, you don't want your hosting service to shut you off because you only contracted for so many hits a month. Look for a plan that offers either unlimited bandwidth or a high enough traffic level that you won't be tempted to stop promoting your site.

- ▶ **Affordable rates.** All of these services come at a cost—and that cost differs wildly from one host to another. Look for the best combination of space, access, features, and price. Don't sign anything until you've checked out several different sites.

- ▶ **Reliability.** The worst thing in the world is to enter your site's URL in your web browser and find that it's down. You want a hosting service with a good reliability record; 95 percent uptime might not be high enough if users access your site for critical information. If possible, evaluate the uptime records from several hosting services; some hosts even guarantee a particular uptime rate.

- ▶ **Easy uploading and maintenance.** When you're shopping for a host, don't overlook ease of use. Look for a site that offers easy uploading either via its own built-in tools, via the uploading function built into your HTML editing program, or with a common FTP client. Consider also any other maintenance tools (such as dead link checkers) that are available free of charge. Many sites offer site maintenance through some form of **control panel.** This is an easy way to access and manage the pages on your site.

- ▶ **Domain name hosting.** If you're creating a professional website, chances are you want to use a unique domain name. Make sure the hosting service handles domain name hosting and consider going with a host that can handle the complete process—from domain name registration through to e-mail forwarding.

- ▶ **E-mail.** Speaking of e-mail, make sure your hosting service offers domain name–linked e-mail and provides its own incoming and outgoing e-mail servers. Also look for web-based access to your domain e-mail; this can come in handy when you travel.

- ▶ **Reporting.** Most hosting services offer a variety of reporting tools so you can track the performance of your site. Look for tools that measure traffic (by day and by specific page) and track **referring sites** (the site from which a visitor just came before he or she entered your site).

- ▶ **Technical support.** If you ever have any trouble with posting or maintaining your web pages, you want to be able to get help—fast. Look for hosts that offer (in addition to web- or e-mail-based support) 24/7 live phone-based technical support, preferably via a toll-free number.

If your site has special needs, you'll also want to take them into account. For example, if you want to sell products on your site, you'll need a host that provides e-commerce tools such as shopping cart and checkout. The key is to find the host that offers the best match of services for your site's particular needs.

Finding a Host

There are literally hundreds of site hosting services on the web. The best way, then, to look for a web hosting service is to use a site that performs the search for you.

Several sites on the Internet offer directories of website hosting services. Most of these sites let you look for hosts by various parameters, including monthly cost, disk space provided, programming and platforms supported, and extra features offered (such as e-commerce hosting, control panels, etc.). Many also offer lists of the "best" or most popular hosting services, measured in one or another fashion.

Among the most popular of these host search sites are the following:

- ▶ HostIndex.com (www.hostindex.com)
- ▶ HostSearch (www.hostsearch.com)
- ▶ TopHosts.com (www.tophosts.com)
- ▶ Web Hosters (www.webhosters.com)

A **website hosting service** is a master site that provides storage of and bandwidth for individual websites.

15.5 SEARCH ENGINE OPTIMIZATION

What Search Engines Look For

How to Improve Your Search Rankings

Once you launch your web page or website, you want to attract visitors. The way most people find new web pages today is by searching, meaning they query Google or Yahoo! for specific information or topics. If your page ranks high in the search engine results, you'll get more visitors. But how do you ensure a high search ranking?

The key to increasing your search engine rankings is to optimize your site for search—that is, to give the search engines what they're looking for. **Search engine optimization** (SEO) involves everything from the design of your site to the text you place on each page to those sites that link back to your site. You have to optimize all these factors if you want to place near the top of the first search results page when someone is searching for what you have to offer.

◀ *SEE ALSO 4.1, "How Search Engines and Directories Work"* ▶

What Search Engines Look For

To know how to optimize your site for search, you need to know what exactly search engines look for when ranking sites in their search results. Fortunately for anyone doing the optimization, a few key factors control the results—and they're pretty much the same factors for every major search engine.

Keywords

One of the most important things to search engines is **keywords**—those words and phrases that their users are searching for. For this reason, all search engines look for keywords on your page and try to determine how important each keyword is.

A search engine does this by seeing where on the page the keyword is used and how many times. A site with a keyword buried near the bottom of a page will rank lower than one with the keyword placed near the top or used repeatedly in the page's text.

Remember, the keyword or phrase is what the user is searching for. If someone is searching for "hammers" and your site includes the keyword "hammers" (or "hammer," singular) in a prominent position—in the first sentence of the first paragraph, for example—then your site is a good match for that search. If, on the other hand, your site doesn't include the word "hammers" at all or only includes it near the bottom of the page, then the search engines will determine that your site *isn't* a good match for that searcher. It doesn't matter if you have a big picture of a hammer at the top of your page (search engines can't read images, only text). Unless you use the keyword prominently and relatively often, you won't rank highly for that particular search.

HTML Tags

A search engine looks not just to the text that visitors see when trying to determine the content of your site. Also important is the presence of keywords in your site's title, which is determined by specific information contained in your site's HTML code.

◀ *SEE ALSO 15.2, "Basic HTML Editing"* ▶

This information includes your site's name and keyword "content," which is specified within the **<META>** tag. This tag appears in the head of your HTML document before the **<BODY>** tag and its contents.

A typical **<META>** tag looks something like this:

```
<META NAME="KEYWORDS" CONTENT="keyword1, keyword2, keyword3">
```

It's easy enough for a search engine to locate the **<META>** tag and read the data contained within. If a site's metadata is properly indicated, this gives the search engine a good first idea as to what content is included on this page.

In addition, some search engines look for information in your page's **<TITLE>** tag. For this reason, your **<TITLE>** tag should contain not only the name of your site but two to three main keywords as well. You want to make sure that your site's most important content is listed within this tag.

Finally, most search engines also seek out the heading tags in your HTML code—**<H1>, <H2>, <H3>,** and so forth. For this reason, you should use traditional heading tags (instead of newer Cascading Style Sheet coding) to emphasize key content on your page.

Links to Your Site

It was the folks at Google who first realized that web rankings could be somewhat of a popularity contest—that is, if a site got a lot of traffic, there was probably a good reason for that. A useless site wouldn't attract a lot of visitors (at least not long term), nor would it inspire other sites to link to it.

So if a site has a lot of other sites linking back to it, it's probably because that site offers useful information relevant to the site doing the linking. The more links to a given site, the more useful it probably is. So if your site has 100 sites linking to it, for example, it should rank higher in Google's search results than a similar site with only 10 sites linking to it.

It's not just the quantity of links; it's also the quality. That is, a site that includes content that is relevant to your page is more important than just some random site that links to your page. For example, if you have a site about NASCAR racing, you'll get more oomph with a link from another NASCAR-related site than you would with a link from a site about Barbie dolls. Relevance matters.

How to Improve Your Search Rankings

Knowing how search engines rank their results, you can now work on optimizing your site to improve its ranking. With that in mind, here are some key factors that are the basis for any serious SEO effort.

Improve Your Content

Of all the methods for SEO, the one that has the biggest impact is improving the content of your website. It's simple: The better your site is content-wise, the higher it will rank.

When it comes to search rank, content is king. The major search engines always find a way to figure out what your site is all about. The higher quality and more relevant your site's content is to a particular search, the more likely it is that a search engine will rank your site higher in its results.

So, even though keywords and <META> tags are important, it's more important to focus on what your site does and says. If your site is about quilting, work to make it the most content-rich site about quilting you can. Don't skimp on the content; the more and better content you have, the better.

Organize Your Site

Here's an important fact: search engine spiders can find more content on a web page and more web pages on a website if that content and those pages are in a clear hierarchical organization.

Let's look at page organization first. You want to think of each web page as a mini-outline. The most important information should be in major headings, with lesser information in subheadings beneath the major headings. One way to do this is via standard HTML heading tags, like this:

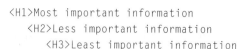

```
<H1>Most important information
   <H2>Less important information
      <H3>Least important information
```

This approach is also appropriate for your entire site layout. Your home page should contain the most important information, with subsidiary pages branching out from that containing less important information—and even more sub-pages branching out from those. The most important info should be visible when a site is first accessed via the home page; additional info should be no more than a click or two away.

Fine-Tune Your Keywords

Just as important as a page's layout is the page's content in terms of keywords. Keywords are important because they're what potential visitors search for and are thus a key factor in how search engines rank your site.

For this reason, you want to make sure that each and every page on your site contains the keywords that users might use to search for your pages. If your site is all about drums, make sure your pages include words like "drums," "percussion," "sticks," "heads," "cymbals," and "snare." Try to think through how *you* would search for this information and work those keywords into your content.

Put the Most Important Information First

Think about hierarchy, think about keywords, and then think about how these two concepts work together. That's right, you want to place the most important keywords higher up on your page. A web crawler will only crawl so far, and you don't want it to give up before key information is found. In addition, searching ranking is partially determined by content; the more important the content looks on a page (as determined by placement on the page), the higher the page's ranking will be.

Create a <META> DESCRIPTION Attribute

When calculating search ranking, most search engines not only consider the visible content on a page, they also evaluate the content of key HTML tags—in particular, your site's **<META>** tag. You want to make sure that you use the **<META>** tag in your page's code and assign important keywords to this tag.

The **<META>** tag, which (along with the **<TITLE>** tag) is placed in the head of your HTML document, can be used to supply all sorts of information about your document. You can insert multiple **<META>** tags into the head of your document, and each tag can contain a number of different attributes. For SEO purposes, the two most important attributes to assign to the **<META>** tag are your site's description and keywords.

We'll start by looking at the **DESCRIPTION** attribute. The text assigned to this attribute is used by some search engines as the description for your web page in their search results. This means you want to think of the **DESCRIPTION** text as a short promotional blurb that describes what your page is about.

The tag works like this:

```
<META NAME="DESCRIPTION" CONTENT="Insert your description here">
```

You insert your own site description between the two quotation marks. For SEO purposes, this text is read as a complete text string—a block of text, as it were. Within this descriptive text, you should make sure to include as many keywords or phrases that fit naturally.

Create a <META> KEYWORDS Attribute

The second key **<META>** attribute is the **KEYWORDS** attribute. This attribute is your opportunity to tell the search engines which keywords your page is targeting.

It's easy to add this tag to your page's HTML code. Just use the following template:

```
<META NAME="KEYWORDS" CONTENT="keyword 1, keyword 2, keyword 3">
```

Separate each keyword or phrase by a comma. You can include as many keywords or phrases as you like; capitalization doesn't matter. It's also important to know that the keywords you include in this tag *don't* actually have to appear on the web page—which makes it a good place to include common misspellings or synonyms for your main keywords.

Solicit Links

One of the best ways to increase your Google ranking is to increase the number of sites that link to your web pages. As far as Google is concerned, the more sites that link to your page—and the higher the corresponding ranking of those linking sites—the higher your page's ranking will be.

To increase your ranking, then, you want to get more higher-quality sites to link back to your site. There are a number of ways to do this, from just waiting for the links to roll in to actively soliciting links from other sites. The latter approach is more effective. You'll need to personally e-mail the webmasters of key sites to ask them to link to your page. (Naturally, you'll promise a link back to their site in return.)

Submit Your Site

While you could wait for each search engine's spider software to find your site on the web, a more proactive approach is to manually submit your site for inclusion in each engine's web index.

Table 15.4 presents the pages you use to submit your site to the major search engines.

TABLE 15.4   SEARCH ENGINE SUBMITTAL URLS

Search Engine	Submit at This URL
Google	www.google.com/addurl
Windows Live Search	search.msn.com.sg/docs/submit.aspx
Yahoo!	siteexplorer.search.yahoo.com/submit/

You can also use a third-party site submittal service to submit your site to multiple search engines and directories; these services handle all the details required by each search engine. Some of the more popular site submittal services are as follows:

▶ 1 2 3 Submit PRO (websitesubmit.hypermart.net)

▶ AddMe.com (www.addme.com)

▶ AddPro.com (www.addpro.com)

▶ Submit Express (www.submitexpress.com)

Use Text Instead of Images

It's important to know that search engines today parse only text content; they can't figure out what a picture or graphic is about unless you describe it in the text. So if you use graphic buttons or banners (instead of plain text) to convey important information, the search engines simply won't see it. You need to put every piece of important information somewhere in the *text* of the page—even if it's duplicated in a banner or graphic.

To work around this limitation, make sure you use the **<ALT>** tag for each image on your page—and assign meaningful keywords to the image via this tag. A searchbot will read the **<ALT>** tag text; it can't figure out what an image is without it.

Similarly, don't hide important information in Flash animations, JavaScript applets, video files, and the like. Remember, searchbots can only find text on your page—all those nontext elements are invisible to a search engine.

WORDS TO GO . . . WORDS TO GO . . . WORDS TO GO

A **keyword** is a word or phrase that users enter when searching the web.
Search engine optimization (SEO) is the process of fine-tuning a web page or website to rank higher in search engine results.

WORDS TO GO GLOSSARY

AAC   Apple's proprietary compressed audio format, used in the iTunes Store and on the iPod and iPhone devices.

adware   Spyware used by advertisers and marketers.

anti-spyware program   A piece of software designed to identify, block, and remove spyware programs.

anti-virus program   A piece of software designed to identify, block, and remove computer viruses.

archives   In a blog, older blog posts.

article   An individual post or message in a Usenet newsgroup.

Atom   A file format used to create site feeds.

Attribute   A subset of some HTML tags that define specific page or text formatting.

avatar   Your physical onscreen representation in a virtual world.

bitrate   The number of bits used to create an audio recording; the higher the bitrate, the better the sound.

blind carbon copy (bcc:)   A copy of an e-mail message sent to a recipient who is not visible to other recipients.

blog   Short for "web blog," a frequently updated online journal containing news, information, and opinions.

blog roll   A list of related blogs.

bloggers   People who post to blogs.

blogging   The act of posting to a blog.

blogosphere   The entire universe of web-based blogs.

broadband   A faster Internet connection than traditional dial-up, typically made via cable or DSL technology.

buddy   Someone with whom you converse via instant messaging (sometimes also called a "friend").

buddy list   Your list of IM buddies.

Buy It Now   An option that lets you purchase fixed-price items on eBay.

cable Internet   A broadband technology that enables fast Internet connections.

carbon copy (cc:)   An e-mail message copied to recipients other than the primary recipient. Recipients of carbon copies are visible to all other recipients of the message.

Cascading Style Sheets (CSS)   Coding used in XHTML to precisely define page elements.

chat room   A web-based forum for public text messaging.

cloud computing   In cloud computing, computer files and programs are not hosted on individual computers, but rather on a "cloud" of computers accessed via the Internet.

commercial software   Computer programs that are available for sale.

comparison shopping site   A site that compares prices from thousands of different online merchants.

compressed audio   This results in smaller files that can be downloaded relatively quickly, although at some sacrifice in sound quality. The most popular compressed audio formats are AAC, MP3, and WMA.

computer attack   Any operation executed over the Internet with the intent to disrupt, deny, degrade, or destroy information on a computer or computer network.

computer virus   A software program designed to do damage to your computer system.

content-filtering software   A computer program that blocks access to websites and web pages that contain inappropriate content.

conversation   An e-mail message thread in Gmail.

cookie   A small text file created by a website and stored on your computer, it records information about your site visit.

cyber bullying   Bullying behavior carried out online.

denial-of-service attack   A type of computer attack that occurs when multiple computers overload a particular computer or web server with thousands of messages at the same time.

dial-up   An Internet connection made via traditional phone lines and limited to 56.6 Kbps.

digital rights management (DRM)   Technology used to prevent unauthorized use of copyrighted music and video files.

digital subscriber line (DSL) Technology that uses standard phone lines to create a broadband Internet connection.

domain name An easily remembered Internet address that is associated with a specific ID address.

domain name system (DNS) On the Internet, where all domain names are registered.

downloading The process of copying a file from a site on the Internet to your computer. (In contrast, uploading a file copies that file from your computer to a site on the Internet.)

e-mail Short for "electronic mail," a means of sending and receiving letter-like messages via the Internet.

e-mail address The identifier for e-mail recipients; all e-mail addresses are composed of the user's log-in name, the @ sign, and the user's domain name.

emoticon A series of symbols used to represent a particular emotion during online chat or instant messaging.

event An item scheduled on a calendar.

eXtensible HTML (XHTML) The next generation of HTML, which provides more control over the look of web pages.

favorite A way of bookmarking a website you wish to visit again in the future.

file archive A website that offers prescreened software programs for downloading.

file attachment A file that piggybacks on an e-mail message.

File Transfer Protocol (FTP) A means of downloading files from dedicated file servers on the Internet.

file-sharing networks Websites that facilitate the downloading of music and video files uploaded by other users; they often have illegal copies of music and movies available.

final value fee (FVF) A fee charged by eBay when an item sells, based on the item's selling price.

firewall A piece of software or hardware that acts as a barrier between an individual computer or network and the Internet to prevent unwanted outside access.

follow A means of subscribing to the "tweets" of a Twitter user.

font face   In HTML, the typeface that defines a font type or family.

freeware   A category of computer programs available for free.

friending   The process of finding new friends on a social network.

function   An advanced formula preprogrammed into a spreadsheet application.

gadget   A page element on a Blogger blog or a plug-in that adds functionality to the Google Spreadsheets application.

Google Earth   Google's 3D mapping software.

grid   The virtual world in Second Life.

high definition (HD)   This type of video reproduces widescreen videos at a minimum resolution of 1280×720 pixels—the same resolution used for HDTV broadcasts.

home page community   A service that hosts personal websites, often for free.

hosting   The process of storing all the files for a website on a web server and then serving those files to other users via the Internet.

hotspot   A public location that offers wireless Internet access.

HTML   Standing for Hypertext Markup Language, it is the coding language used to create all web pages.

HTML editor   A software program that creates sophisticated web pages in a WYSIWYG environment.

HTTP e-mail   Web-based e-mail.

hyperlink   A piece of text or a graphic on a web page that, when clicked, links to another page on the web.

Hypertext Markup Language (HTML)   The coding language used to create all web pages.

identity theft   A crime that involves the illegal use of your individual identity or personal data.

IMAP   The Interactive Mail Access Protocol.

IMAP servers   Used by ISPs to receive POP e-mail messages.

incremental reveal   Used in Google Presentations to animate individual elements on a slide.

instant messaging (IM)   A process that enables two users to send text messages to each other in real time over the Internet.

Internet Protocol (IP) address   Used to identify each server and device connected to the Internet.

Internet service provider (ISP)   A company that connects individual users to the Internet backbone—for a fee.

Internet telephony   Enables users to place phone calls directly from their computers over the Internet.

Java   A programming language used to develop full-blown applications and sophisticated web page applets.

JavaScript   Scripting language used to insert special effects into web pages.

keyword   A word or phrase that users enter when searching the web.

latency   The lag time between when a command is sent and when it is received; you want low latency when playing online games.

layer   Consists of specific data or points of interest overlaid on a Google Earth map.

Linden Dollars   The virtual currency in Second Life.

listing fee   The fee charged by eBay when you list an item for sale; it is based on the item's starting bid price or fixed price.

malware   A piece of malicious software such as a computer virus or spyware.

massively multiplayer online role-playing game (MMORPG)   Another phrase for a virtual world.

message window   The pop-up window where you enter and view your IM conversations.

micro-blogging   A feed of short text posts that updates others on one's current activities; Twitter is the web's most popular micro-blogging service.

modem   A piece of equipment used to connect a computer to the Internet by modulating and demodulating an analog signal to and from digital format.

MP3   The most popular compressed audio format, compatible with just about every music player program and portable music player device.

multiplayer games   These let multiple users play against each other online.

newsgroup   A Usenet online discussion forum; newsgroups are organized in hierarchies by topic.

newsreader   A software program used to read and post Usenet newsgroup articles.

office suite   A collection of software programs that typically includes applications for word processing, spreadsheets, and presentations.

online auction   A process that enables interested buyers to bid up the price of an item for sale via the Internet, such as those on the eBay site.

online chat   A public exchange of text messages with a group of other users.

online classifieds   The web-based version of traditional print classified ads, connecting local buyers and sellers.

PC-to-PC calls   Made from one computer to another computer over the Internet.

PC-to-phone calls   Made from a computer to a traditional landline or mobile phone over the Internet.

phishing   A type of scam that extracts personal information from the victim using a series of fake e-mails and websites.

placemark   A place of interest on a map that you create yourself.

places of interest (POI)   Specific locations, such as restaurants or hotels, overlaid on a map.

podcast   An audio blog.

pop-up window   A typically unwanted web page in a browser window that opens automatically when a page is viewed. Pop-ups are usually used to display advertisements.

post   A single blog entry.

Post Office Protocol (POP)   One technology used to send e-mail over the Internet via dedicated e-mail servers; POP e-mail requires the use of special e-mail client software.

private browsing   A mode of browsing in which no record is kept of the sites you visit.

profile page   On a social network, this displays a user's personal information—and is the home page for comments and messages.

protocol identifier   That part of a URL that identifies the protocol used by a given site or server; it's the http:// part of a website URL.

proxy bidding software   This automates the bidding process for online auctions; you specify the highest amount you're willing to pay, and the software bids the minimum amount necessary to win the auction.

range   A group of more than one contiguous cells in a spreadsheet.

Really Simple Syndication (RSS)   A file format used to create site feeds.

residents   The other players in the Second Life virtual world.

resource name   The second part of a URL (to the right of the //); it contains the domain name.

router   A piece of equipment that connects all the computers on a network; wireless networks use wireless routers.

search engine   This scours the web to create an index of web pages that can then be searched by users.

search engine optimization (SEO)   The process of fine-tuning a web page or website to rank higher in search engine results.

search index   The database of web pages assembled by search engines.

search operators   These enable users to fine-tune their queries within the search box.

second-level domain   That part of a domain name, to the left of the dot, assigned to a specific server or website.

secure server   A type of web server, typically used by online merchants, that encrypts your credit card information to provide a safe online shopping experience.

server   A computer connected to the Internet that serves information and services to users.

shareware   The category of computer program that you can download for free, but that you are encouraged to support with your financial donation.

shopping cart   A means of virtually storing the items you intend to purchase at an online store until you're ready to check out and complete your purchase.

site feed   An automatically updated stream of a blog's contents.

smiley   Another word for an emoticon.

SMTP   The Simple Mail Transfer Protocol.

SMTP servers   Used by ISPs to send POP e-mail messages.

sniping   The process of placing a single last-second bid in an online auction.

social networking   Enables people to share experiences and opinions with each other via community-based websites; the most popular social networks today are Facebook and MySpace.

software-based banking   Enables you to access and manage your bank account via a financial management software program such as Quicken or Microsoft Money.

spider   Software used by search engines to crawl the web.

spyware   A type of program that installs itself on your computer and surreptitiously sends information about the way you use your PC to a third party.

stop words   Small words, such as "and" or "the," that are automatically removed from a search query.

streaming audio and video   These let you listen to music and watch movies in real time without first downloading the complete file to your computer.

Street View   In Google Maps, this displays street-level photos of select locations.

tabbed browsing   Lets you open multiple web pages within a single browser window, with each page displayed on its own tab.

tag   An HTML code used to insert instructions that define the look and content of a web page.

template   A predesigned combination of text styles, document formatting, and graphics used to create new documents.

theme   A predesigned collection of background images, color schemes, and fonts that are applied to every slide in a Google Presentations presentation.

thread   A collection of messages and replies about a given topic.

top-level domain   That part of a domain name, to the right of the dot, that identifies the type of website or server.

tweet   A text update on the Twitter service.

universal search results   These display all matching media for a search query, not just web pages.

uncompressed audio   Reproduces exactly what you hear on a CD—but results in files too large to be downloaded from the Internet.

uniform resource locator (URL)   The full address of a website or server, including the protocol identifier and the resource name.

Usenet   That part of the Internet that hosts online discussion groups called newsgroups.

virtual world   An online environment that is part multiplayer role-playing game, part online chat room.

Voice over Internet Protocol (VoIP)   The technology that enables Internet telephony.

web browser   A software program that enables you to access the web and display specific web pages. Popular web browsers include Internet Explorer, Mozilla Firefox, Google Chrome, Opera, and Apple's Safari.

web directory   A collection of websites organized by human editors.

web e-mail   Sends and receives e-mail over the web using any web browser.

web group   A web-based community for users devoted to a particular topic or hobby; the two biggest web group communities are Google Groups and Yahoo! Groups.

web page   A single document on the web, typically housed on a website.

web server   A computer that hosts one or more websites.

web-based application   An application housed on and run from computers connected to the Internet; you access web-based applications using your computer's web browser via any Internet connection.

web-based banking   Enables you to access and manage your bank account from any web browser.

webcam   A small camera that attaches to your computer and records video, audio, and still pictures. The word "webcam" also refers to hardware webcams connected to the Internet that stream continuous images or video to other computer users.

webcast   Streaming video sent from a webcam over the Internet.

website   An organized collection of pages on the web.

website hosting service   A master site that provides storage of and bandwidth for individual websites.

whisper   A private conversation initiated from a public chat room.

WiFi   The 802.11x wireless networking standard used in home and public networks.

wildcards   A means of substituting specific characters in keyword searches.

WMA   Microsoft's compressed audio format that is compatible with the Windows Media Player software.

word stemming   Technology that automatically searches for all forms of a word with no wildcards necessary.

World Wide Web   A collection of linked websites and pages hosted on servers connected to the Internet.

zombie computer   A computer that has been hijacked by a virus or spyware and used to attack another computer by remote control.

367

INDEX

I